THE STORY OF
OXFORD SPEEDWAY

THE STORY OF
OXFORD SPEEDWAY

ROBERT BAMFORD & GLYNN SHAILES

Front cover: Hans Nielsen in action. (Courtesy of Mike Patrick)

First published 2007

Stadia is an imprint of
Tempus Publishing Limited
The Mill, Brimscombe Port,
Stroud, Gloucestershire, GL5 2QG
www.tempus-publishing.com

© Robert Bamford and Glynn Shailes, 2007

British Library Cataloguing in Publication Data.
A catalogue record for this book is available from the British Library.

ISBN 978-0-7524-4161-0

Typesetting and origination by Tempus Publishing Limited
Printed in Great Britain

CONTENTS

ACKNOWLEDGEMENTS

Grateful thanks are extended to the following persons for their advice, help and assistance: Les Aubrey, Chris Broadway, Ian Charles, Colin Clarke, Jeff Davies, John Gaisford, John Hall, Paul Hawthorne (Willow Print 92 Ltd.), Phil Hilton, John Jarvis, Keith Lawson, Peter Morrish, *The Oxford Mail & Times*, Geoff Parker, Mike Patrick (www.mike-patrick.com), Peter Shiston, John Somerville, Mark Tregale and Alf Weedon. Also to those who are regrettably no longer with us: Tom Bromley, Henry Chandler, Ralph Jackson, Alf Viccary and Wright Wood.

In the production of this book, several images have been used where the photographer is unfortunately unknown and all efforts to try and trace them have failed. The authors would also like to place on record their grateful thanks to these photographers.

With regard to much of the photographic content herein, many C.F. Wallace, Wright Wood, Trevor Meeks and Peter Morrish images are now available as digital photolab produced photos – most of them from the original negatives. Contact John Somerville: 35 St Ninians Road, Linlithgow, West Lothian, EH49 7BN, or email john.somerville@blueyonder.co.uk, or telephone 01506 844315 for a free CD with 10,000 contact sheet images and price list.

FOREWORD

Oxford Speedway has been part of my life for more years than I care to remember and, whilst I am not involved with the club these days, I still think of myself as a keen supporter and am proud to be involved with the sport in other ways, namely through the Speedway Riders' Benevolent Fund.

It was a great honour to be asked to write a foreword for this publication on Oxford Speedway and I can think of no one person better qualified to be involved in the compilation of this than our former press officer Glynn Shailes. It was John Payne and myself who, having been appointed co-promoters of Oxford Speedway by stadium owner David Hawkins in 1983, were happy to hand Glynn the post.

I would like to say here that for John and myself the job of being speedway promoters seemed a daunting task, but it was made easier thanks to the 'apprenticeship' we both served under Dan McCormick. We owed much to Dan, who not only taught us what we needed to know, but, when we were team building, tipped us off that, following the closure of his club Birmingham, Hans Nielsen was available. We took action, and the rest as they say is history.

As for the appointment of Glynn as our press officer, we never regretted it for one moment. Glynn would send out press releases to over fifty contacts each week, and remember this was in the days before computers. The press release had to be typed out and then put in envelopes. Those envelopes had to be addressed, stamps stuck on and then put in the post box. This was quite a task, but it was done every week, without fail. As far as John and I were concerned, the publicity we had for Oxford Speedway just couldn't be bettered. And now Glynn, together with prolific speedway author Robert Bamford, has been burning the midnight oil again to produce this latest book on the story of Oxford Speedway. It's a work that brings back a host of happy memories, most certainly for me, and I'm sure for all the people who supported the club over many years. In my case, there is the memory of visiting Cowley with my father to lend support to the Cheetahs. It is well known that my favourite rider was Jim Gregory and, at a time when Oxford weren't doing too well, he always gave his best. Years later, at one of our many reunions, I was able to meet Jim and right up until the close of the 2006 season, he was still taking part in old-time demonstration races.

The rider reunions that over the years have been so successful at Oxford were organised by Glynn, together with the late Ron Hoare, the secretary of the Veteran Speedway Riders' Association. They both played an important part in putting together 'those do's', as Ron called them. In 2005, Glynn was responsible, along with Pete Seaton, for getting those riders who were members of the 1985 and 1986 league title-winning sides back together for a grand reunion at the stadium. It was great to see these former Cheetahs and, of course, the details of this have found their way into this book. Glynn never stops telling me that I was team manager of a side, who, in 1986, created a record that perhaps may be equalled, but never beaten – that of going through the entire league programme and never tasting defeat. Ah happy days! Believe me, they were wonderful times; we had a fine team on the track and a good back-up team off it. Nothing, in my view, can equal them.

So do enjoy a good read that chronicles the Cheetahs of yesteryear, all of whom made a contribution in making Oxford Speedway 'tick'. The club has had its ups and downs over the seasons, but it's always come through and long may it continue to do so. Happily, those two scribes, Glynn and Robert, have got it all written down for your enjoyment!

Bernard Crapper
February 2007

INTRODUCTION

I completed my first book on Oxford Speedway in 1991, and in recent years I had often thought that perhaps the time was right for an updated version. However, it was only in the last couple of seasons that I really considered getting down to it, as it were, so when Tempus Publishing contacted me I was only too pleased to begin work again.

It was an event in 2004 and another in 2005 at Oxford that really convinced me. In 2004, Peter Seaton was busy arranging a reunion of former riders and things really took off when I realised the scheduled date for this was 23 July. It was on this date in 1949 that Swindon first opened for speedway at their Abbey Stadium home, with a challenge match against Oxford. In 2004, the two teams were going to meet again on 23 July, but on this occasion at Cowley.

I joined Peter in his quest and began concentrating on contacting ex-Oxford and Swindon riders, with a view to inviting them to Cowley. I was very fortunate to be able to contact four riders who had actually appeared in that very first meeting at Swindon, namely Dennis Gray, Alf Viccary and Jimmy Wright, who all represented the Cheetahs, and the Robins' own Ivor Atkinson. All four of these lads were able to get along to the reunion and joined in the fun, reliving their memories of old times.

The event generated great publicity, particularly on television. On a beautiful evening, Victoria Bennett of Central News Sport was interviewing both the then Oxford promoter Nigel Wagstaff and me. With a flick of the switch to the local BBC South Today channel, viewers were able to watch sports reporter Jerome Sale covering the event as well. All in all, it was a wonderful evening of nostalgia.

Then, in 2005, I was delighted to be involved in tracing Oxford's 1985 and 1986 league title-winning sides for another reunion. This was a very enjoyable experience, with many former Cheetahs coming along to watch a meeting at Cowley, followed by a golf tournament and a celebration meal the next day. It was wonderful to see the former lads who, in 1986, went through the entire league campaign without losing a single match. It was true that two home meetings fell victim to inclement weather, but that brilliant Oxford team did win all their away fixtures and took the Championship by 6 clear points from Cradley Heath. Someday, a side may equal that remarkable record, but of course a 100 per cent success rate can never be beaten.

Apart from Marvyn Cox and the late Simon Wigg, the rest of the 1986 team were present, but it was a particular honour to welcome Simon's widow, Charlie, to the event, along with their two children, Abigail and Ricki. Everyone knew Simon was also present in spirit, and what a pleasure it was to welcome Hans Nielsen, Per Sorensen, Andy Grahame, Jon Surman and Nigel De'Ath back to the scene of so many of their triumphs. Yes, a wonderful and unforgettable evening, which had the desired effect – I just had to write the book!

For this purpose, I engaged the help of prolific author Robert Bamford, not just for his computer skills, but also to draw upon the vast knowledge of the sport he has acquired over the years. Chris Broadway, John Jarvis and Geoff Parker were particularly helpful in allowing us access to their marvellous photograph collections, and also their ability to check information from their personal libraries, often without any prior notice.

I wish to thank my wife, Christine, for all her support, help, encouragement and ever-readiness to check my copy, especially on those days when things just weren't going very well!

I can't close without relating an amusing story from the 1986 season. The then co-promoter Bernard Crapper had a wicked sense of humour and I recall the occasion when I had received a letter from a lady in Sheffield who requested a photograph of the title-winning side, along with one of Bernard, who also doubled as the team manager. I duly came across him in the pits one evening and said: 'A lady wants a picture, BC, will you see to it please?' 'Of course my boy,' came the reply, and the following week sure enough there was an envelope passed on to me from Bernard, with the message, 'You wanted a picture Glynno.' I opened the envelope to find a photo inside, indeed it was a very nice picture of... Didcot Power Station! It served me right for asking!

Enjoy what I trust is a good read, as Oxford Speedway continues along another era, happily known as the Cheetahs once more.

Glynn Shailes
February 2007

1939

The cinder sport first came to Cowley on Easter Saturday, 8 April 1939, when the Oxford Motorcycle Speedway Club, under their hardworking secretary Ted Mander, moved their racing activities from their old grass circuit at Sandford-on-Thames. Much of the credit for establishing speedway at Oxford Stadium was due to the aforementioned Mr Mander, who described the new raceway as 'a short circuit rider's dream of a perfect track.' The new raceway, very different from the old grass circuit at Sandford-on-Thames, comprised of sandy soil, and was 370 yards in length. Following an inspection by Mr Laughborough, the secretary of the ACU, the Oxford club received the following compliment: 'There is no amateur club in England that has a place of such magnificence and you are to be congratulated upon securing it.'

So, on that April evening in 1939, Oxford Speedway was born, and little did Ted Mander know that he and his club were starting something that, a few years in the post-war period apart, would grow in stature and still be going strong some sixty-eight years later. To Roy Duke goes the honour of winning the first ever meeting, and throughout the summer of 1939, regular events were held on Saturday evenings. Riders usually practised on race days from 6.30p.m. to 7.30p.m., with racing starting at 8p.m., and the leading riders of the day flocked to Oxford. Not only were there individual meetings, but there was team racing as well. Although there was no league competition as such, the Oxford club contested matches against Smallford, Wisbech, High Beech and Reading. To add further interest, composite teams would sometimes be selected from the competitors on show, the first of these being Buster Yeoman's team versus Geoff Godwin's side on 1 July. Despite the declaration of the Second World War, the club continued its regular Saturday race meetings, with the final of the so-called 1939 Speedway Championship taking place on 29 October, when Geoff Godwin was triumphant. The following week saw the last meeting of the season, when a team captained by Danny Lee met opposition led by Ron Clarke.

1940

Racing resumed on 28 April 1940, when Jim Boyd, who was to join Oxford twelve years later, led his team against another captained by Geoff Godwin. Meetings were held until 9 June, when the Speedway Championship final was won by Ron Clarke, who was to become the captain of Bradford in the post-war period.

1941

Although the Second World War was far from over, the Oxford club were back in action in 1941, but the season didn't last long. In fact, just two meetings were held, on 4 May and 1 June. On the latter date, secretary Ted Mander announced that racing at the stadium would

**OXFORD MOTOR-CYCLE
SPEEDWAY CLUB**
(Affiliated to the South Midland Centre A.C.U.)
DIRT TRACK RACING
at the
OXFORD STADIUM, COWLEY, OXFORD
EVERY SATURDAY EVENING
8 p.m. till 10.15 p.m.

**AMPLE AND IDEAL ACCOMMODATION
FAST TRACK**

**ADMISSION 1/- & 1/6 (incl. Tax)
Children 6d.**

OPENING   MEETING—APRIL   8th
Gates Open at 7.0 p.m.
Hon. Secretary:——Ted Mander, 6, Barrett St., Osney, Oxford.

An advert from *Motor Racing* dated 8 April 1939 shows that dirt-track racing was held at Oxford Stadium on Saturday evenings throughout that year.

Geoff Godwin, who was a star at Oxford in the pre-war meetings. For the greater part of the hostilities, Godwin served with the Navy and rose to the rank of Lieutenant Commander.

be suspended for the duration of the war, and although peace was declared in 1945, it wouldn't be until 1949 that the roar of the speedway machine was again heard at Cowley Stadium. The final track record for the old circuit was 74.4 seconds, set by Bill Kitchen, who was to become captain of the famous Wembley Lions in the post-war speedway boom. Kitchen was one of the many riders to appear at Oxford in the early days who went on to reach the very top in league racing when it became properly established in 1946.

1948

Speedway had enjoyed the most successful period in its history in the immediate post-war period, with meetings attended by huge crowds. Indeed, it was reported in 1946 that a match between Wembley and West Ham had attracted a gate of some 85,000! Having seen racing successfully staged before the outbreak of hostilities, stadium owner Les Calcutt wanted Oxford to be part of the new boom. He promptly applied to the ACU and the Speedway Control Board for a licence and a place in the new speedway league, a Third Division having been formed in 1947. Regrettably, Mr Calcutt's efforts at that time bore no fruit, and it was not possible to obtain the necessary licences for all the alterations to the stadium that were deemed necessary by officialdom before any further speedway racing could take place, so the idea was temporarily suspended.

Promoter Les Calcutt, whose determined efforts eventually brought speedway back to Sandy Lane in 1949.

In the autumn of 1948, Mr Calcutt tried again, and this time the Speedway Control Board accepted the plans submitted by the Oxford boss. It was a major step forward, but there was still the question of obtaining a building licence, and the plan to re-launch Oxford Speedway received a setback, when, in the first instance, the application for the necessary licence was turned down.

1949

Les Calcutt wasn't a man to take a setback without a fight, and due to great efforts on his part, the authorities eventually had second thoughts and granted the necessary building licence, but not until the end of January 1949. Thus began the great seventy days when the stadium was virtually transformed. Offices, a medical room, track shops and, most importantly, a racing strip had to be constructed. Some 400 tons of earth also had to be moved in order to make proper spectator accommodation available. For the go-ahead management were hoping for, at least 10,000 regular supporters needed to back their new venture.

Whilst the Oxford management, combined with their helpers and contractors, worked around the clock to transform the stadium, there was another problem to overcome, namely the entry of the club into Third Division league speedway. Having achieved so much in such a short space of time, Mr Calcutt, together with his fellow directors, Russell Chaundy and Archer Giles, was not going to see Oxford as simply a non-league side. Their persistence eventually paid off and Oxford were accepted into the National League Division Three, with the first home league match scheduled for Thursday 21 April 1949, when the Oxford Cheetahs were born. The name Cheetahs came from the public themselves, as a result of a competition held by local newspaper, the *Oxford Mail*, to find a suitable name for the new team. Over 500 entries were received, with Cheetahs emerging as the clear winner. It was agreed that the colours for the Cheetahs would be dark blue with a yellow sash. Plans moved forward towards the opening day, when Her Grace, the Duchess of Marlborough, and Ron Johnson, the captain of New Cross Speedway, would declare the track open. But before that, the new Cheetahs would, in fact, be in action as a team, since their first match, a league encounter, was to be held at Exeter on Monday 18 April 1949.

So it was at Exeter that Ron Bear, who had joined Oxford as speedway manager, and Alf Elliott, who, like the new manager, had come from Poole, paraded the Oxford Cheetahs for the first time. Elliott had played a master role in laying the revamped track at Cowley and was also the proud skipper of the new side. It was small wonder that Oxford, who had never ridden as a team before, were heavily beaten 60-24 by high-flying Exeter, with Bert Croucher and Dennis Gray heading the Cheetahs' scorechart, yielding 9 and 7 points respectively. Three days later, Oxford were ready to perform on their own track, and just under 4,000 enthusiasts turned up to cheer their team in league action against Hastings. Rain did its best to spoil the opening, but the gods smiled on the new Cheetahs and the inclement conditions cleared in time for the ceremonies to proceed.

The printed programme, a simple twelve-page production, outlined details of the opening ceremony on page three, with music provided by the Morris Motors Band. This was followed in turn by the official opening performed by Her Grace, the Duchess of Marlborough. Ron Johnson, the famous international rider who was skipper of First Division New Cross, had been scheduled to assist with the opening ceremony but due to an injury was unable to attend, so West Ham's Australian international Aub Lawson fulfilled the role instead. The Duchess soon had those in attendance cheering when she accepted a lift on the back of Lawson's steed, although, as a result of the weather, there was little doubt she would have subsequently had a bill to pay for the cleaning of her coat. Following this, it was finally time for the racing to commence, albeit some thirty minutes late, but nobody seemed to mind.

Above: Bert Croucher was a member of the very first Cheetahs team that took to the track at Exeter on 18 April 1949. The photograph shows the Southampton-born rider in practice prior to the start of the season.

Right: Programme cover from the Cheetahs' first home match against Hastings on 21 April 1949.

OXFORD *Stadium*

OXFORD
v.
HASTINGS

National League Division 3

21 APRIL, 1949

Official Programme 6d.

Above left: West Ham's Australian star Aub Lawson assisted with the opening ceremony at Cowley in 1949.

Above right: Hastings rider Jock Grierson, who took victory in heat one of the Cheetahs' very first home meeting.

The Oxford team had one change to the programmed line-up, with Ernie Rawlins, who, like Bert Croucher, had arrived via Southampton, replacing Johnny Fry. Heat one saw Alf Elliott and Bob Aldridge represent the Cheetahs, while Dan English and Jock Grierson were the Hastings pairing. This resulted in an even share of the points, with the two Oxford lads following Grierson home. The victor was timed at 75.2 seconds, which was good considering the conditions and of course, was the first track record. In heat two, it was Ron Clark who raced away to win in a faster 73.6 seconds, with his partner Buddy Fuller in second spot and the Cheetahs' Dennis Gray third. Incidentally, Ron Clark is not to be confused with the rider who had ridden for Oxford prior to the war, whose name was Ron Clarke with the additional 'e'. Continuing with the opening meeting, Croucher won heat three, giving the home supporters a first race win to enthuse over, although this was somewhat muted since the visiting riders filled the minor scoring positions to share the points. The next win for the homesters occurred in heat five and it was a beauty that had the fans cheering themselves hoarse. It was a triumph for Alf Viccary, who was on Grierson's exhaust pipe for two laps before making his move and speeding by for an epic success. As the match went on, the Cheetahs did well to keep in the hunt, although time and again they found the Saxons sharper from the gate. In heat twelve, however, came a first 5-1 for Oxford, with Rawlins taking the chequered flag and Croucher holding the visiting duo at bay. There was to be no fairytale ending, though, and the extra experience of the visitors saw them through to victory by 47 points to 37. Although beaten, the Cheetahs certainly weren't disgraced. The scorers from this momentous meeting in the club's history were, for Oxford: Bert Croucher 10; Dennis Gray 8; Alf Elliott 6; Alf Viccary 4; Bill Downton 3; Ernie Rawlins 3; Bob Aldridge 2; Maurice Hutchens 1. For Hastings: Ron Clark 11; Jock Grierson 10; Ken Middleditch 10; Ken Smith 6; Buddy Fuller 5; Harold Tapscott 3; Dan English 1; Ken Tidbury 1.

Bristol-born Alf Elliott was responsible for
constructing the new track at Cowley and was also
the first skipper of the Cheetahs. He was to score
73.5 points in the club's first season of league activity.

Off-track, there were problems for the club to contend with as the season rolled on. Speedway manager Ron Bear left the club in July, but thankfully Henry Chandler, the greyhound racing manager, was available to take over and went on to do a fine job in charge of the Cheetahs' fortunes. Meanwhile, riders came and went. Alf Elliott, the first Oxford captain, who had played an outstanding off-track role in laying the circuit, lost form and retired in the same month that Bear departed. Meanwhile, Bob Aldridge, Maurice Hutchens and Bill Downton, all of whom had ridden in the early matches, soon disappeared from the Oxford scene. Jimmy Wright arrived from Cradley Heath in May, and Bill Kemp was another Heathen to join the Oxford camp in June, while New Zealander Frank Boyle was an additional June arrival. All three became regulars in the Cheetahs team, but showed their best form only in flashes, although Boyle became a great favourite with his wholehearted efforts. Jim Coy, on loan from Wimbledon, and Australian Bill Reynolds were other riders given opportunities, but neither were the answer to Oxford's need for team strengthening and it was not until mid-August that the Cheetahs signed a rider who could answer their need for heat-leaders. The rider concerned was a tubby little New Zealander named Bob McFarlane, who arrived via Southampton on 18 August and celebrated with 10 points against Exeter. Unfortunately, the Cheetahs lost the match by a single point, although the Kiwi's arrival had coincided with an injury to Bert Croucher, so it was a few weeks before Oxford could field a side that contained their three best riders, namely McFarlane, Croucher and Dennis Gray.

Prior to the arrival of Bob McFarlane, a very special match was raced on Saturday 23 July, when the Cheetahs provided the opposition for the very first meeting at Swindon's Abbey Stadium home. The Robins were embarking on a series of challenge matches as a non-league side, with a view to entering the Third Division in 1950. Riding at number one for Swindon was Bill Downton, who had begun the season as an Oxford rider, but had been released following a loss of form. He was to net 5 points in the match and also created his own little bit of history as it meant he had appeared in the opening meetings at both Oxford and Swindon, riding for the home team in each case. The Cheetahs ran out winners of the Blunsdon opener by 45 points to 39, with Bert Croucher heading their scoring on 11 points, while Jimmy

Wright tallied 10. Wright had received a very bad injury whilst representing Cradley Heath in a match at Exeter the previous year, but he'd made a splendid recovery after joining the Cheetahs to re-start his racing career. The rivalry between Oxford and Swindon began on that warm summer's evening and it is something that exists to this day.

On 8 September, in a league match against Leicester, the Cheetahs raced to a fine win by 48 points to 36. Bert Croucher, who had taken over the captaincy from Alf Elliott, was still absent, but Bob McFarlane was in cracking form and recorded maximum points. In the same match, Dennis Gray racked up 11 points, as well as establishing a new track record of 68.8 seconds.

No one could have predicted it at the time, but the Cheetahs were to visit Swindon again on 24 September for a league encounter, the Robins having joined the Third Division earlier in the month following the unfortunate closure of Hull. The Wiltshire outfit had taken over the fixtures of the defunct Angels and the second match-up between the two local rivals was to be a real thriller, with Swindon eventually winning by a single point, 42-41. Having won his previous three outings, the unbeaten Dennis Gray fell in the final race and although he remounted and tried to push home for the odd-point that would have clinched a draw, the effort of trying to cover the remaining 300 yards or so within the time limit proved too much, giving the Robins the narrowest of victories.

Swindon also appeared at Oxford in 1949, in a challenge match on 20 October. This resulted in a hefty 56-28 win for the Cheetahs, although the meeting was run in terrible conditions, with the rain never letting up. Both Bert Croucher and Jimmy Wright made light of the treacherous track to wrap up 12-point maximums, but it has to be said that there is no way a match would be raced in such conditions today. However, things were very different in 1949. Some years later, co-author Glynn Shailes mentioned the meeting in conversation with Henry Chandler, who remembered it well. Mr Chandler said: 'The conditions were really bad and I did consider cancelling it, but my riders came to me, pleading with me to keep it on and even offering to ride for half the regular points money!' He continued: 'Well, it went on and they raced all fourteen heats, but the second half was cancelled. I had said to them, if it goes ahead, then you ride and finish it – no six races and then off. Well, they promised – both sides – and they did complete the match, and I must tell you I paid them full points and start money so they didn't lose out. Would they have ridden for half pay? I expect so, but there was no way the Speedway Control Board or Jack Parker, the riders' representative, would have allowed it I'm sure.'

Dennis Gray, whose RAF posting was cancelled so that he could continue riding for Oxford Speedway. The Londoner headed the Cheetahs' scoring in 1949, gleaning 292 points from the league programme.

There is an interesting story about Dennis Gray, since it was well known that he was doing his National Service in the RAF during his time with Oxford. It transpired that he had been posted and, to all intents and purposes, this would have meant putting his speedway career on hold. One can, therefore, imagine Gray feeling somewhat bewildered when he was informed that the Station Commander wished to see him. As he made his way to the CO's office, he racked his brain trying to think what he'd done that could possibly result in being summoned to see the top brass. He was shown to the CO's office, saluted and then, almost to his horror, asked to sit down. 'My heart was beating faster and faster,' he later commented, 'to be summoned before the CO was one thing, but to be asked to sit down when in his presence was something else.' The CO said: 'I don't know who you know Gray, but it's somebody in high places. Your posting is cancelled and whenever possible we will take you by plane on Thursdays particularly and deliver you as near as we can to Oxford. That's all Gray, you can go.' Sometime later, the rider/airman was able to solve the mystery of his non-posting. 'When I first told Les Calcutt about the posting, he wasn't very pleased,' explained Gray, 'Oxford were bottom of the league and he was trying to strengthen his side. I was fortunate in that I was scoring a few points, but if I wasn't available he had more work to do in finding a replacement. Anyway, Mr Calcutt, as a local businessman and a member of the Chamber of Commerce, knew everyone in Oxford, including the local MP, one Quintin Hogg, who later became Baron Hailsham of St Marylebone. I believed it was he who might have whispered in the right ears on Les Calcutt's behalf. Whether I had got it 100 per cent right I wasn't sure, but many years later I learned that I had. My CO hadn't been quite right when he inferred that I knew somebody in high places as I didn't, but Mr Calcutt certainly did!'

Getting back to the story of the 1949 season, it had been one of success and disappointment. The success was the support for the sport of speedway racing, which saw the Oxford public respond in magnificent fashion, with crowds increasing throughout the year. Meanwhile, the obvious disappointment was the fact that the Cheetahs finished as wooden spoonists in the league table. In a mammoth league campaign consisting of forty-eight matches, the side had won on just eleven occasions, while suffering thirty-six losses and drawing just once. There is no doubt that of their eleven victories, the one that gave both supporters and riders the greatest satisfaction was the win over visiting Yarmouth on 14 July. The Bloaters were riding high in the league table at the time and came to Cowley confident of success, but it was Oxford, with Croucher, Viccary, Kemp and Boyle riding with great tenacity, who emerged as the winners by 43 points to 41. At the time, it was only the third league success of the year for Oxford, but it was a victory to savour.

The general failure of the team to click as a unit was understandable, being summed up by their speedway manager, Henry Chandler, in this way: 'The Cheetahs were born into league speedway racing, almost before it was possible to do any preliminary teamwork at all. We looked around and got together whatever riders were available, and many of them did not quite make the grade.' Mr Chandler's words were true, of course, as it took the Oxford management some time to get a settled side together. Injuries to Bert Croucher, who was a great success, and the absence of the inspiring Dennis Gray, due to RAF duties, certainly did not help the Cheetahs' cause. Both riders, who came on loan from Southampton and Wimbledon respectively, held their team places on merit, while Alf Viccary, who came on loan from Harringay, also held a regular team spot. He wasn't quite as successful as either Croucher or Gray, but he had his moments during the season, which included a fine 12-point tally against Liverpool. Viccary was, in fact, the one rider in the Cheetahs line-up with a 100 per cent record of league appearances. Briefly looking at the statistics, Gray was the team's leading scorer over the Third Division campaign, totalling 292 points. Support came from Croucher (262) and Viccary (227), whilst Frank Boyle (154), Jimmy Wright (131) and Bob McFarlane (129) made useful contributions.

Promoter Les Calcutt remained determined to put the year's problems behind him and plan for the future. Writing in the final programme of the season, a challenge match against

Alf Viccary arrived at Oxford on loan from Harringay in 1949 and held down a regular team spot throughout the season. He had a very good campaign, scoring 227 points in the league and giving great support to the side's top two of Dennis Gray and Bert Croucher.

Walthamstow, he stated: 'We intend to carry out a strengthening up process, by adding to the existing team, new riders of proven calibre during the closed season, and look forward to the 1950 Cheetahs being a truly formidable force in league racing.' Little did Mr Calcutt know how true his words would turn out to be!

NATIONAL LEAGUE DIVISION THREE

Team	Mts	Won	Drn	Lst	For	Agn	Pts
Hanley	48	35	1	12	2,336	1,674	71
Yarmouth	48	35	1	12	2,330	1,676	71
Tamworth	48	33	0	15	2,294	1,722	66
Halifax	48	28	2	18	2,212	1,792	58
Plymouth	48	28	2	18	2,096	1,917	58
Poole	48	27	0	21	1,962.5	2,053.5	54
Exeter	48	24	0	24	2,038	1,973	48
Hastings	48	21	1	26	1,936	2,080	43
Liverpool	48	19	0	29	1,842	2,172	38
Leicester	48	17	1	30	1,878	2,140	35
Swindon	48	15	1	32	1,809	2,207	31
Rayleigh	48	14	0	34	1,708	2,295	28
Oxford	**48**	**11**	**1**	**36**	**1,637.5**	**2,377.5**	**23**

NOTE: Swindon took over the results and fixtures of Hull, who withdrew after completing thirty-five matches.

1950

During the winter of 1949 and the spring of 1950, the Oxford bosses began team building for the forthcoming season. The matter became urgent when they learned their top three scorers from the previous year, all of whom were loaned, would not be available. Bert Croucher decided to retire from racing in order to concentrate on his business affairs, while both Wimbledon and Harringay had noted the progress of Dennis Gray and Alf Viccary, so they had to return to their respective parent clubs. That meant replacements had to be found and Oxford made a great start when they signed Harry Saunders from Tamworth. The rider had scored 430.5 league points during 1949 and was one of the Third Division's leading riders. His transfer fee was £750, which was a huge amount of money at the time, but Mr Calcutt figured he was worth it and quickly made him captain of the 1950 Cheetahs. Another signing, and a rider with plenty of experience too, was Bill Osborne from Walthamstow. Meanwhile, a former cycle speedway rider also came on board from Wembley whose name was Raymond Brown, although everyone knew him as Buster. At the pre-season trials, the large crowd which gathered to see the riders go through their paces saw a tough-looking, fair-haired speedster lapping the Cowley circuit at some speed. This was surely no young hopeful, they thought – and they were right. It was an experienced rider named Eric Irons, who had sat out the 1949 campaign after two very successful seasons with Cradley Heath. It didn't take Les Calcutt long to get his signature on a contract and make him a Cheetah.

Pat Clarke was a big signing for the Cheetahs in 1950, having been snapped up for £250 from Rayleigh. The Londoner proved a brilliant acquisition, top-scoring for the club with 326.5 points from their National League Division Three fixtures.

Another acquisition, and perhaps the most important of all, was the £250 spent to bring 1949 Rayleigh skipper Pat Clarke to Sandy Lane. Unfortunately, Clarke's clearance wasn't received from the Control Board in time for him to appear in the club's opening meeting of the season, a challenge match against Poole. Instead, the frustrated rider had to view the action from the pits. Oxford, however, had suffered cruel luck even before the season had got underway. Harry Saunders had looped-the-loop at the starting gate during practice, and in the process received a back injury that was to sideline him until June. As if that wasn't enough, after winning his opening race against Poole, Bill Osborne took a nasty fall in his second outing and suffered a broken leg, so he too was out of action for a spell. It is interesting to note at this time that, despite the great success the side went on to achieve in 1950, at no time were they able to track their strongest line-up. Oxford went on to win the opening challenge fixture against Poole by 48 points to 34 with some solid scoring throughout the side. The Pirates, though, were too reliant on just two riders, with Dick Howard bagging a 12-point full house and Cyril Quick notching 11 points. Quick only lost out on a maximum to Eric Irons in heat nine, while Howard had surely never ridden better in the colours of the Dorset side.

The following week saw a National Trophy tie against Liverpool. Pat Clarke had been cleared to ride for the Cheetahs and did so, as second reserve. He was clearly pleased to make his debut and celebrated with 11 points in a crushing 76-32 victory. The rest of the side also contributed with points all down the line, the pick of the bunch being Eric Irons, who romped to a five-ride maximum.

Happily, the Cheetahs were led from the front by Pat Clarke, Bob McFarlane and Eric Irons, and together with great improvement from many of the riders retained from 1949, they soon became a side to be feared. Wherever the team went, so did a huge following of fans proudly sporting the club's blue and yellow colours, be it in the form of scarves, hats, badges or all three.

Harry Saunders linked with the Cheetahs for a transfer fee of £750 from Tamworth in 1950 and was handed the club captaincy. Following an injury setback, he was to tally 151 points from Oxford's league fixtures that season.

Although many matches raced by the Cheetahs provided excellent racing and gave the supporters much to cheer, it was the encounters with old rivals Swindon that caused the most excitement. Having disposed of Liverpool in the National Trophy, Oxford drew the Robins in the next round, and the first of the two legs saw the Cheetahs entertain the Wiltshire side on 20 April. The road between Oxford and Swindon was packed with coaches carrying the Robins' supporters to Cowley. What made things even more exciting was the fact that Swindon had also begun the season in cracking style, and certainly in the early weeks of the campaign, both teams were up there at the top of the league table. The crowd that filled the Oxford stadium saw a good meeting, with the Cheetahs eventually winning 62-46. It certainly looked encouraging, being able to take a 16-point advantage to Blunsdon two days later. Oxford's scoring was again solid, with their two New Zealand boys in tip-top form, Frank Boyle netting 14 points, while Bob McFarlane tallied 13. For Swindon, George Craig was outstanding with 14 points, whilst former Cheetah Bill Downton enjoyed a good evening, scoring 9 points. Next in line was Danny Malone, who contributed 8 points, but the rest did very little.

The journey to Swindon for the return match on 22 April was equally as exciting as the Robins' visit to Sandy Lane. Buses streamed into the Blunsdon car parks, and there were, as with the first leg, a number of supporters who made the trip by train. A gate, reported by the Swindon promoter, of 13,000 in round figures, crammed into the Abbey Stadium to witness the home side fight back and force a last-heat decider. After heat seventeen, the score stood at 106-103 to Oxford on aggregate and, although Danny Malone streaked away to win the final race, the Cheetahs' pairing of Pat Clarke and Eric Irons rode sensibly to keep the other home representative, Reg Lambourne, at the back. The duo's efforts meant Oxford had won by 3 points and thereby qualified to meet Exeter in the next round.

The Cheetahs subsequently defeated the Falcons by 136 points to 78 on aggregate and progressed to meet Tamworth in the final of the qualifying round. They were in a mean mood when they visited the Fazeley venue for the first leg, hammering the Tammies by 70 points to 38. Believe it or not, the Tamworth lads rode much better at Cowley, but were still beaten 67-41 all the same. Having won 137-79 overall, Oxford qualified to meet Second Division Halifax in the eliminating competition. When the Dukes visited Sandy Lane, they found the Oxford boys in very good form. Indeed, a wonderful display saw them claim a 68-40 success thanks to a 15-point tally from Frank Boyle, who was the only home rider to defeat the immaculate 'Black Prince' Arthur Forrest. In truth, the Yorkshire outfit relied too heavily on Forrest and one can only wonder how they would have fared without his 17-point contribution. In the return match up at The Shay, the Oxford riders found the banked sweeping bends difficult to master. In spite of this, they put up a terrific fight before going down by 71 points to 37. Halifax owed much to reserve Al 'Pancho' Allison, who posted an 18-point maximum, while the leading performers for the Cheetahs were Bob McFarlane and Eric Irons, both of whom recorded 8 points. McFarlane, in fact, clocked the fastest time of the evening, but it was the Dukes who proceeded to the next round courtesy of a 111-105 aggregate victory.

Following their exit from the National Trophy, Oxford were left to concentrate on their league programme and they did well too. However, there was a bit of a shock when Poole came to Cowley on 29 June and forced a 42-42 draw. The match culminated in a last-heat decider and saw Pat Clarke race to the flag, while in the battle for third place Eric Irons held Terry Small at the back to ensure that honours ended even. There was little doubt that Oxford were as able a side on their travels as they were at Cowley, and there were a number of victories on their opponents' circuits to savour, but the sweetest of them all was the hammering of near neighbours Swindon at Blunsdon by a 54-30 scoreline. The Cheetahs knocked up six 5-1s to the Robins' one, and there was just a single drawn heat, which occurred in the very first race of the match. Harry Saunders had, by this time, made a track return, marking the occasion with 11 points in a 51-33 success over visiting Tamworth. However, he had a bad night at Swindon and failed to score. This was more than compensated for by his teammates, though, who collectively were bang on form.

On 13 July, it was the turn of Oxford to welcome the Robins to Cowley for what proved to be another marvellous advert for the sport, played out before a huge attendance. Making his debut for the Cheetahs was local boy Frank Johnson, riding as reserve for the absent Buster Brown. Unfortunately, 'Johnno' failed to score in his two outings, but he gave his opponents a few anxious moments, nevertheless. Johnson was to serve many clubs in his speedway career and was a real crowd pleaser, with speedway folk flocking to see him in action. Going back to the match, the home fans were horrified when, with just one heat to go, Swindon held a two-point lead. The final race of a pulsating meeting was to be memorable for both sets of supporters; firstly there were the superb efforts of Frank Evans to win the match for Swindon, and countering that was the outstanding team riding of Pat Clarke and Frank Boyle, who came from behind to card a 5-1 and, more importantly, snatch a 43-41 victory from the jaws of defeat.

On 28 July, the Cheetahs appeared in a league fixture at Exeter and, regrettably, Frank Boyle was involved in a bad crash, which left him with a broken ankle and meant his season was over. Small wonder that Oxford lost 48-36 as Boyle was enjoying a superb year in the saddle. Although he was to make a full recovery, he never again showed his consistent brilliance on the track, instead he tended to be up one week and down the next.

The loss of the popular ginger-haired Frank Boyle was eased somewhat because Bill Osborne was ready to return to the saddle, and to further strengthen his side, Mr Calcutt dipped into the Oxford coffers to purchase Brian Wilson from Tamworth. The incoming rider had enjoyed a productive season with the Tammies, but in the event, he was to never really settle at Cowley. This was unfortunate, but at least the Cheetahs' supporters could see that the club's management weren't afraid to spend money when it was thought necessary.

Poole returned to Sandy Lane and lost a real thriller by a single point, the result being Oxford 42.5 Poole 41.5. Then came a match to remember on 24 August, when Leicester were the visitors. In truly awful conditions, the Hunters emerged victorious by 45 points to 39. Jock Grierson raced to a 12-point maximum, while Lionel Benson and veteran Harwood Pike hit 9 points apiece. The three seemed to excel in the rain, as their side adapted much better to the dreadful conditions than the Cheetahs. Brian Wilson made his Oxford debut and netted 4 points, but Harry Saunders, Eric Irons and Ernie Rawlins were all badly off form, totalling just 6 points between them.

Winning form returned for the following month, with Oxford still topping the league standings. There was one match to forget though and this occurred at Leicester on 8 September, when the Cheetahs went down to an unbelievable 64-17 defeat, with only Bob McFarlane recording a race win for the under-fire visitors.

As the season drew to its close, a three-team competition was arranged involving Oxford, Swindon and Poole. This was entitled the Autumn Cup and saw the three clubs racing each other on a home and away basis. The Cheetahs entertained Swindon on 5 October and convincingly won 53-31. Both Pat Clarke and Harry Saunders posted 12-point maximums, but the real talking point was the performance of Ernie Rawlins, who registered two storming wins from the reserve berth. The excellent form of these three Cheetahs continued for their visit to Blunsdon two days later, when Oxford went to town with a vengeance. Clarke recorded another unbeaten 12-points and, for good measure, set a new track record of 75.2 seconds. There were also 12-point maximums for both Saunders and Rawlins, plus a tally of 8+2 from Eric Irons. A dejected Swindon side had just one race win, which came from George Craig in heat eight. At Poole on 9 October, the Cheetahs gave a good account of themselves, but were beaten 49-35, with Rawlins top scoring on 10 points as his purple patch continued. The final match at Cowley had the programme printers, Hall, again producing an excellent souvenir issue, with the spires of Oxford shown on the cover in all their glory. Poole provided the opposition, but the meeting resulted in a 48-36 win for the Cheetahs and the Autumn Cup was theirs. Clarke once more led the scoring with 10+1 points, losing only to Ken Middleditch in the opening race. His bonus point came in the final heat when he finished second to teammate Bill Osborne.

Oxford Cheetahs 1950. From left to right, back row: Buster Brown, Pat Clarke, Bob McFarlane, Ernie Rawlins, Bill Kemp, Eric Irons, Frank Boyle. Front, on bike: Harry Saunders.

With the trophy in his hand, Pat Clarke gets pushed off on his celebration lap after taking victory in the Third Division Riders' Championship at Walthamstow on 23 October 1950.

Perhaps Pat Clarke's finest hour occurred at Walthamstow on 23 October in the Third Division Riders' Championship. He recorded a 15-point maximum to win the event and proved he was a worthy Champion. Not only was he the best rider on view, but in one of his races he still took victory despite having a puncture. The prestigious meeting took place before a crowd of 23,000, which was Walthamstow's largest ever paid gate for the sport.

So, with the league title and promotion being theirs, Oxford also had the Third Division Riders' Champion. This was a remarkable achievement in only the club's second season of post-war racing. Fittingly, it was Pat Clarke who headed the team's league scoring over the course of the season, finishing with a tally of 326.5 points. Backing his wholehearted efforts were Bob McFarlane (243) and Eric Irons (222), while Bill Kemp (182), Frank Boyle (171), Harry Saunders (151), Buster Brown (123) and Ernie Rawlins (109) also topped the century mark. Those now far off days of 1950 were truly special, when the crowds at Cowley were tremendous. Indeed, it was estimated that between 800 and 1,000 people had turned up for a pre-season practice! The atmosphere was always electric, and it was commonplace for the Cheetahs' supporters to be in their favourite spot soon after six o'clock because if they weren't, someone else would have bagged it!

NATIONAL LEAGUE DIVISION THREE

Team	Mts	Won	Drn	Lst	For	Agn	Pts
Oxford	**36**	**26**	**2**	**8**	**1,711.5**	**1,297.5**	**54**
Poole	36	23	3	10	1,625.5	1,392.5	49
Leicester	36	21	0	15	1,637.5	1,372.5	42
Swindon	36	19	1	16	1,514	1,497	39
Aldershot	36	18	1	17	1,526.5	1,481.5	37
Tamworth	36	17	0	19	1,432	1,580	34
Exeter	36	16	1	19	1,533	1,481	33
Liverpool	36	14	1	21	1,383	1,626	29
Rayleigh	36	12	0	24	1,318	1,699	24
St Austell	36	9	1	26	1,380	1,634	19

1951

For supporters of the Oxford Cheetahs in 1951, the start of the season couldn't come quickly enough. After just two years of post-war league racing, the team was about to embark on a campaign in the Second Division of the National League, having gained that right the proper way; by promotion as a result of winning the Third Division title.

Most of the riders who had played a part in the 1950 success were available for selection, the exceptions being Buster Brown and Jimmy Wright. This was because Wright moved to Cardiff, while Brown initially returned to his parent club, Wembley, before going on loan to Swindon. To add strength to the side, promoter Les Calcutt shelled out a tidy sum to purchase Poole skipper Cyril Quick. This looked like good business as Quick was a rider of considerable experience, having joined Bristol in 1948, prior to linking with the Pirates towards the end of that same season. He went on to be Poole's captain and leading scorer in both 1949 and 1950, having recorded respective league tallies of 386.5 and 322 points. He appeared to be the ideal man to add a bit of bite to the Oxford team.

The Cheetahs opened the season with a challenge match at Swindon on 24 March and won an exciting track battle by 44 points to 40. The success was largely thanks to a 10-point haul from Ernie Rawlins, who showed that the brilliant form he'd discovered at the end of

Bill Kemp enjoyed a fruitful campaign for the Cheetahs in 1951, scoring 187 points from the league programme.

1950 would be ongoing. The match marked the club debut of Cyril Quick, who notched 5+1 points, while Bill Kemp looked particularly sharp with an identical tally from his two programmed rides. Kemp also won the Cheetahs' Scurry race in the second half, beating teammates Colin Clarke, Brian Wilson and new boy Quick.

The following Monday, 26 March, Oxford opened their doors with a challenge match against Leicester, but the meeting was to prove disastrous for the home supporters. As at the end of the 1950 season, the Hunters showed they still had an Indian sign over the Cheetahs as they raced to a runaway win by 55 points to 28. Every one of eight fast-starting Leicester lads registered at least one race win, with Oxford having no answer whatsoever. Frank Boyle headed a disappointing home scorechart with 6 points, his total including one of only two heat wins secured by the side. Bob McFarlane gained the other, with the 3 points being his total score for the evening. Cyril Quick scored just 4 points, but then so did Bill Osborne and Ernie Rawlins. Having also been well and truly beaten earlier in the day at Leicester by a 62-22 scoreline, the Oxford team and their supporters were, with some justification, sick of the sight of the Hunters.

On 29 March, the Cheetahs entertained Hanley in another challenge fixture and on this occasion the homesters rode more like the team of old, winning 45-38. Pat Clarke, who'd ridden at Leicester and scored just 1 point, having missed the Oxford opener, was back in the side and revealed all his old form to notch 10 points. Looking down the line, Cyril Quick carded his first win in the Cheetahs' colours, when taking heat three. Despite this success, he only added a further 3 points to his total and really looked unhappy. Also, the Sandy Lane fans noted the performance of Bill Kemp in the second half of the programme, when he knocked up a couple of wins and a second-place finish. His inclusion in the team surely wouldn't be long in coming.

Southampton visited Cowley on 5 April for a Kemsley Shield encounter, a competition for all the Second Division teams, split into three regions, North, Midland and South, with Oxford in the latter group. Bill Kemp was brought into the side at reserve, replacing Eric Irons. Riding for Southampton, also in a reserve berth, was 1949 Oxford captain Bert Croucher, who was having another bash at speedway following a season's retirement. The Cheetahs won the meeting 48-35, with Frank Boyle leading the scoring on 10 points, while Kemp justified his selection, scoring 4 points from two outings. Regrettably, yet again Cyril Quick was a failure, netting just 3 points and Mr Calcutt could be forgiven for wondering if there was an Oxford jinx. Good money had been spent on Brian Wilson in 1950 and Quick in the current season, yet both rode the Cowley circuit as if they had never seen it before. However, both, when visiting Oxford in the past, had performed well.

When the very strong Norwich team visited Cowley for a Kemsley Shield fixture, Cyril Quick was down as the second reserve, and with no Ernie Rawlins, Oxford rode out of their skins to defeat the Stars 50-34. Second-half trials were given to Herbie King of Newcastle, who actually lived in Ascot, with a view to signing the rider, but that evening's success, with Frank Boyle and Bill Osborne outstanding, did show that when the Cheetahs were all on form as a team, they could beat anyone.

Oxford went on to surprise many folk in speedway by winning the Kemsley Southern Shield, and it has to be said they were deserved winners at that. There was no big star as such in the Cheetahs' line-up, but what they did have was eight riders who were all capable of scoring at least half-a-dozen points in a match. Following the victories over Southampton and Norwich, they carved out further successes over Coventry (53-30) on 19 April and Yarmouth (52-32) seven days later, before wrapping up their home programme by defeating Walthamstow 49-35 on 3 May. On their travels, a narrow 43-41 defeat at Southampton was followed by excellent wins at Coventry (47-37), Walthamstow (45-39) and Yarmouth (48-36). Having done enough to win the competition, the Cheetahs completed their Kemsley Shield fixtures at Norwich on 12 May, losing 51-33.

In the National Trophy, Oxford entertained Exeter in a first round tie on 10 May. The Cheetahs again hit form collectively and slaughtered the unfortunate boys from Devon by 80 points to 28. They all scored well, with Ernie Rawlins and Pat Clarke outstanding. Only Exeter's Don Hardy offered any resistance to the onslaught, recording 8 points from his six rides.

On Whit Monday 14 May, Oxford journeyed to the County Ground for the second leg of their National Trophy tie. After winning his first outing, disaster struck for Pat Clarke in heat six when he fell and sustained a fractured leg, which was to keep him out of the saddle for the rest of the season. Reserve Eric Irons filled in for Clarke and rode as well as he'd ever done for the Cheetahs to score 12 points, an effort that saw his team safely through on aggregate, even though Exeter took the honours on the night by 60 points to 47.

Oxford met Yarmouth in the second round of the National Trophy and travelled to the 'Bloater Pond' on 22 May. Riding for the home side was Cyril Quick, who had been released to try his luck elsewhere, as indeed had Brian Wilson, who linked with Aldershot. The match resulted in a 63-44 win for the Bloaters, with Quick netting 11 points and looking the sort of rider that Oxford had hoped he would have been.

The Cheetahs had moved to sign Herbie King from Newcastle, and he'd made his debut in a league match against Southampton on 17 May – unfortunately failing to score. In the home leg of their National Trophy tie with Yarmouth, King netted 5 points, but it was former Oxford rider Cyril Quick whose victory in heat seventeen made certain that the Bloaters would proceed to the next round. The final result on the night was Oxford 53 Yarmouth 47.

A league match at home to Hanley on 31 May saw another signing, Roger Wise, make his debut for Oxford, having joined via Bristol. The Swindon-born racer had lost his team place with the Bulldogs amidst the cut and thrust of the First Division, but his wealth of experience was just what the Cheetahs needed and against the Potters he notched a creditable 8+1 points in a 49-35 victory.

A memorable league encounter took place on 7 June when Edinburgh arrived in town, led by Jack Young, the brilliant Australian. In a great all-round team performance, the Cheetahs defeated the Monarchs by 45 points to 38, with Ernie Rawlins showing great form. In heat seven, he even led Young until the Aussie went through a gap that almost wasn't there. However, despite the crowd getting a trifle upset, the sporting Rawlins made it clear that Young hadn't touched him. He beat him fair and square. Young was to visit Oxford again on 12 July for a World Championship qualifying round and he swept to victory with a superb 15-point maximum. It is fair to say that the Oxford supporters in attendance weren't surprised when he eventually took the world title at Wembley on 20 September, in the process becoming the only rider from a lower league ever to do so.

Oxford entertained their 'nearest and dearest' Swindon in a challenge match on 14 June. There were no league meetings between the two sides during the season, just a couple of challenge encounters and this was one. The Cheetahs had won at Swindon in the opening match of the season, and in this encounter they really went on the rampage to triumph 58-26 with Bill Kemp recording a paid maximum. Good wins over Liverpool, Newcastle and Cradley Heath thrilled the Oxford public, while Coventry forced a 42-42 draw on 28 June. Newcastle's visit took place on 19 July and during the second half Swedish rider Bertil Carlsson had some outings and showed himself to be well up to Second Division standard. The success over Liverpool occurred on 21 June, when the final result stood at 50-34, and in the second half the Oxford management arranged a special attraction, which saw Ernie Rawlins face Wimbledon wonder boy Ronnie Moore in a series of match races. Moore showed his undoubted class to comfortably take victory by two races to nil and proved a very popular visitor to Cowley.

There was a setback when Norwich stole the league points from a visit to Oxford on 9 August. A couple of engine failures for Bill Osborne cost the side dearly, as they slumped to a 44-40 defeat. Prior to that, the Sandy Lane regulars were surprised during Motherwell's visit on 2 August, when, in the last heat of the match, Keith Gurtner was a good winner in a track record time of 66.0 seconds. The Eagles' representative was chased hard throughout by Harry Saunders, who himself had clocked a fast time of 66.6 seconds in the opening race. Another Scottish side, Glasgow, came on 30 August, when a Festival of Britain contest was held in the second half. Saunders took a nasty toss in the evening's opening race and, following his second outing, was ruled out of the remainder of the match. However, Herbie King enjoyed his best ever meeting for the Cheetahs with a 10-point score, while Roger Wise tallied 9 points courtesy of three excellent heat wins. Their efforts helped Oxford to a 47-37 success and Wise carried his good form into the second half by winning the Festival of Britain trophy.

Motherwell's Australian rider Keith Gurtner established a track record time of 66.0 seconds at Cowley in the last heat of a league encounter on 2 August 1951.

On 1 September, a Test match at Swindon pitched the England 'C' team against New Zealand. Both Bob McFarlane of the Cheetahs and Coventry's Charlie New were selected for the Kiwis, but there was a snag. The Coventry promoter, Charles Ochiltree, refused to release New, claiming, with justification, that he had spent £600 to buy the rider from Sheffield, and that the fee had been paid for New to score points for the Bees and not New Zealand in a junior Test match. By coincidence, that same day Oxford were visiting Coventry in the Midland Cup and the attitude of the Cheetahs' bosses was that if the Bees would release New, then they would reciprocate by releasing McFarlane. However, Coventry refused, so Oxford instructed McFarlane to report to Brandon instead of Blunsdon. The Bees went on to win the match 59-37 and New headed their scorechart with 14 points. McFarlane, meanwhile, was the Cheetahs' best performer on 13 points. Oxford had secured a 58-38 first-leg victory at Cowley on 16 August, but it was Coventry who went through by the narrowest of margins, 97-95 on aggregate. Over at Swindon, the Kiwis defeated England 57-51 in a real thriller, with Bruce Abernethy, who rode in place of New due to a special dispensation, topping the victor's scoring with 12 points. Last-minute selection Laurie Holland, who arrived late, still totalled 8 points and played an important part in New Zealand's success.

After a home meeting against Yarmouth on 6 September, the Oxford team embarked on a northern tour, taking in matches at Motherwell, Edinburgh and Fleetwood. Upon their return they originally had an open date on 13 September, but in an effort to give the supporters a meaningful meeting the management approached First Division Bristol to try and arrange an inter-league challenge match. However, upon learning of this the Oxford riders refused to appear in such a meeting for their usual Second Division pay rates. Henry Chandler reported that he had never dreamt rates of pay would be an issue for his riders. Indeed, if there was a problem over money, he expected it to come from the Bristol lads, who mightn't have been keen to race for Division Two rates. This wasn't the case, though, and apparently the top-flight side were happy to oblige. The reason behind the decision of the Oxford riders was because the Speedway Riders' Association had been actively trying to establish that Division One rates of pay should apply for all riders engaged in any sort of racing where riders from the top-flight were participating. The Oxford bosses, in line with other promoters, did not agree that any arrangement had ever been made by what were described as proper negotiations between the promoters and the SRA. The whole matter, according to the Cheetahs' management, remained in abeyance for early settlement at the highest level. The Oxford riders were, therefore, acting in accordance with the advice from their own association, so it was wrong to suggest, as many did, that there was a 'terrible rift' between them and their promotion. Regrettably, with no agreement forthcoming, the proposed meeting was cancelled and the date of 13 September remained a blank day in the Cheetahs' calendar.

Yet another side from north of the border journeyed down on 22 September, when Ashfield arrived complete with Ron Johnson in their line-up. The Australian had lost form, so was trying to establish himself with the Glasgow-based club, but he failed to score in the match at Cowley. It was indeed sad to see a once great rider struggling, but at least he received a warm welcome from the terraces.

The penultimate home match of the season was against Walthamstow on 27 September, and again the Oxford lads showed their displeasure at wet conditions. The only rider bearing the Cheetahs' blue and yellow colours to master the tricky circuit was Roger Wise, who posted 7 points as the Wolves ran out 47-33 victors. The season ended with a league fixture versus bogey side Leicester on 4 October, when a fine souvenir programme was again on sale, produced by Hall the Printers Ltd. Regrettably, from an Oxford perspective, the Hunters were right in the groove, with visiting captain Len Williams scorching to a fine 12-point maximum and receiving solid support from Les Beaumont and Lionel Benson. Meanwhile, with 9 points apiece, Bill Kemp and Bill Osborne were the highest scorers for the Cheetahs as the side crashed to a hefty 52-32 defeat.

Above left: Londoner Bill Osborne was Oxford's leading rider in 1951, with 203 points to his name from the league campaign.

Above right: Jack Young pictured with the World Championship trophy at Wembley Stadium on 20 September 1951. Oxford promoter Les Calcutt always introduced the Australian as 'Jack Maximum Young', such was the high regard in which he held him. It wouldn't have at all surprised Mr Calcutt when 'Youngie' took the sport's most prestigious honour as a Second Division rider with Edinburgh.

All things considered, Oxford could be satisfied with their first season of Division Two racing and a final position of twelfth place in a sixteen-team league. They recorded twelve wins, two draws, and tasted defeat on sixteen occasions to leave everyone wondering how different things might have been if Pat Clarke had been fit. Early in the year, despite a poor start, the Cheetahs had ridden with confidence and some solid performances saw them win the Kemsley Shield. Henry Chandler juggled with his side, and it is interesting to note that for much of the campaign Oxford did in fact operate a squad system, giving every rider on the books a chance to make good. In the scoring stakes, Bill Osborne reached the heady heights of pole position, totalling 203 points in the league. Not far behind, both Bill Kemp (187) and Ernie Rawlins (183), who were reserves for much of 1950, came on in leaps and bounds to fully merit their team places. Skipper Harry Saunders was next in line with 155 points, and while the form of Frank Boyle (113), Eric Irons (107) and Bob McFarlane (105) could be described as patchy, they still topped the ton mark. Off track, the Oxford Supporters' Club was booming, with meetings every Sunday night at The Cape of Good Hope for billiards and darts or just a drink and a speedway chat.

No promoter was willing to spend money if the need arose more than Les Calcutt, and he must have been frustrated when riders like Brian Wilson and Cyril Quick, who had good reputations, failed at Cowley. Another rider who ought to have shone but didn't was Australian Doug Ible, who appeared in two league matches and didn't score a point, yet in 1950 he had recorded 245 league points for Aldershot. Regrettably, he was another major disappointment, although nobody could say that Mr Calcutt didn't try, and try hard, to strengthen the team.

NATIONAL LEAGUE DIVISION TWO

Team	Mts	Won	Drn	Lst	For	Agn	Pts
Norwich	30	24	0	6	1,526	990	48
Leicester	30	19	0	11	1,350	1,169	38
Edinburgh	30	18	0	12	1,333	1,179	36
Coventry	30	16	3	11	1,311	1,199	35
Walthamstow	30	17	0	13	1,394	1,116	34
Halifax	30	17	0	13	1,300	1,219	34
Motherwell	30	16	1	13	1,277	1,237	33
Ashfield	30	16	0	14	1,287	1,228	32
Hanley	30	15	0	15	1,242	1,268	30
Glasgow	30	14	1	15	1,303	1,215	29
Yarmouth	30	13	1	16	1,158	1,355	27
Oxford	**30**	**12**	**2**	**16**	**1,183**	**1,330**	**26**
Liverpool	30	12	1	17	1,211	1,300	25
Fleetwood	30	9	2	19	1,049	1,453	20
Cradley Heath	30	9	0	21	1,139	1,372	18
Newcastle	30	7	1	22	1,039	1,472	15

NOTE: Sheffield withdrew prior to riding a single league match; Southampton withdrew after completing seven fixtures, with their record expunged from the table.

1952

The supporters had every reason to be optimistic at the beginning of the 1952 season, as the Oxford promotion attempted to assemble a winning side. There were the usual comings and goings, but most importantly Pat Clarke had fully recovered from his broken leg. On the downside, New Zealander Bob McFarlane would be missing, having decided to remain in his homeland, where he was reported to be rhubarb farming. Off the track there were some changes too, with Dickie Worth and Fred Beckett joining the promoting company, who traded simply as 'Oxford Speedway'.

The train really came off the rails when, out of the blue, Pat Clarke shook the management by requesting a transfer, stating that he wanted to compete in Division One racing. Needless to say, it wasn't long before he was snapped up, with West Ham gaining his signature. However, Russell Chaundy, who had taken over the main promotional responsibilities when Les Calcutt unfortunately fell ill, reacted by purchasing Jim Boyd from defunct Walthamstow. Boyd was a rider of great experience, who had often ridden at the Sandy Lane circuit before the Second World War. He was seen as just the man to replace the departing Clarke, and with most of the other Oxford favourites available, things all of a sudden perked up again down Cowley way. One rather surprising change was that Harry Saunders ceased to be the Cheetahs' captain, this honour for 1952 was given to Bill Osborne. Meanwhile, aside from Bob McFarlane, another rider not returning to the camp was Eric Irons, who instead linked with Wolverhampton.

Oxford opened the season with a fine 51-30 victory over Cradley Heath, with Harry Saunders racing to a 12-point maximum. The soon to be departing Pat Clarke scored 6 points, while new boy Jim Boyd tallied 5. Then there was a visit from Leicester, who again put one

Jim Boyd hailed from Maidenhead in Berkshire and joined the Cheetahs from defunct Walthamstow in 1952. He enjoyed an excellent season to head the Oxford scoring with 264 points from the league programme.

over the Cheetahs from both a racing and the weather point of view. Run on a mud bath, the visitors won 45-38, with the Hunters' skipper Len Williams carding 11 points. For Oxford, Boyd hit 10 points, while Clarke bade farewell with just 2.

On 11 April, the Cheetahs travelled to Leicester with a seven-man team, including novice Tony Wintour. Just prior to the racing they signed Ron Wilson, a rider who had lost his place in the Hunters' side and was available for transfer. Although Oxford lost by 50 points to 34, Wilson showed good form at his old home base, scoring 7. Leading the way was Harry Saunders with 9 points, while Bill Osborne scored 8. However, it was on Easter Monday afternoon that Oxford rode a match in the wet, which was to shake the speedway world. This occurred at Poole, who had won the Third Division Championship in 1951 and had begun their days in the next rung up the speedway ladder with away successes at Liverpool and Edinburgh. The Pirates were a formidable outfit at Wimborne Road, but on the night the Oxford boys rode their hearts out. Poole held a 38-34 advantage after heat twelve, only for Bill Kemp and Herbie King to level the scores at 39-39 courtesy of a magical 5-1. In the last heat, Osborne streaked away to win, and complete a superb paid maximum, thereby securing a wonderful 42-42 draw. Looking in a little more detail at the Cheetahs' performances on the night, Frank Boyle failed to score and had three machine failures, while Saunders was a non-starter in three of his heats and he too failed to score. Kemp had three race wins and an engine failure, and Ernie Lessiter suffered a couple of falls, yet Oxford still claimed a league point. As things were to pan out, the significance of this became more obvious. Poole went on to win the Second Division Championship, hammering most sides that visited the Wimborne Road raceway, with the Cheetahs being the only team to come away with a point. However, as the record books show, it was Oxford who finished the 1952 campaign with the wooden spoon!

Despite the draw at Poole, the management realised further strengthening was necessary, and for the home match against Coventry on 24 April, Jim Gregory made his debut and scored 6+1 points in a 44-40 win. The signing of Gregory, who arrived via Wimbledon, was to prove a winner as the season progressed, for while other riders puzzlingly lost form, he most certainly didn't. As time went on, Gregory's fine riding endeared him to a fifteen-year-old schoolboy, who was supporting the Cheetahs with his father. Little did that young boy realise at the time, but he was later to play a major role in Oxford's success of the 1980s – his name was, of course, Bernard Crapper! As team manager, he would establish a record in speedway, which may one day be equalled, but can never be beaten.

Oxford drew Poole in the second round of the National Trophy and, all things considered, wished they hadn't. The first leg took place at Wimborne Road on 9 June, when the Pirates went on the offensive to triumph 78-30. The return leg, on 19 June, saw Poole again take victory by 55 points to 53. Thus, the Dorseteers completed two successes at Cowley, having won the league match on 22 May, when Brian Crutcher, the Poole whizz kid, scorched to a 12-point maximum.

Prior to the cup matches against Poole, there was an interesting happening on 5 June, when Oxford rode to a close 44-40 win over Liverpool. Looking for more team strengthening, the Cheetahs gave trials to Wimbledon novices Barry Briggs and Len Glover. Both had been offered to Oxford on loan, but the young Kiwi, Briggs, did not impress, and some reports even said he was 'a trifle wild and dangerous'. There must have been some red faces in the years that followed as 'Briggo' went on to become one of the most brilliant riders in the history of the sport, winning the World Championship on four occasions! Glover, meanwhile, was signed, but never did much other than ride as a reserve. A feature of the fixture versus Liverpool, which didn't please the Oxford public, was the riding of Frank Boyle. He scored 5 points in the match and looked all at sea. In the second half, however, he was a different rider – winning the Scratch Race final from visiting number one Peter Robinson, who had registered a 12-point maximum in the main match. It wasn't just Boyle who displeased the Cheetahs' supporters during the season, since several other team members were to suffer from indifferent form. Harry Saunders, in particular, was inconsistent to say the least.

There was a treat for the faithful Oxford fans on 3 July, when Cowley hosted an international match between Great Britain and the Overseas. It was the second of five Test matches, with Jim Gregory picked to represent GB in the main body of the side, while Bill Kemp occupied a reserve berth. Keeping the Oxford flavour, Frank Boyle was selected as reserve in the Overseas team. Gregory netted 11 points and formed a very strong partnership with Derek Close, who tallied 16, as the British lads ran riot to win 70-38. Kemp didn't get a ride, but Boyle did for the Overseas, scoring 2 points. Most impressive for Britain was Glasgow's Tommy Miller, who rode to a superb 18-point maximum. A week later, on 10 July, the enigmatic Harry Saunders gave a terrific display to win a World Championship qualifying round, beating sensational Swede Olle Nygren in heat twenty to take the winner's cheque; both riders having been unbeaten going into the race.

Leicester visited Sandy Lane on 24 July and yet again they left with the league points, thanks to a 47-37 win. Jim Gregory headed the Oxford scoring with 8 points in a match ridden on a very rough circuit. Thankfully, winning form returned for the next home match against Ashfield on 31 July, the result being 52-32.

Regrettably, promoter Les Calcutt passed away on Sunday 3 August at the Acland Nursing Home in Oxford. He'd had an operation and appeared to be recovering, only to suffer a relapse. No one person had done more to ensure that speedway came to Oxford, and he had worked so hard to ensure it was a success. He and, indeed, his fellow initial directors, Russell Chaundy and Archer Giles, established the sport, built a team that won the Third Division Championship in only their second post-war season and had never been afraid to spend money to strengthen the side.

So, the season progressed with an air of gloom hanging over the Cheetahs. On 4 August, they again went to Poole for a Second Division fixture, and as one really disgruntled Oxford supporter remarked as 5-1 followed 5-1 for the homesters, 'if this was boxing, they'd stop it.' The Cheetahs had Harry Saunders and skipper Bill Osborne as reserves, and it was the latter of the two that stopped the rot when he finished second in heat eight. Prior to that, the Pirates

Jim Gregory was a great servant to Oxford Speedway during his spell with the club in the 1950s. Amazingly, he was still competing in vintage races many years later and achieved his ambition of taking a final ride at Cowley on 27 September 2006.

had won the first seven races with successive 5-1s. The maximum advantages began again until heat twelve, when Osborne secured another second place. In the very next race, Saunders and Ron Wilson kept out Poole's Allan Kidd for a share of the points, but it was back to a 5-1 to finish the match as the Pirates comprehensively completed a 66-18 rout. Just why Osborne wasn't given an extra ride was a real puzzle, since three of his teammates failed to score. As it was, Messrs Osborne, Saunders, Boyle and Wilson all scored 4 points each, with Jim Gregory's tally of 2 completing a sorry-looking scorechart.

There was some brightness as Oxford did at least beat Wolverhampton in the first round of the Midland Cup. However, in a tight finish on 14 August, Motherwell snatched the league points from Cowley, winning 43-41. Coventry then provided the opposition for a league engagement at Sandy Lane on 21 August, when a fabulous effort saw the Warwickshire side defeat Oxford by 52 points to 32. Jim Gregory was the Cheetahs' best performer with 7 points, and he followed this by beating Coventry rider Vic Emms in a match race, before again defeating the same rider in the Dorchester Scratch Race final.

With their home form sliding in the wrong direction, the Cheetahs could only scrape a 42-42 draw against Ashfield in a match full of thrills and spills on 28 August. The frustration of the Cheetahs' fans boiled over as, on a night when the Scottish outfit suffered all the bad luck going, Oxford really ought to have won. In the second half, the riders competed for the Leydon Cup, which was duly presented by the Sheriff of Oxford. It was the winning of this trophy by Harry Saunders that provoked rather unpleasant scenes. The Cheetahs' rider had scored only 3 points in the match and, in general, didn't seem to put himself about. However, it was a different story in the second half, when Saunders revealed his known form to win the Leydon Cup. As with the riding of Frank Boyle in the home match versus Liverpool on 5 June, the supporters weren't happy at all, with jeers and boos greeting Saunders when he received the trophy. The attitude of the fans was understandable and the outcome was that the Oxford promoters suspended Saunders. There was a swift response to this from Jack Parker, the rider representative of the SRA, who said: 'If Oxford feel aggrieved by Saunders, they should report him to the Control Board. Only the board may suspend a rider. Our association have told Oxford they must reinstate Saunders and compensate him for any loss of earnings.' This affair just about summed up the Cheetahs' season, one that frustrated the loyal Oxford public. Saunders was reinstated, but didn't show any worthwhile form as the season petered out. At the end of the campaign, he left the club and joined Wolverhampton, but by the end of 1953 had retired for good. It was a sad ending for a rider who in the past had ridden brilliantly for the Cheetahs and had also been inspiring as team captain.

Coventry came back in the Midland Cup semi-final on 4 September and the Oxford fans watched in horror as the Bees went to town, claiming a crushing 71-25 success. With 8 points, Jim Gregory was the only home rider to give the Coventry lads any trouble. It was around this time that the speedway press indicated that both Wilf Plant and Peter Orpwood, riders of experience, would be joining Oxford. They were wrong though and neither man arrived at Cowley. By now, things were very troubled in the Cheetahs' team, and they weren't helped when Poole romped to a 60-24 success at Sandy Lane on 17 September.

Jim Gregory had to report for Z reservists training with the forces in the last week of September and whilst he was absent Glasgow plundered a 49-35 victory at Cowley. By the time Stoke came for the final home match of the season on 2 October, Oxford had gone seventeen matches without a win. Out of the blue, in a top-class display, the Cheetahs raced to victory by 51 points to 33, and still without Gregory, they looked like the Oxford of old, with Frank Boyle scoring a wonderful maximum.

So, the season ended and Oxford fans could be excused if they welcomed the finish of a campaign which had achieved nothing. Jim Boyd recorded 264 points from the league programme, while Jim Gregory totalled 247. Both were exempt from criticism as they had given their all and set an example, which in the main, the others failed to follow. Yet, in a season when Oxford finished bottom of the Second Division standings and suffered some hammerings at Cowley, they did do something that no other team in the league could accomplish, namely taking a point at the home of champions Poole. Continuing on the rider front, Bill Osborne (236) and Harry Saunders (218) were also double centurions despite some patchy performances, while Frank Boyle (174), Bill Kemp (165) and Ron Wilson (129) topped the hundred mark. Looking much further down the line, Ernie Rawlins, who had shown such excellent form during 1951, missed almost all of the season due to injury. In fact, he rode in only four league matches, scoring a meagre total of 6 points. It came as no surprise when, before the 1953 season began, he secured a transfer to his hometown team Southampton.

NATIONAL LEAGUE DIVISION TWO

Team	Mts	Won	Drn	Lst	For	Agn	Pts
Poole	44	31	1	12	2,217	1,477	63
Coventry	44	25	5	14	1,938	1,756	55
Leicester	44	25	2	17	1,882	1,808	52
Cradley Heath	44	24	0	20	1,870	1,821	48
Glasgow	44	23	1	20	1,837	1,853	47
Edinburgh	44	21	4	19	1,926	1,763	46
Ashfield	44	19	3	22	1,752	1,940	41
Motherwell	44	19	2	23	1,825	1,861	40
Yarmouth	44	20	0	24	1,812	1,883	40
Stoke	44	18	1	25	1,774	1,916	37
Liverpool	44	16	3	25	1,726	1,967	35
Oxford	**44**	**11**	**2**	**31**	**1,587**	**2,101**	**24**

1953

The promotion was listed as Russell Chaundy, Archer Giles and Oxford Speedway Club in 1953. Following the awful year they had endured in 1952, Oxford applied for and were granted permission to return to the Southern League, which was formerly known as the Third Division. Thus, the travelling that had cost so much in terms of expense, and often proved tiring to the riders, was considerably reduced. With no long distance hauls to Scotland, this sphere of racing also offered more local derbies, especially against the 'auld enemy' Swindon.

Henry Chandler, who had worked so hard for the club, departed to take up the greyhound racing manager's job at Swindon, where dog racing had only begun on 1 November the previous year. Mr Chandler had taken over as speedway manager at Oxford when Ron Bear quit midway through 1949, and had done a tremendous job, but greyhound racing was his first love. His post was taken over by John Deeley, the former manager of Walthamstow.

On the team front, the great news from New Zealand was that Bob McFarlane would be returning from his rhubarb farm. The two Jims, Boyd and Gregory, remained on board, as did the long-serving trio of Bill Kemp, Bill Osborne and Frank Boyle. Meanwhile, Herbie King and Ron Wilson were also back at Cowley, and there were new signings in Bill Codling from Norwich, and Ray Moore, who arrived via New Cross. Moore was to be described in one of John Deeley's programme columns as one of 'speedway's problem children'. He had joined New Cross after the Second World War and had held down a team place with no problems at all. He made such progress that he was picked for an England Test team, but a loss of form had seen him join Norwich in 1952. Unfortunately, he wasn't able to rediscover his touch with the Stars, scoring just 15 league points for them. Surely, thought Deeley, he would recover his form in the Southern League with Oxford. Regrettably, this was not to be. Moore couldn't find his golden touch at Cowley and was gone in a short space of time. Meanwhile, Ron Wilson was another rider to struggle and, after a few weeks, was given a free transfer.

Going back to the beginning of the campaign, the Oxford doors first opened on 3 April, when John Deeley's side locked horns with old rivals Swindon in a league fixture. It turned out to be a terrific encounter, with the Cheetahs snatching a 42-42 draw, thanks to the last-heat heroics of Jim Gregory and new boy Bill Codling, who recorded a 4-2 advantage after visiting reserve Bob Wells had fallen. That took Gregory's total to 8+1 points, while Herbie King also chipped in with an identical tally. Next in line, Jim Boyd recorded 6+1 points and 'Bobby Mac', on his return to Cowley, scored a useful 6 points. However, the Oxford star of the evening was Bill Kemp, with a tally of 10+1 points. Unfortunately, both Bill Osborne and Frank Boyle were missing, the former having wintered in New Zealand and not yet returned, while the latter was subject to an airport delay on his way from South Africa. With justification, Deeley was sure that if these two riders had been present, then the Cheetahs would have tasted victory.

The second meeting of the season saw the visit to Oxford of Swedish touring side Filbyterna, giving the loyal Sandy Lane supporters a first sighting of a blond-haired rider named Ove Fundin. The young and brilliant Swede was to produce a truly wonderful performance, recording a maximum in the match, before going on to win his heat and the final of the Scratch Race in the second half – what more could anyone hope to see? His showing led the tourists to a 43-41 success on a night when Jim Boyd and Bob McFarlane were the homesters' leading lights with 8 points apiece. Oxford had looked like claiming the win as they held a 39-33 advantage with two races remaining, but it wasn't to be as the Swedes finished with a flourish, netting successive 5-1s. Riding at number four in the Filbyterna side was a lad called Per Tage Svensson, who several years later, in 1962, would proudly wear the blue and yellow colours of the Cheetahs.

Above left: Brilliant Swede Ove Fundin made his debut appearance at Cowley with Swedish touring side Filbyterna in 1953, recording a maximum and then taking victory in the second-half event.

Above right: New Zealander Frank Boyle was unfortunately hit by injury in 1953 and it was to be his final year of racing.

On 14 April, Oxford journeyed to Southampton for a Southern League fixture, only to find the Saints on-song. Appearing for the home side was former Cheetah Ernie Rawlins, who rode with great skill to register a paid maximum (10+2 points). With unbeaten tallies also coming from Maury Mattingley and Brian McKeown, the poor Cheetahs found themselves on the end of a 60-24 hiding. Only Kiwis Bob McFarlane and Frank Boyle showed any resistance for an under-fire Oxford side, scoring 6 points each.

Unfortunately, the Cheetahs still had the blues when Rayleigh visited Sandy Lane for a league match on 16 April. Bill Osborne had now returned to action and recorded 5 points, but Bob McFarlane and Frank Boyle were right off form, scoring just 2 points apiece. To be fair, each suffered a fall, but whilst Oxford generally struggled, the visiting Rockets fought hard and deservedly secured a 44-39 victory. By this time, Ray Moore had gone after some below par performances.

The Cheetahs got back to winning ways when they entertained Plymouth in a National Trophy tie on 23 April, thrilling their fans with an excellent 66-42 victory. Jim Gregory was at his best, heading the scorechart with 13 points. Jim Boyd supplied top-notch support with 12 points, while Bob McFarlane and Frank Boyle roared back to form, tallying 11 apiece. Most speedway pundits thought the Oxford boys wouldn't have much of a chance in the return leg the following day, but happily they were wrong. Led by Jim Gregory's fabulous 16-point haul, the lads in blue and yellow fought like tigers to draw the match 54-54 and progress to the next round. The Plymouth side incidentally contained a certain Bill Thatcher, who was to link with Oxford in 1954.

London-born Benny King joined Oxford via Wolverhampton during the 1953 season and he was to total 86 points in the side's Southern League fixtures.

A large number of fans followed the Cheetahs to Swindon for a league engagement on 2 May and although their favourites went down to a defeat, they saw some entertaining fare. Oxford had no one to match either Bob Wells (12) or Ian Williams (11+1), who both went through the card unbeaten, although Jim Gregory and Bill Osborne certainly couldn't be accused of throwing in the towel. At heat nine the score stood at 36-17 in favour of the Robins, but a determined Oxford comeback had reduced the homesters' advantage to 41-35 four races later. Wells and Williams duly completed their maximums in heat fourteen, giving Swindon victory by 46 points to 36. Gregory headed the Cheetahs' scoring with 9 points, while Osborne tallied 8. Bill Codling, riding from a reserve slot, is also worthy of a mention as he netted 7+2 points from four starts.

When Southampton came to Cowley on 7 May, they met an inspired Oxford side that simply raced away to triumph 56-28, with Bill Osborne bagging a 12-point full-house. The margin of victory could have been even more, since Jim Gregory fell in the opening race, and Jim Boyd lost points when he suffered a seized motor while leading heat ten. Unfortunately, the win was marred by injuries to Bob McFarlane and Frank Boyle, which would cost the side dear. Two days later, the Cheetahs appeared at Rayleigh in the second round of the National Trophy, but they crashed to a 67-41 reverse. With their two New Zealanders missing through injury, Oxford had recalled Ray Moore, who, in the event, failed to turn up, although it is doubtful if his presence would have made any difference to the result. In the second leg at Cowley on 14 May, Rayleigh really dug deep and, thanks to a fine 14 points from Gerald Jackson, secured a 57-51 success to win 124-92 on aggregate.

Wolverhampton were Oxford's opponents in the Queen's Cup at Cowley on 21 May and in an exciting encounter the visitors claimed a 57-51 success. Benny King had now joined the Cheetahs, ironically from Wolverhampton, and he top-scored against his former club with 12 points. Oxford had needed to record a 5-1 from the final heat to force a draw, but Jim Gregory, who had 11 points under his belt, was excluded following a three-man pile-up and bang went their chances. Meanwhile, a returnee to Sandy Lane for the match was Harry Saunders, who, from the reserve berth, notched 8 points for the Wolves. This was to be one of his best returns for the West Midlands outfit, since in the league he scored just 9 points from six matches for them before hanging up his leathers. It was a great pity that he left Oxford under such a cloud at the end of the 1952 season, as he had put in many match-winning rides for the club during his stay and was indeed a fine team captain.

A great contest at St Austell on 19 May saw Oxford go down by 50 points to 34. Bill Osborne with 8 points and Jim Gregory with a fighting 7 were the Cheetahs' best performers on this occasion. Moving on to 28 May, Jim Boyd and Gregory were the stars of the World Championship qualifying round at Cowley. Boyd eventually came out on top with a 14-point tally after defeating his club colleague in the final heat of the meeting. Sticking with the individual theme, Birmingham's Graham Warren gave a vintage performance, scoring 14 points to triumph in a qualifier for the Midland Riders' Championship at Sandy Lane on 4 June. Meanwhile, Boyd again performed well, taking second place with 13 points.

On 8 June, a wonderful 12-point maximum from Jim Gregory at Exeter made for an interesting match at the County Ground, although his sterling efforts couldn't prevent Oxford from slipping to a 54-30 defeat. Three days later, on a Cowley circuit made heavy by rain, the Cheetahs beat Ipswich 49-35. Once again the two Jims were on song, with a four-ride maximum for Boyd and a paid full-house for Gregory. Oxford were now serving up some excellent racing, both at home and away. All the problems and poor form experienced in 1952 were now a distant memory, and the addition of just one good rider would, it was thought, propel the side to new heights.

At Wolverhampton on 26 June, the Oxford lads rode like demons to restrict the home side to a 51-45 victory in the Midland Cup. Jim Boyd, now riding at his very best, romped to a 15-point maximum, and there had also been a tally of 11 for him against Plymouth the night before in a league fixture at Cowley. The Coronation Best Pairs at Cowley on 9 July resulted in a win for Jim Gregory and Bill Osborne with 18 points. Unfortunately, the meeting didn't create much interest, since Oxford were staging the final round in the competition, which had already been won by Exeter. No matter, it was a home victory to cheer. A week later, the Sandy Lane regulars welcomed back former favourites Pat Clarke and Ernie Rawlins for an Oxford Past and Present versus New Zealand match. The powerful Kiwis, who included Ronnie Moore, Barry Briggs and Geoff Mardon in their line-up, also had home riders Bob McFarlane and Frank Boyle at reserve and it was no real surprise that they won 62-46. Clarke notched 11 points, while Boyd top scored with 14 points for the Cheetahs' select. Meanwhile, Moore raced to a superb 18-point maximum for New Zealand in what was a tremendous night's entertainment.

Moving on a month and 13 August brought Swindon to Oxford for league activity, and as usual a very good crowd, with the Cheetahs showing they meant business by taking four maximum heat wins in the first five races. Heat three, believe it or not, resulted in 5-1 to Swindon, courtesy of Ron Swaine and Danny Malone. Supplying the thrills was local boy Frank Johnson, who had come back to Oxford following Cardiff's premature closure. His signing was greatly assisted when the Supporters' Club made money available from their 'Penny on the Bike' fund. There was nothing to equal Johnson for excitement and he was wonderful 'box office'. The final score of 49-35 to the Cheetahs certainly sent the fans home happy, with Bob McFarlane (11), Jim Boyd (9) and Bill Osborne (8+3) leading the scoring.

The month brought some good fortune for the Sandy Lane supporters, although it wasn't such good news for speedway in general. Second Division Liverpool were forced to close down and the Cheetahs wasted no time in making a bid for their captain Peter Robinson, an Oxfordshire boy who was still in business in the area. There were many approaches for the rider's services, but 'Robbo' wanted to join his local club and there was never any doubt about it. So, it was on 20 August in the second leg of the Midland Cup tie versus Wolverhampton that Robinson donned the colours of the Cheetahs. His 8-point tally helped the side to win 53-42 and thus qualify for an exciting match in the next round against Birmingham.

Peter Robinson joined the Cheetahs from Liverpool late in the 1953 campaign. During the Second World War, he had served in the RAF as a Flight Lieutenant with Bomber Command and remarkably completed 2,000 flying hours.

In a league match at Exeter on 24 August, the Cheetahs lost by 57 points to 27, and followed it up with a 47-37 defeat at St Austell the following night. However, when they came back to their Cowley headquarters on 27 August, they went to town against the Gulls in the return fixture. With a 12-point maximum from Peter Robinson and a tally of 10 from Bill Osborne, Oxford roared to victory by 60 points to 23.

On 3 September, the Cheetahs clinched a hard-fought 44-40 success over Southampton in a league encounter at Cowley. Jim Boyd was at his best with an 11-point tally, while Peter Robinson backed him up with 10. In a good, close meeting it was the Oxford reserves who swung the result their way, with Frank Johnson and Herbie King tallying 7 points between them and proving far superior to their counterparts in the Saints' line-up.

There were home and away matches against Ipswich, which both resulted in losses, before Oxford travelled to Birmingham for the first leg of their Midland Cup encounter on 12 September. Unfortunately, they were soundly beaten 73-23, with guest Jim Tolley of Wolverhampton, who appeared in place of the injured Jim Gregory, heading the Cheetahs' scoring on 12 points. That meant the second leg was academic on 23 September and although the Oxford lads gave their all, they couldn't prevent the Brummies from winning 59-37 and thereby securing victory on aggregate by 132 points to 60. Peter Robinson with 10 points and Tolley, again as a guest, with 9 were the Cheetahs' top performers on the night. In between the Midland Cup fixtures, Oxford had appeared in the first leg of the Supporters' Cup at Swindon on 19 September. This went down to the wire, before Swindon narrowly scraped home by 49 points to 47. Keeping Oxford in the hunt for an overall success were super guest Tolley with 12+1 points and the excellent Robinson, who tallied 11. Although the fans fancied the team's chances of an aggregate win prior to the second leg on 1 October, it wasn't to be. The Robins looked in a serious mood and went on to win 52-43 for an overall triumph by 101 points to 90. Once more, the Cheetahs were best served by Tolley (10+1) and Robinson (10).

There were changes on the management front as the season reached its conclusion, with Dickie Worth and John Deeley named as the promoters in the race-day programme from 1 October.

Cardiff's withdrawal had left eight teams in the league and Oxford's finishing position was sixth, having won just nine of their twenty-eight fixtures. True, it was nothing to write home about, but at least there was the promise of better things to come. For a second year running, Jim Boyd was the side's most productive rider, totalling 236 points from the league campaign. The excellent Jim Gregory amassed 210 points, while Bob McFarlane (144) and Bill Osborne (116) were the only other team members to reach three figures.

SOUTHERN LEAGUE

Team	Mts	Won	Drn	Lst	For	Agn	Pts
Rayleigh	26	21	1	4	1,259	919	43
Exeter	26	20	1	5	1,244	939	41
Ipswich	28	13	2	13	1,183	1,165	28
Swindon	28	13	2	13	1,137	1,209	28
Southampton	28	12	2	14	1,184	1,159	26
Oxford	**28**	**9**	**1**	**18**	**1,118**	**1,228**	**19**
St Austell	28	9	0	19	996	1,348	18
Plymouth	28	8	1	19	1,096	1,250	17

NOTE: Cardiff withdrew from the league after completing twelve matches, with their record expunged from the table; Rayleigh *v.* Exeter (first match) was deleted from the records following a protest by Rayleigh over the make up of the Exeter team; Exeter *v.* Rayleigh (second match) was also deleted from the records, following another protest by Rayleigh over the steward's decision not to allow them to change their team pairings.

1954

The 1954 season saw Oxford competing in the Second Division of the National League, due to the merger of the previous season's Division Two with the Southern League. Bristol dropped down from the First Division and in the early planning stages the new league set-up boasted no fewer than sixteen teams. However, this happy situation didn't last very long, as Yarmouth never actually got going. Then Glasgow finished after a couple of Northern Shield matches, while Wolverhampton closed before their league campaign started. These were dark days for speedway, yet at Oxford things looked bright and support was actually on the increase.

On the team front, Jim Boyd, after top scoring for the club in 1953, announced his retirement from the sport, as did Bill Kemp and Benny King, while Frank Boyle returned to his native New Zealand. Manager John Deeley looked around for replacements, and one of his first signings was New Cross asset Ronnie Genz, who had assisted Yarmouth in 1953. This was to prove one of the best ever signings made by Oxford, for 'Genno' was to give great service to the Cheetahs for many seasons and proved to be the most loyal of club servants. To back the youth and enthusiasm of Genz, Mr Deeley looked for experience and from West Ham came Fred Curtis, who had been known as 'Kid' in his heyday. Also incoming via Swindon was Bob Wells, who'd had considerable experience with Wembley before joining the Robins in 1952. So, with these three newcomers to back the scoring efforts of Jim Gregory and Peter Robinson, plus old favourites Bill Osborne, Bob McFarlane and Frank Johnson, things were humming at Oxford when the Southern Shield competition opened the season.

Above left: The spectacular Frank Johnson unfortunately didn't enjoy the best of seasons for Oxford in 1954, netting just 32 points in the league.

Above right: Bob Baker added some much-needed strength to the side after being signed in 1954. He went on to tally 99 points from the league programme and finished third in the club's end-of-season statistical rundown, behind Peter Robinson and Ronnie Genz.

The Cheetahs' start in the Southern Shield was not particularly good, so with Yarmouth a definite non-starter, the experienced Bob Baker was signed in order to add further strength to the side. Perhaps the most important fixtures in this competition were against Swindon, as far as the fans were concerned anyway. The Cheetahs travelled to Blunsdon on 17 April and went down to a 46-38 loss in a cut-and-thrust encounter. In defeat, Jim Gregory was a giant, recording a 12-point maximum, while Ronnie Genz totalled 11. They lacked support, however, and with scoring all the way down the line in the Robins' camp it was easy to see why Oxford were the losing side.

The return match against Swindon in the Southern Shield took place at Cowley on 22 April, when, disastrously as far as the Oxford fans were concerned, the Robins stole away with a 46-37 success under their belts. Only Bill Osborne with 10 points and Jim Gregory with 9 could really escape criticism from the terraces, while Swindon had maximum man Ian Williams (12), together with Bob Roger (9+1) and Mick Holland (8+2) leading them to victory.

Oxford again visited Swindon on 26 June, this time for a Second Division fixture, and suffered their third loss to the old enemy, going down 45-39. Not one rider reached double figures for the Cheetahs, with Peter Robinson and Ronnie Genz heading the side's scoring on 8 points apiece. For the victorious Robins, Bob Roger (10+1) and Danny Malone (9) were the main contributors on the night.

West Ham-born Ronnie Genz was to be a loyal servant to Oxford Speedway for many years. His first season for the side was in 1954 and he enjoyed a good term, scoring 149 points in the league.

Plymouth withdrew from the league in early July, and the closure of the Devon track resulted in another Oxford signing, with New Zealander Bill Thatcher duly arriving at Cowley on 22 July for the match against Southampton, and just missing out on a maximum on his debut. Regrettably, the arrival of Thatcher coincided with a couple of unfortunate happenings for the Cheetahs. Bill Osborne broke a leg at Leicester in a freak accident, and Jim Gregory lost form and asked to be left out of the team. This was a real blow for the club, since Osborne was proving a reliable second string, and Gregory had scored well in the Southern Shield competition, his best performance undoubtedly being the maximum he notched at Swindon.

So, for the Cheetahs' home match against Swindon on 29 July, the popular Jim Gregory was in the second half of the programme. It was a memorable match, firstly because the Cheetahs won 47-36, but also for the second-half performance of Dennis Newton. The rider had made a sensational start at Swindon in 1951, but had suffered a badly broken thigh, which sidelined him for most of that year. He came back in 1952, and was dubbed the 'Golden Boy', but was injured again and his form deserted him. Newton, who had begun to rebuild his career, had signed for Wembley in 1953, but was still struggling to find his form. He was subsequently loaned to Oxford in 1954, and in the match against his former club, Swindon, he'd come in as a late replacement for Bob McFarlane but failed to score. However, in the second half, he won both the Cumnor Scratch Race and the Botley Scratch Race in fast times, beating Gregory, Bob Wells and the Swindon reserves Ray Harris and Gordon Leigh. It was the beginning of a real comeback for Newton, who went on to become a useful scorer, but the meeting really signalled the end of Gregory's career as a Cheetah, and it wasn't long before he retired from active racing.

The Cheetahs continued to do reasonably well in the league campaign. Peter Robinson had a good season and top scored with 172 points, while Ronnie Genz had a great time in his first year at Oxford, notching 149 points. The team finished midway in the final league table, winning ten matches and also losing ten. All in all, it was a reasonable campaign, with the old team spirit successfully rekindled by John Deeley, and, perhaps most importantly, increased support through the turnstiles.

To close the season, Oxford again faced Swindon in the Supporters' Cup. The first leg was held at Sandy Lane on 7 October and, in a meeting when neither side gave an inch, it was the Robins who grabbed a narrow 49-47 success. Peter Robinson headed the Cheetahs' scoring with 12 points, while Bob Baker tallied 10+2. For Swindon, Ian Williams was the hero, his 14 points including a decisive win in the final heat, which sealed the Wiltshire side's victory. The return leg was staged at Blunsdon two days later and saw the Robins overwhelm Oxford by 69 points to 26 to win 118-73 on aggregate. George White (12+3), Williams (11+1) and Bob Roger (10+2) all remained undefeated for the homesters, while Peter Robinson (7+1) and Bob Wells (7) topped the Cheetahs' dismal scorechart.

Finally, at a rain-swept Belle Vue on 16 October, Peter Robinson represented Oxford in the Second Division Riders' Championship. He went on to occupy fourth place overall in a meeting won by Poole's Ken Middleditch. Second place went to Swindon's Ian Williams, while another Poole rider, Terry Small, filled third spot.

NATIONAL LEAGUE DIVISION TWO

Team	Mts	Won	Drn	Lst	For	Agn	Pts
Bristol	20	14	0	6	908.5	769.5	28
Poole	20	12	0	8	896.5	781.5	24
Swindon	20	11	0	9	870	789	22
Leicester	20	11	0	9	829	765	22
Ipswich	20	10	0	10	873	806	20
Exeter	20	10	0	10	851	827	20
Oxford	**20**	**10**	**0**	**10**	**807**	**868**	**20**
Coventry	20	10	0	10	807	869	20
Southampton	20	9	0	11	800	878	18
Motherwell	20	9	0	11	759	819	18
Rayleigh	20	4	0	16	725	954	8

NOTE: Glasgow and Wolverhampton withdrew from the league before racing any matches; Plymouth withdrew after two matches, with their record expunged from the table; Edinburgh withdrew after four matches, with their record also expunged from the table; the match between Motherwell and Leicester was abandoned after heat eight. Motherwell declined to re-run the fixture, so Leicester were awarded two league points.

1955

The 1955 season saw the Oxford Cheetahs still being members of the Second Division. The year also saw the introduction of the tactical substitute rule, which was perhaps the most important rule change ever. It's one of the few rules that has stood the test of time, although the modern-day slant has given it a new meaning. However, its introduction most certainly led to more exciting matches. There were other changes too: after many years of eight-man teams, there was now just one reserve instead of two, and the league matches were run over sixteen heats instead of fourteen. This meant the main team-men would have five programmed rides each, while the reserve was scheduled for just two outings. The Second Division welcomed a new member in Weymouth, promoted by former Exeter, Swindon and Cardiff boss Bill Dutton. Regrettably, as things turned out, the newly formed Scorchers didn't last long, and by May they had closed down. Another closure, which hit speedway hard, was that of Bristol, the 1954 League Champions, in June.

Despite the doom and gloom that threatened to engulf the sport, things were looking good at Oxford. Reg Trott had arrived on loan from Wimbledon, and Dennis Newton had returned following a new loan agreement with Wembley. Two new faces arrived in the form of the Courtnell brothers, Terry, who had enjoyed experience with Yarmouth and West Ham, and his younger sibling, Maury, who created a lot of interest with his Teddy boy gear. It was all there too, including the drainpipe trousers, the shoes and the special haircut and, as can be imagined, he was quite a hit with the Cheetahs' young female supporters.

There had been departures from Cowley, with Bob McFarlane remaining at home in New Zealand, while Frank Johnson had surprisingly been allowed to link with Weymouth. This was a puzzle since Johnson was a trier second to none and had no equals as a thrill-maker. There was no Bill Osborne either, since he was recovering from the broken leg he had sustained at Leicester the previous year. On the plus side, many of the old favourites were back for more, namely Peter Robinson, Bob Baker, Ronnie Genz and Bill Thatcher. The two veteran riders, Bob Wells and Fred Curtis, also came back for another season, but really they had had their day and in the end they scored just 100 points between them, respectively totalling 60 and 40.

New Zealander Bill Thatcher had a good season for the Cheetahs in 1955, recording 205 points from the side's National League Division Two campaign.

Going back to the start of the season, Oxford opened their campaign with a league match against old rivals Swindon at Cowley on 8 April. This lived up to expectations and had all the ingredients of a local derby, but the wrong result as far as the Cheetahs' supporters were concerned, with the Robins winning narrowly by 49 points to 47. Bob Baker was in great form and his 12-point tally was a sign of things to come, since he was to enjoy a terrific term. Meanwhile, Peter Robinson contributed an 11-point score and Ronnie Genz recorded 9+2. A return of 8 points from Fred Curtis was a fine effort on the day, but unfortunately he couldn't keep it up, and it was evident as the season progressed that he was reaching the end of his speedway career. The return match at Blunsdon the following evening saw Swindon knock the stuffing out of the Cheetahs, as they meted out a 71-25 drubbing. Oxford's best performer on a dismal evening was Baker with just 6 points. Emphasising their dominance, the Robins' scorecard included unbeaten performances from Ian Williams (14+1), Ron Swaine (13+2) and George White (12+3).

The following week saw Leicester at Cowley and another outstanding match resulted in a fine win for the Cheetahs by 55 points to 41. The scoreline might suggest it was plain sailing for the Oxford lads, but really that wasn't the case. The visiting side put up quite a fight and every point was keenly contested, with Bob Baker and Dennis Newton, especially, winning many of their points from the back. Two races were particularly brilliant: firstly, in heat eleven, when Peter Robinson rode a blinder to beat the Hunters' big two of Ken McKinlay and Len Williams, and secondly, in heat fifteen, when the Bob Baker/Ronnie Genz combination team rode to a 5-1 over Johnny Green, with McKinlay relegated to last place. It was a different story when Oxford rode up at Leicester on 22 April, however, with the Hunters gaining revenge by 63 points to 33. Genz was just brilliant with 13 points and Baker scored a dozen, but the rest of the Cheetahs were poor indeed. Small wonder that one match report called the encounter 'a dull as ditchwater' event.

Things were far more exciting when newcomers Weymouth were the visitors to Sandy Lane on 28 April. The Scorchers had two ex-Cheetahs in their side in Frank Johnson and Ernie Lessiter. Both lads put in plenty of effort, although this wasn't reflected in their returns of 4 and 3 points respectively. The real star of the Weymouth side was former Exeter and Birmingham rider Ron Barrett, who carded 12 points and really put himself about. By and large he fought a one-man battle as Oxford rode to a 62-34 success and there was no stopping Ronnie Genz from thundering to a 15-point maximum. Providing solid backing, Bob Baker recorded 13 points, despite his poor gating, and Peter Robinson tallied 12. Regrettably, the league points gained didn't do the Cheetahs any good in the end as the result was expunged from the record books when Weymouth closed down at the end of May.

As the weeks came and went, there was much in the way of good speedway to enjoy at the home of the Cheetahs, with Reg Trott and Dennis Newton giving support to the side's heat leaders. It was only in the reserve berth that the Oxford team were somewhat suspect, but to be fair, manager John Deeley gave Maury Courtnell every opportunity to make the grade. The month of May had opened well for the Cheetahs with home and away matches against Rayleigh. The home fixture, on 5 May, resulted in a fine Oxford victory by 63 points to 33, with 15 points from Ronnie Genz, 13 from Peter Robinson and 12 from Bob Baker. Two days later the return match featured a wonderful display from the Cheetahs, who rode like their lives depended on it to triumph 51-44. Baker and Genz kept going where they had left off at Cowley, and in a thrilling final heat Bob Wells called on all his experience to keep the Rayleigh riders behind him and follow Baker across the line for a magnificent 5-1.

It was National Trophy time at Cowley Stadium on 12 May, with Coventry supplying the opposition. Once more, the Cheetahs put in a great performance to win 66-42. Peter Robinson was beaten just once on his way to 17 points, while Bob Baker again starred with 15 and Genno tallied 11. It was a different story two days later at Coventry, however, and in a rain interrupted match the Bees pulled out all the stops to win 75-33, thereby progressing through on aggregate. With 12 points, only Ronnie Genz offered any resistance to the flying home side.

Oxford carved out good home wins over Ipswich (55-41), Poole (52-44) and Southampton (56-40), although in a sobering experience they suffered a 74-22 thrashing at Poole on 23 May, but then most teams came away from Wimborne Road on the back end of a hefty defeat. The score may have been bad, but the Cheetahs were heartily congratulated by the press as they never gave up the fight. On 9 June came a match that was eagerly awaited by everyone, the first leg of the Supporters' Trophy against Swindon. After eighteen heats of cut and thrust action, it was the Robins who had edged victory by 56 points to 52. Bob Baker was tremendous in registering 17 points, losing only to Jimmy Gooch in heat seven. Meanwhile, lower down the order, Maury Courtnell worked hard for an excellent 5-point tally. At Blunsdon in the second leg on 11 June, Swindon raced to a 69-39 win to secure an aggregate success by 125 points to 91.

Bristol then came to Cowley on 16 June and the Oxford lads returned to form, winning 50-46. Bob Baker led the way with 13 points, while Ronnie Genz bagged 12. Neither could hold star visitor Dick Bradley, who showed his liking for the Sandy Lane circuit with a wonderful 18-point maximum. Fellow Bristol rider Jack Unstead also rode well to rack up 14 points, while at number seven the Bulldogs tracked the one and only Frank Johnson, who had joined the club following the closure of Weymouth. As ever, he showed a penchant for the Oxford raceway, scoring 10 points from six rides in his own inimitable fashion. He even caused quite a stir in the pits, although it was nothing to do with him in reality. Bristol manager Bill Hamblin had sent Johnson out for a sixth outing in heat fifteen and straight away an argument ensued, with the meeting official left to decide whether a reserve rider could have six rides if his team were less than six points in arrears. Suffice to say Johnson took his sixth outing, although the debate surrounding its legality was rendered purely academic soon afterwards when Bristol closed down. Like their earlier victory over Weymouth, the points won by Oxford were again deleted from their total. Left without a track for the second time in the season, Johnson went off to Belle Vue for trials.

Leicester, with Split Waterman as a guest, arrived at Cowley on 23 June and left with nothing, Oxford winning 54-42. Peter Robinson, having missed a 59-37 defeat at Exeter three days earlier, returned with 10 points, but it was Ronnie Genz who top-scored on 13. The leading rider for the visitors was Gordon McGregor with 15 points and no doubt the Oxford bosses marked his card for the future. On 25 June, Oxford travelled to First Division Belle Vue for a challenge match against the Manchester club's reserve team. The home side included old friend Frank Johnson and were scheduled to be strengthened by Billy Hole, also late of Bristol. In the event, Hole didn't show and the Cheetahs cantered to a 61-35 victory. In defeat, Johnson enjoyed what must have been his finest hour in the sport, scoring 17 points and losing only to Bob Baker. To put his performance into perspective, his tally represented almost half of his side's total on the night.

On 30 June, an excellent win over Coventry by 61 points to 35 kept the Cheetahs in the league title hunt, but they quickly returned to earth with a bump, losing 60-36 at Swindon on 2 July. The Oxford boys just couldn't adapt to the Blunsdon track, and furthering their plight the local side included Bert Roger from First Division West Ham as a guest for the injured George White. He recorded a paid maximum (14+1), as did his brother, Bob, and the two gave solid support to Swindon's on-loan signing from Wembley, Jimmy Gooch, who hit a superlative five-ride full-house.

In a break from team racing, the World Championship qualifying round at Cowley on 7 July saw the home lads do well. Ronnie Genz won the meeting with a 15-point maximum, ahead of Norwich's Harry Edwards (14), Bob Baker (13) and Reg Trott (11), with Peter Robinson also up with the leaders on 10 points. League activity was back on the agenda on 14 July, when a good scrap resulted in Oxford beating Exeter by 56 points to 40. Visiting speedster Neil Street showed great form for the Devonians, scoring 15 points and recording a time of 66.2 seconds in the opening heat – the fastest time since Keith Gurtner had established the track record in 1951. The result marked a return to winning ways for the Cheetahs, who had again been hammered mercilessly at Poole by a 76-19 scoreline on 11 July. Little can be said about the match, with Genz topping the Oxford scoring on 5 points. Among their problems on the night, Baker failed to arrive and Wimbledon, as they were permitted to do in those days, had recalled Reg Trott to ride for them. To make up their side, Oxford borrowed Ernie Brecknell, the Poole number eight, but could only muster 1 point in the face of the onslaught.

Regrettably, Oxford lost Ronnie Genz during a Midland Riders' Championship qualifying round at Cowley on 21 July, when the popular rider fell and fractured a collarbone. Jointly finishing on top of the pile were Birmingham's Doug Davies and Coventry's Charlie New with 13 points apiece. The best performer in the home camp was Bob Baker, who totalled 12. Genno's accident meant that guests were used until his recovery and for the match at home to Rayleigh on 4 August, it was Bert Roger's turn to fill the vacancy. He did a great job too, heading the Cheetahs' scoring with 14 points in a 52-44 win. This followed a 52-44 loss to Southampton on 28 July, when guest Harry Edwards topped Oxford's scoring on 13 points. Jim Tolley was booked in as a second guest for Baker, but he disappointed with just 1 point, costing the Cheetahs dearly.

There were two matches for Oxford the following week, at home against local rivals Swindon and away at Rayleigh. The home fixture on 11 August was a cracker, and a big crowd witnessed the Cheetahs snatch a narrow success by 49 points to 47. The victory was only secured in the last race courtesy of a marvellous 5-1 from Dennis Newton and the returned-from-injury Ronnie Genz. At Rayleigh, though, it all went wrong two nights later. The Rockets put Oxford to the sword and romped to a 71-25 win, with only Bob Baker and Genz troubling the home lads, scoring 7 and 6 points respectively.

Matches against Leicester had shown what every fan knew, that Oxford were in the main formidable at home, but rather suspect away from Sandy Lane. However, in a Midland Cup encounter between the two sides at Cowley on 18 August, it was the Hunters who took victory by 53 points to 49. The match began in breathtaking fashion with Ken McKinlay setting a new track record in the opening race, only for Derek Close to go even faster in heat two, when clocked at 65.6 seconds. It was reported that the starting gate had been shortened before the meeting and this seemed to upset the Oxford lads. Up at Leicester, in the return match the following evening, the home side were in dominant mood and the Cheetahs crashed to a 73-29 reverse as they unceremoniously headed out of the competition.

A good match at Southampton on 23 August saw a battling Oxford side lose by 56 points to 40, with Peter Robinson in good form for a 10-point tally. Then came the big meeting of the year when a first-class field of riders met for the Kings of Oxford Trophy on 25 August. Unfortunately, the contest was marred by a heat one accident, which saw Jack Young crash down after his frame had broken in two. In trying to avoid the stricken rider, Ronnie Genz also took a spill, with both subsequently ruled out of the meeting. Sensational Swede Ove Fundin went on to take top spot with a 15-point maximum, ahead of Barry Briggs (14), Ronnie Moore (13) and the Cheetahs' own Peter Robinson (11).

Although honours ultimately eluded the team, Dennis Newton carried the Oxford colours with pride in the Midland Riders' Championship final at Leicester on 26 August, scoring 11 points to finish fourth in a meeting won by home star Ken McKinlay.

There was an inter-league challenge fixture on 8 September, when the Cheetahs met First Division West Ham, with track specialist Dick Bradley bolstering the side as a welcome guest. It proved to be a close match and although the sides raced to a 53.5-53.5 draw, it was rather spoiled by heavy rain. Bob Baker produced the ride of the night in heat thirteen, when he split the Jack Biggs/Split Waterman pairing right on the line, forcing a dead heat for second place. Biggs was credited with the win on his way to a marvellous 18-point maximum, while Baker and Waterman gained 1.5 points each from the race. Heading the completed scorechart for Oxford was Bradley with 10 points, while Bill Thatcher tallied 9.

Following a 54-42 loss at Southampton on 27 September came a home match that all of Oxford wanted to see, versus Poole two evenings later. It looked as though the Pirates meant business when Ken Middleditch lowered the track record to 65.4 seconds in the opening race. But the Cheetahs, solid throughout, dug deep and ran out victors by 59 points to 37. Revenge was sweet, particularly as Poole became League Champions. On 6 October, the final home meeting was against Coventry and the Oxford side ended a good season on a winning note, 54-41. Bob Baker ended a fine campaign with 13 points, while the Bees relied too heavily on New Zealander Charlie New, who tallied 17 and lost only to Dennis Newton.

This has to be looked upon as a good season, with Oxford for a time challenging for league honours. The side eventually finished fourth in the nine-team division, with four riders topping 200 points. These were Bob Baker (261), Peter Robinson (256), Ronnie Genz (249) and Bill Thatcher (205), while two others made very useful contributions, namely Dennis Newton (151) and Reg Trott (108).

Reg Trott was born in Mitcham, Surrey and scored 108 league points for the Cheetahs in 1955. After retiring from racing some years later, he was to stay very much involved in the sport when he became a referee.

NATIONAL LEAGUE DIVISION TWO

Team	Mts	Won	Drn	Lst	For	Agn	Pts
Poole	32	23	0	9	1,689	1,380	46
Coventry	32	19	0	13	1,534	1,535	38
Rayleigh	32	15	2	15	1,573	1,495	32
Oxford	**32**	**15**	**1**	**16**	**1,424**	**1,644**	**31**
Southampton	32	15	0	17	1,445	1,621	30
Ipswich	32	13	3	16	1,537	1,531	29
Leicester	32	14	0	18	1,539	1,529	28
Swindon	32	14	0	18	1,515	1,556	28
Exeter	32	13	0	19	1,553	1,518	26

NOTE: Weymouth withdrew after seven matches, with their record expunged from the table; Bristol withdrew after fourteen matches, with their record also deleted from the league table.

1956

After a satisfactory season in 1955, when, for a while, the Cheetahs were up there challenging for the league title, the Oxford supporters eagerly looked forward to the tapes rising in 1956. Unfortunately, it was to be a case of 'after the Lord Mayor's show', since right from the off, when they lost their opening league match against Swindon, the Cheetahs struggled in the main. Despite this, much to the Oxford bosses surprise and gratitude, the crowd stayed loyal and gate numbers were very pleasing. Peter Morrish, the well-known speedway journalist and photographer, endorsed this when he wrote: 'There was none of the atmosphere usually associated with a poor team.'

Oxford Cheetahs 1956: From left to right, back row: Peter Robinson, Jim Tebby, Pat Clarke, Bob Baker, Howdy Byford, Dennis Newton, Bill Thatcher. Front row: Maury Courtnell, Ronnie Genz (on bike), Terry Courtnell.

On the team front, both Bob Wells and Fred Curtis unsurprisingly retired, as did Bill Thatcher, although he subsequently returned to the saddle for nine matches. Reg Trott was recalled by Wimbledon, who then sold him on to Norwich, but it wasn't all about departures. Pat Clarke, one of Oxford's most famous sons, returned to Cowley following the closure of West Ham. The popular rider had been injured whilst training at Oxford in 1955, but was now fit and hoped a return to his old stomping ground would help boost his form. Meanwhile, Roy Bowers, who was reckoned to be a good prospect, also came on board after gaining experience with Harringay and Yarmouth. Another to join the Cowley ranks was one of the sport's greatest characters in Howdy Byford. Known as 'The Champ', he too arrived via West Ham and was to settle down well with the Cheetahs, although he admitted that the racing in the Second Division was every bit as tough as it had been in the top flight. The other tried and tested Cheetahs were back at Cowley for the season, namely Ronnie Genz, Bob Baker, Dennis Newton, Peter Robinson and the Courtnell brothers, Terry and Maury.

Perhaps the biggest disappointment as the season unfolded was the failure of Bob Baker to get going. He had been the club's leading scorer in 1955, when recording 261 points from the league programme. He had also proved a master at coming through from the back. However, his golden touch almost completely vanished and he retired in the summer having tallied just 58 points – over 200 down on the previous year. He did give speedway another go in September, but was just a shadow of the rider who had performed so brilliantly in 1955. At the close of the 1956 campaign, he retired again – this time for good.

The opening meeting of the season against Swindon took place at Sandy Lane on Good Friday 30 March, when no quarter was either asked for or given. After fifteen gruelling races the scores were level, only for Swindon to grab a final heat 4-2 courtesy of Ray Harris and George White to win 49-47. Ronnie Genz was the Cheetahs' best performer with a dozen points, while Bob Baker and Peter Robinson each tallied 11+1. However, Pat Clarke just couldn't get going and failed to score from two starts. The Oxford public were aware that he had suffered some bad injuries in the past and knew what he could do, so they were content to be patient. For Swindon, the best performances came from Ron Swaine (12) and Bob Roger (10).

At home, meetings tended to be close, with the Cheetahs really fighting to ensure they didn't lose points but away, it is sad to say, they never looked like winning any matches. In the main, when on opponents' tracks, it was usually a case of the homesters hitting 60 points and the best that Oxford could do was at Swindon when they lost 55-41 on 12 May. Ronnie Genz was magnificent with 15 points from six outings, while Howdy Byford notched 10+2. The Robins boasted three men in double figures on the night, with Ian Williams unbeaten on 14+1 points, while Bob Roger (12) and George White (10) lent solid top-end support.

Swindon visited Cowley again in the Supporters' Club Cup on 24 May, but on this occasion Oxford produced a fine performance to triumph 62-45. A wonderful display saw Peter Robinson head the scoring with 15+1 points, while Ronnie Genz (13+1) and Howdy Byford (10+2) also did very well. The Cheetahs were to lose in the second leg at the Abbey Stadium two days later, but despite suffering defeat, this was a meeting in which the team covered themselves in glory. After heat sixteen, the overall scores stood at 103-100 in Swindon's favour. Could the Cheetahs do it? Regrettably not, as the Robins recorded 5-1s in each of the last two heats to take an aggregate victory by 113 points to 102. Bob Roger completed a marvellous 18-point maximum for the homesters, while Ian Williams also remained unbeaten in scoring 16+2. Oxford's best on a night to remember was Genz with 12 points.

On 31 May, the Sandy Lane racing strip hosted the Midland Riders' Championship qualifying round, which was won in great style by Alan Hunt of Birmingham with a 15-point maximum. Ronnie Genz filled the runner-up position on 14 points, while three other Cheetahs all totalled 11, namely Dennis Newton, Peter Robinson and Howdy Byford. In the programme from this meeting, Supporters' Club secretary Reg Timms' notes revealed that John Deeley would be departing from Oxford. Deeley had done much to revive the fortunes of the club, and on 21 June, following a league match versus Swindon, he handed over his duties to Ted Flanaghan. He went out on a winning note with Oxford putting up a spirited display to beat the Robins by 51 points to 45. It was indeed a fitting way for the Cheetahs to say cheerio to Deeley and wish him well. Once again, it was Genz who led the scoring with 13+1 points, while both Newton and Robinson plundered 10 apiece. Genz was the only rider to beat Swindon skipper Ian Williams, who returned 17 points. Their heat two race was a cracker, with Genno winning by a whisker. Backing Williams once again for the Robins was Bob Roger, who notched 13 points.

The following week, 28 June, for a league match against Coventry, it was the turn of Ted Flanaghan to welcome the patrons to Cowley as their new promoter and team manager. The incoming boss was a man of great experience, having been in the sport for many years at Sheffield and Leicester as a manager. On track, the Cheetahs supplied a good start for their new promoter, winning 59-37. It was perhaps as good a team performance as they gave all season, since they scored solidly from one to six. Both Ronnie Genz and Howdy Byford posted 12-point tallies, while Terry Courtnell scored 11. Only Bob Baker, down at reserve, didn't show any form, registering just 1 point. It wasn't pretty to see Baker in action; all the fighting spirit that was a feature of his riding in 1955 was missing and it was, therefore, no surprise when he announced his retirement.

Ted Flanaghan, who took over as promoter and team manager at Oxford following the departure of John Deeley in June 1956.

On 3 July, Leicester's Ken McKinlay retained the Midland Riders' Championship at Coventry. The Cheetahs were represented by Ronnie Genz and Dennis Newton, with Howdy Byford qualifying as first reserve. Unfortunately, they all finished well down the field, Genz scoring 5 points, while Newton tallied 3 and Byford just 1.

On 21 July, Oxford travelled to Swindon for a second time in the league and went down by 56 points to 39. Both Bob Roger and Ian Williams were again on fire for the Robins, plundering brilliant 15-point maximums. For the Cheetahs, Dennis Newton showed excellent form with 12+1 points, with Ronnie Genz (7+2), Terry Courtnell (7+1) and Pat Clarke (7+1) next in line. Why, the reader may ask, are the Oxford scorers against the Robins so significant? The answer is simple really, because Swindon became League Champions of the Second Division, while the poor old Cheetahs were the wooden spoonists. Proof, if proof were needed, that the rivalry between the two clubs was as keen as ever and both sides tried that little bit more in these local derbies. Pride as well as points was at stake.

There were to be more problems for Oxford in what was a troubled season. Pat Clarke, who was trying hard to regain his touch, crashed and was hurt again on 26 July in a home match versus Ipswich. He was out of action for a while, but returned only to break a leg in heat four of a Best Pairs meeting at Cowley on 20 September, an event won by Peter Robinson and his partner from Leicester, Charlie Barsby. Unfortunately, Clarke had endured nothing but bad luck since his return to Oxford, and wisely he retired from active racing. Nevertheless, the supporters always fondly remembered his fine riding from the Championship-winning season of 1950.

So, going into the final weeks of the season, Oxford had lost the services of Pat Clarke, whilst both Howdy Byford and Roy Bowers were also out through injury. On top of that, Bill Thatcher had disappointed in his comeback and now retired for good. Likewise, Bob Baker, whose form loss was a complete puzzle, especially to the rider himself. To plug the gaps, Ted Flanaghan had secured Tommy Miller from Coventry, although, frustratingly, the Scotsman was but a shadow of the rider who some years before had taken the Second Division by storm when riding for Glasgow. He contributed little to the Oxford cause and recorded just 35 points from seven league matches.

It must have been strange for a Swindon rider to be called a Cowley track expert, but that is what the Robins' skipper Ian Williams became known as. Oxford were forced to call upon guest riders due to their injury problems and Williams represented the side on 27 September, when he rode unbeaten for a superb six-ride maximum in a challenge match against Coventry. Regrettably, his efforts didn't lead to an Oxford win and it was the Bees who took victory by 52 points to 44.

Swindon were the final visitors of 1956 in a challenge match on 11 October, when Oxford tracked two guests in Ken McKinlay and Gordon McGregor. The pair of guests from Leicester couldn't prevent Swindon from winning 50-46, although McKinlay did all that could possibly be asked in netting a 15-point maximum. Ronnie Genz gave great backing to the Scotsman to net 12+2 points, while Swindon's best were yet again Bob Roger and Ian Williams with 12 apiece. It must have been strange for Williams, since he had been cheered from the rooftops when he landed an 18-point maximum for the Cheetahs against Coventry, yet on this occasion he was given the 'bird'.

Looking at the Cheetahs' record for 1956, there can be little doubt that all the injuries cost the team dearly, and despite all the trials and tribulations, the fans stayed loyal in the knowledge that the team members were trying hard and giving of their best. Briefly touching on some of the other meetings that took place during the year, Swindon's Bob Roger was the victor in the Kings of Cowley Trophy on 13 September, the meeting having been rained-off seven days previously. In the Inter-Division matches, Oxford performed brilliantly to overwhelm Bradford by 60 points to 36 on 14 June in what was quite their best showing of the campaign. Understandably, it wasn't the same fairytale story when they came up against Belle Vue and lost 59-37 on 4 October. Meanwhile, in the National Trophy, they lost out on aggregate to Rayleigh by 142 points to 74.

The Cheetahs ended up seventh in a seven-team league. The numbers had been reduced as Poole had been promoted as a result of winning the Second Division Championship, while Exeter had closed their doors to the sport. As far as Poole were concerned, one staunch Oxford fan was heard to say: 'I cried crocodile tears when they were promoted, because visiting there with the Cheetahs over the years was usually good for a real hiding. It's as though they never forgave us for taking that league point in their opening home match of 1952!' Statistically speaking, Ronnie Genz was the club's leading scorer with 279 points from the league programme. Looking down the line, Dennis Newton occupied second position in the scoring stakes with 152 points, while Peter Robinson (144) and Howdy Byford (112) were the only others to reach a ton.

Tragedy struck during the year when former Oxford rider Ernie Rawlins lost his life following an accident in the final meeting of the season at his home track, Southampton. The meeting was an inter-league challenge versus Birmingham on 18 September and the accident happened in heat two, with the popular rider passing away four days later as a result of his injuries. Unfortunately, there was another note of sadness on 17 November, when news came through that Terry Courtnell had lost his life in a road traffic accident in South Africa, having been on a working holiday in the land of the Springbok.

NATIONAL LEAGUE DIVISION TWO

Team	Mts	Won	Drn	Lst	For	Agn	Pts
Swindon	24	16	0	8	1,196	1,102	32
Southampton	24	15	1	8	1,223	1,081	31
Rayleigh	24	14	1	9	1,248	1,053	29
Ipswich	24	13	0	11	1,151	1,149	26
Coventry	24	12	0	12	1,150	1,149	24
Leicester	24	6	1	17	1,088	1,214	13
Oxford	**24**	**6**	**1**	**17**	**996**	**1,304**	**13**

1957

An icy blast swept through the sport of speedway before the 1957 season got underway, with three major clubs announcing they wouldn't be running. These were Bradford, Poole and the world famous Wembley, and it is interesting to note that all three were members of the old First Division. The closures left just four teams in the top flight, which meant there was no way the league could operate efficiently. The Control Board, therefore, did the only thing that could be done: they amalgamated the two divisions and formed a National League of eleven sides. However, there were some anxious moments for a couple of the old Division Two teams as well, namely Oxford and Rayleigh.

The company promoting speedway at the home of the Cheetahs went into liquidation and Oxford were only saved when Dickie Worth formed a new administration with Ted Flanaghan, known as Worth's Speedway (Oxford) Ltd, enabling them to continue looking after the running of the club. It would have been a sin if Oxford hadn't operated as support for the club had always been good, even if on-track results disappointed at times. As far as Rayleigh were concerned, a former rider, Vic Gooden, came forward with an offer to take over as promoter of the Rockets, allowing not only supporters of the club, but those in general to breathe a huge sigh of relief.

Australian ace Jack Biggs arrived at Oxford in 1957 and scored 158 points from the club's National League fixtures.

One item of really good news occurred in the April Budget of 1957, when the ridiculous Entertainment Tax was ended. This was a welcome move, but if it had happened a few years earlier the sport would surely not have reached the stage where just eleven tracks were left in business. This year also saw the Control Board do away with race times, or at least they weren't announced as it was claimed they didn't encourage team riding. This was based on the absurd notion that a rider who was leading a race would rather try to better the track record than assist his partner. However, this wasn't well received by the fans and race times were back by June, and they stayed back. Guest riders, always a thorny subject, were also done away with, but this change didn't last long either.

There were, as was to be expected, the usual comings and goings within the Oxford team. Peter Robinson, Pat Clarke and Tommy Miller all retired, and with seven former Second Division sides now in what was effectively a higher sphere of racing, much attention was given to proper equalisation of team strengths. Fans of the Cheetahs were quite happy for almost any rider to be allocated to the club, since after the year they had endured the only way Oxford could go was up. The riders who were allocated to the Sandy Lane set-up were, most certainly on paper, excellent acquisitions. From Poole came the Australian star Jack Biggs, who had been very much the number one with the Pirates in 1956. Also joining was another Aussie, Ray Cresp, who was a protégé of Biggs' and had made such progress the previous term that Wembley had signed him. Meanwhile, from Leicester came Gordon McGregor, who had guested for the Cheetahs in the last match of 1956 and scored a good 7 points in the defeat by Swindon. He was a rider of considerable experience and, having netted a total of 240 league points for the Hunters, he was just the sort of rider Oxford needed. Happily, a number of the lads who had represented the club during 1956 were back and raring to go. These were Ronnie Genz, now the cornerstone of the Cheetahs, Howdy Byford and Dennis Newton. Thrillmaker-in-chief Frank Johnson was also about, as was Roy Bowers, and both were determined to make a real effort to secure a permanent team place.

Scotsman Gordon McGregor joined the Cheetahs via Leicester in 1957 and went on to register 144 league points in his first season for the side.

Early season visitors were of course the team's oldest rivals, Swindon, for a challenge match on 25 April. The Robins had strengthened their line-up with the addition of former Poole skipper Ken Middleditch, who was always a great performer at Cowley. They had also signed a riding mate of Ray Cresp's at Wembley in Mike Broadbank, who was to go on and become the Wiltshire club's longest-serving rider. The match saw Oxford put on a battling display to triumph 55-40, with two of their new acquisitions netting excellent tallies, Jack Biggs scoring 12 points and Gordon McGregor 9+2. However, the real star of the evening was Howdy Byford, who, despite a fall, still recorded 13 points. Mention should also be made of Frank Johnson, who registered 6+1 points, which included a fine win over George White in a re-run heat twelve.

The Cheetahs faced the Robins again at Blunsdon two days later, when the home side gained revenge with a 53-43 success. The Swindon programme stated it was the first leg of the Supporters' Trophy, but this was incorrect. Both these matches were in fact raced in September. Jack Biggs was Oxford's best performer with 13+1 points, while Dennis Newton scored 9+2. For the Robins, Bob Roger went through the card unbeaten (14+1), with Ken Middleditch (11+1) and George White (10) providing valuable support.

After some good showings early on, and with things looking particularly promising at Cowley, Oxford's form regrettably became inconsistent. The fans just never knew what to expect when the tapes rose, with new boys Jack Biggs and Gordon McGregor being prime examples. On their day, both could beat anyone on any circuit, but equally if they weren't on song they could lose to anyone, be it a heat leader or a reserve. On the other hand, one man who continued to lead the Oxford scoring by example was Ronnie Genz. When the points were totted up at the end of the season it surprised no one that Genno was perched on top of the pile.

As far as official matches were concerned, the season had kicked-off with the Britannia Shield, which was split into north and south divisions. Surprisingly, Oxford were in the north section, along with Belle Vue, Leicester, Birmingham and Coventry. The group was eventually won by Belle Vue, who met southern section winners Norwich in the final.

The league programme commenced at Cowley on 6 June, when Oxford endured a defeat that was hard to swallow. Local rivals Swindon came away with a 59-37 success, but the one thing that beat the Cheetahs more than their on-form visitors was the Sandy Lane circuit. It was very dry, with hardly any shale on top and, according to reports, just wasn't good at all. The Robins didn't let the poor track worry them, whereas the Oxford lads were unhappy, complained a lot and generally let themselves become psyched out. Only two Oxford riders actually won a race throughout the entire meeting, these being Ronnie Genz in heat four and Jack Biggs in heat thirteen. Biggs went on to top his side's scoring with 10 points, while Swindon's power-packed scorechart was headed by unbeaten tallies from Ian Williams (15) and Ken Middleditch (14+1). Also weighing in with double figure for the rampant Robins were Neil Street (12+1) and George White (11+3).

Two matches then took place against Belle Vue, the first on 20 June at Cowley. This was a tight affair, although Oxford sent their fans home happy with a 50-46 victory. Jack Biggs and Ronnie Genz led the scoring with tallies of 12 and 10 points respectively. The Aces took revenge in Manchester on 22 June, winning by 60 points to 36. However, the Cheetahs had been taken aback when they saw Arthur Forrest and Eddie Rigg, both formerly of Odsal, in the Belle Vue line-up. Between them, the duo netted 11 points, Forrest scoring 9 and Rigg 2. The home side claimed that they were replacements for injured riders Peter Williams and Dick Fisher. This was done with the sanction of both the Speedway Control Board and the meeting referee, so it could be argued that Oxford's protest was merely a token gesture. Forrest, however, had refused to go to Leicester when the pre-season allocation of former Odsal riders took place, and to all intents and purposes had retired. It wasn't until much later that a decision was made by the Control Board, who ruled that the Forrest transfer be nullified, while Rigg's move was supported. Despite this, the result of the meeting was allowed to stand because Forrest had been given prior approval to ride on the night.

One of the most exciting matches of the season took place at Southampton on 25 June. The Saints were without Brian Crutcher, but nothing should be taken away from the Cheetahs, who were desperately unlucky. Indeed, Oxford began in style with a 5-1 from Ronnie Genz and Gordon McGregor. Then Genz and Frank Johnson repeated the dose in heat four, before Genno and Mac gained another 'fiver' three races later. Southampton fought back and it was level pegging with one race remaining. Against all the odds, Johnny Hole and Bill Holden combined for maximum points over Genz and Ray Cresp, giving the Saints victory by 50 points to 46. Never was a side more glorious in defeat, with McGregor heading the Cheetahs' scoring on 12+2 points.

On 26 June, Bradford, who later replaced Birmingham in the league, staged a Best Pairs event. This resulted in a win for the Cheetahs' twosome of Ronnie Genz and Dennis Newton, who did their club proud. With the happenings at Southampton in mind, Oxford enjoyed better luck at Rayleigh, where they secured a 48-48 draw on 20 July, but the away win that shook everyone occurred at Wimbledon nine days later when they triumphed 49-46.

Maury McDermott had joined Oxford from Rayleigh, but whilst he was a trier, he wasn't a heat leader and that was what the side desperately needed following a broken ankle suffered by Dennis Newton. The latter's injury occurred on 1 August, when the Cheetahs entertained Ipswich in the National League. Visitor Junior Bainbridge shed a chain in one race and Newton was unable to avoid a collision with the stricken rider's machine. At first it was thought Newton had received only bruising, but it was later reported that he had in fact fractured an ankle.

The Cheetahs once more travelled to Swindon for a league fixture on 17 August, but the Robins again had the upper hand, comfortably winning 61-35. Only Ronnie Genz with 13 points and, to a lesser degree, Ray Cresp with 9+1 saved Oxford from a real roasting in what was effectively a one-sided contest. Bob Roger hit a 15-point maximum for the home side, while Neil Street (12+1), Mike Broadbank (10+1), Ken Middleditch (9+4) and George White (9+2) also scored heavily.

Ray Cresp, like teammate Jack Biggs, hailed from Melbourne in Australia. Having joined the Cheetahs in 1957, he was to score 104 points in the league.

On 19 August, Oxford made the journey to Exeter for a challenge match. The Devon raceway had closed down at the end of the 1955 season, but Cyril Roger (a former Falcons rider now racing for Ipswich) and Geoff Pymar (formerly of Bristol) had reopened the circuit on an open licence. On the occasion of the Cheetahs' visit, Swindon's Neil Street and Dick Bradley of Southampton were brought in to head the Exeter challenge. Meanwhile, Oxford tracked Swindon's Ian Williams as a guest in place of Jack Biggs. The star of the evening in a 52-46 win was Ronnie Genz with a superb 15-point maximum, while Roy Bowers impressed with a tally of 10. Both Williams and Ray Cresp chipped in with 9 points apiece, with the Cheetahs being deserved winners of a closely fought encounter. In the second half, Oxford met Exeter in a midget car match and again came out on top. Driving for the visitors was former Cheetah Jimmy Wright, who in 1948 had suffered a very bad injury when riding at the County Ground circuit for Cradley Heath. Regrettably, he had more trouble whilst driving, losing control of his car coming off the pits turn and careering across the greyhound track, before tearing down a number of lengths of fencing. It was later learned that the damage to the dog circuit caused a meeting to be cancelled and this resulted in midget car racing being banned at Exeter. Geoff Pymar, writing in the match programme for the following week, claimed that 'repairing the damage could cost a small fortune.'

The following evening, 20 August, the Cheetahs appeared in another challenge fixture, this time up at Yarmouth. There were no guests in the Oxford team, but the Bloaters, who were operating as a non-league outfit in a similar manner to Exeter, had former favourite Billy Bales in their side, along with the likes of Danny Dunton, Peter Moore, Harry Edwards and Al Sparrey. It was little surprise that the home side ran out victors by 66 points to 30, with Ronnie Genz's 13 points heading the Cheetahs' disappointing scorechart. Ray Cresp gave some support with 8 points, but the remainder of the Oxford lads were out of touch on the tricky Caister Road circuit. For the Bloaters, Bales showed that he knew every inch of the track by registering a fine 15-point maximum. Meanwhile, Moore also notched a 15-point full-house and his battle with Genz in heat twelve was the race of the night until the top Cheetah unfortunately took a tumble. He wasn't hurt, thankfully, and remounted to claim third place.

For a home league encounter versus Rayleigh on 22 August, Swindon's Bob Roger came into the side as a guest for the injured Jack Biggs. He was a more than able deputy in registering 13 points as Oxford took victory by 57 points to 39. Another injury, an ulcerated eye, kept top man Ronnie Genz out of the Oxford team for a while, so guest riders were again called upon. Against Coventry at Cowley on 29 August it was another Swindon rider, Ian Williams, and he netted 12 points in the 54-42 defeat of the Bees, with the returned Jack Biggs heading the scoring on 13.

The first leg of the Supporters' Club Cup versus Swindon was held at Sandy Lane on 5 September. The Robins were once again in the ascendancy and claimed a narrow 50-46 win. This was despite a magnificent score of 17 points from Jack Biggs, along with 13 from guest Barry Briggs. Swindon's scoring was headed by Neil Street's 11-point return, although they had no real star, instead relying on solid scoring right down the line. In the second leg at Blunsdon two days later, Biggs came in for some justified criticism as Oxford were crushed 71-25. The Australian appeared to just tour the track and seemingly wasn't interested as he recorded a 2-point tally. Guest Harry Bastable topped the Cheetahs' scoring with 5+1 points, while Ray Cresp notched 5. In stark contrast, the Swindon section of the completed programme made for impressive reading, with three men undefeated in Mike Broadbank (14+1), Bob Roger (14+1) and Neil Street (13+2). Meanwhile, a fourth team member, Ken Middleditch, also recorded double figures, scoring 10+3 points.

The one and only Peter Craven was Oxford's guest when they entertained Southampton in a challenge match on 12 September. He was replacing Ronnie Genz and helped the Cheetahs clinch a 48-48 draw. On 26 September, Oxford gained a 51-45 success over Norwich in a further challenge fixture at Cowley. Genz returned to action to top the scoring with 11 points, while guests Ken McKinlay and 1957 World Champion Barry Briggs starred with 15 points apiece for the Stars. The match also marked the return of Dennis Newton following his broken leg and the Londoner did well, scoring 6 points. Genz's good form continued in the league match at Bradford two days later, when he led the Oxford attack with 16 points as his side went down to 58-37 defeat.

In a bid to strengthen the team, the Oxford promoters tried hard to sign German rider Josef Hofmeister, who appeared in the World Final at Wembley Stadium on 21 September, but failed to score from five starts. Regrettably, their efforts came to nothing, as Hofmeister was able to earn more money by competing in lucrative long-track meetings in his own country. Thankfully, Dennis Newton returned to the side before the season finished and on 28 September he rode for the Cheetahs at Bradford, scoring 6 points.

Briefly, going back to the World Final, the Oxford fans almost had a rider to cheer on the night… but not quite. Jack Biggs was second reserve for the big event, but unfortunately didn't get a ride. It is interesting to note that, with Wembley not operating as a league side, this was the first time the final could be said to be held on a neutral circuit.

Peter Craven posted a 15-point maximum to take the Kings of Oxford Trophy on 3 October, proving he was the master of the Sandy Lane raceway. Craven was again a visitor on 10 October for the staging of a Best Pairs contest. Gordon McGregor and Southampton's Brian Hanham emerged as the winners after Craven had crashed and retired from the meeting. Thankfully, the Belle Vue rider escaped without any broken bones. In between Craven's back-to-back appearances at Cowley, Oxford rode in a league match at Coventry on 5 October, when Arthur Forrest guested in place of the injured Jack Biggs. The Bees comfortably won the match 60-36 and Forrest netted 10 points, with reports stating he rode hard for his return. Indeed, only the former Odsal rider and McGregor, the side's top scorer with 11 points, extended the Coventry riders.

The campaign closed with a challenge match against Swindon at Cowley on 24 October and the Cheetahs signed off in style with a hard-earned 50-46 victory. Guests Dick Bradley and Ron Mountford both scored 10+1 points for Oxford, while Bob Roger charged to a five-ride full-house for the Robins.

Ronnie Genz was the top Cheetah during the season, scoring 171 league points, and he was definitely the man to beat around Oxford. Jack Biggs was next best with 158 points, whilst Gordon McGregor tallied 144 and Ray Cresp notched 104, which was a good effort in only his second season of British racing. The Cheetahs finished ninth in the league table, which meant that they'd improved on their 1956 position by a couple of places. The speedway press had described them as being a 'team without a star', which wasn't quite true, for Genz was a very capable rider indeed. What the Cheetahs desperately needed was someone to back Genno's efforts consistently. All in all, though, it wasn't a bad season with plenty of good racing to cheer the fans.

NATIONAL LEAGUE

Team	Mts	Won	Drn	Lst	For	Agn	Pts
Swindon	20	15	1	4	1,103	817	31
Belle Vue	20	15	0	5	992	830	30
Wimbledon	20	12	0	8	997	919	24
Norwich	20	11	0	9	1,015	905	22
Leicester	20	10	1	9	938	977	21
Southampton	20	9	0	11	1,002	911	18
Bradford	20	9	0	11	884	939	18
Coventry	20	9	0	11	868	1,050	18
Oxford	**20**	**7**	**1**	**12**	**880**	**1,036**	**15**
Ipswich	20	6	0	14	885	1,032	12
Rayleigh	20	5	1	14	885	1,033	11

NOTE: Bradford took over the results and fixtures of Birmingham, who withdrew after completing nine matches.

1958

When the season dawned, the speedway press described the Oxford team as 'the mixture as before', with obvious reference to the side of 1957. That turned out to be correct, since the Cheetahs were ninth in an eleven-team National League in 1957, and in 1958 they were to finish eighth out of the ten competing sides. But let's start at the beginning of the year. As far as the league was concerned, Bradford, who had taken over from Birmingham following the Midland side's closure the previous season, were non-starters, while Rayleigh moved lock, stock and barrel to Poole, where they had, in fact, staged a couple of 'home' meetings during 1957. With Poole returning to the league, Jack Biggs moved back to the scene of his former triumphs in 1956, while Ray Cresp went to Ipswich, so the Cheetahs needed replacements. These came in the form of Eric Boothroyd and Arthur Wright, both formerly of Bradford, and Reg Duval, who arrived via Coventry. Unfortunately, Howdy Byford suffered a fractured skull before the league campaign got underway and with top man Ronnie Genz enduring more problems with an eye infection, further replacements became an urgent necessity.

Kiwi Charlie New was in dispute with Coventry, where he had been a top scorer, and thankfully he joined the Oxford camp giving them an acceptable replacement for the departed Biggs. However, the team still lacked a top-class heat-leader with the high-scoring Ronnie Genz often absent. The Cheetahs' management therefore made overtures for the South African ace Doug Davies and the Swedish international Dan Forsberg, who had ridden briefly with some success for Birmingham in 1957. Regrettably, despite all the publicity and razzmatazz, neither of the signings materialised and Oxford had to keep going with the riders they had. Eric Boothroyd had filled a heat-leader berth at Birmingham/Bradford in 1957, but yet again it was a case of an established rider losing form when he arrived at Cowley, as Boothroyd struggled to find form in the Cheetahs' colours. The same could be said of Reg Duval, who had scored 121 league points for Coventry the previous year. At Oxford, his tally for league matches was 85, just 2 points less than Boothroyd, who netted only 87!

It is not particularly well known, but prior to the season Oxford had been allocated the services of former England international Eddie Rigg, who had ridden for Belle Vue the previous year. However, it was announced that the rider had in fact retired. Despite this, Rigg did appear for the Cheetahs as a guest in a Britannia Shield fixture at Belle Vue on 12 April, when he scored 4 points in a 58-40 defeat. Meanwhile, Eric Boothroyd excelled with 13 points, while another guest, Jack Biggs, gave fine support with 12. It is disappointing to relate that Boothroyd never displayed such great form for Oxford again. Despite the allocation of Rigg, he never became an official Oxford rider and later on in the season he rejoined his preferred club, Belle Vue.

There were some things to keep Cowley fans happy though. Gordon McGregor enjoyed a much better season, totalling 159 points from the league programme. He was far more consistent and he frequently headed the Cheetahs' scoring. Charlie New gave him excellent backing in recording 146 points, while Arthur Wright also had a good season to tally 122. Meanwhile, despite his eye trouble, Ronnie Genz still weighed in with 109 points. Unfortunately for Oxford, no other rider managed to top three figures. Things might have been better on the team front if Dennis Newton had ridden to his true potential, but he was another rider to struggle and it was no surprise to anyone when he upped and left after a row with the management.

Halifax-born Eric Boothroyd linked with Oxford in 1958 and recorded 87 league points. After retiring from racing, he was to promote the sport at his hometown track.

New Zealander Charlie New joined Oxford from Coventry in 1958 and enjoyed an excellent campaign, scoring 146 league points to finish second in the club's end-of-term statistics, just behind Gordon McGregor.

An interesting match took place at Cowley on 24 July, when Coventry visited for a league fixture. Former Bees Charlie New and Reg Duval both rode well to net 10 points apiece, in the process supplying excellent backing to Gordon McGregor, who top-scored for the Cheetahs with a tally of 11. With just a couple of heats to go, it had looked as though Oxford were heading for victory, but Coventry gained 5-1 and 4-2 advantages to force a 48-48 draw. Jack Young certainly showed he still knew the quickest route around the Sandy Lane circuit, recording an unbeaten 15-point maximum for the Bees.

The Cheetahs enjoyed but a single away success during the 1958 campaign, at Ipswich on 23 August, when they won 51-45. However, the Witches were unbelievably poor and most teams won there. In fact, Ipswich only won once and drew once during the whole season! At home, Oxford managed four wins and two draws, their best victory being a 54-42 success against those Witches from Ipswich on 11 September. A 48-48 draw with eventual Champions Wimbledon was a fine effort, but Leicester, Norwich and Swindon all took league points from the Cheetahs' lair during the campaign. Oxford at least got some publicity for pulling off what can only be described as the stunt of the season, when, with guest riders permitted for the top riders, they succeeded in using Barry Briggs (top point-scorer in the league with Wimbledon) as a guest for Howdy Byford!

Matches against Swindon were keenly contested as ever, the first meeting of the two adversaries occurring at Sandy Lane on 22 May, when the Robins claimed a narrow 49-47 success in a league encounter. The Cheetahs had led in the early stages, but a 5-1 from Neil Street and George White put Swindon ahead in heat eight and the visitors managed to keep their noses in front for the rest of the evening. Leicester's Jack Geran made a guest appearance for Oxford and he led the home side's scoring with 11 points, while Gordon McGregor chipped in with 10. For the Robins, Ian Williams totalled 14 points, with Street (13+1) and

Mike Broadbank (11) giving them a three-pronged attack. The return league encounter against Swindon was held at Blunsdon on 14 June, when the Robins raced to a more comfortable 56-40 success. Street sped to a 15-point maximum on this occasion, receiving excellent backing from guest Brian Hanham of Southampton (11+2) and the diminutive White (10+2). Oxford, meanwhile, were too reliant on Eric Boothroyd and Charlie New, who tallied 14+1 and 11 points respectively from six rides apiece.

Surprisingly, Oxford engaged in combat with Swindon on only one other occasion during the season, when they entertained the Robins at Cowley on 18 September in the Supporters' Trophy. The Cheetahs took a grip on proceedings right from the off and by heat six, had stormed into a 28-8 lead. They went on to win 55-41, their scorechart headed by Ronnie Genz with 12+2 points, while Arthur Wright notched 10+2. Swindon owed much to brilliant skipper Ian Williams, who recorded 15+1 points from six starts, with Neil Street also taking half a dozen rides to tally 11+1.

NATIONAL LEAGUE

Team	Mts	Won	Drn	Lst	For	Agn	Pts
Wimbledon	18	12	2	4	991	737	26
Norwich	18	12	0	6	945	782	24
Southampton	18	11	0	7	909	818	22
Leicester	18	11	0	7	869	858	22
Belle Vue	18	10	0	8	908	819	20
Swindon	18	10	0	8	875	851	20
Coventry	18	9	1	8	893	833	19
Oxford	**18**	**5**	**2**	**11**	**783**	**943**	**12**
Poole	18	6	0	12	754	973	12
Ipswich	18	1	1	16	707	1,020	3

1959

The 1959 season will always have special memories for Oxford fans. The Cheetahs didn't accomplish anything of note in their quest to climb the league table, but what made the year so memorable for everyone was the signing of the Danish Champion Arne Pander. There was no doubt that manager Ted Flanaghan took a mighty gamble when he signed Pander, because in those days the Danes were comparatively untried in British racing. However, from the off, Pander showed that he was of heat-leader class, and how he thrilled the Cowley public. At long last, the Cheetahs had a speedster who could take on and beat the world-class riders who featured in National League speedway. Among the top stars of the day were, of course, Peter Craven (Belle Vue), Ken McKinlay (Leicester), Ove Fundin (Norwich), Brian Crutcher (Southampton) and Ronnie Moore (Wimbledon), and Oxford now had a rider of equal calibre in Pander.

There were the usual team changes before the season commenced, which saw Eric Boothroyd move to Leicester, while Charlie New was a non-starter, preferring to remain in his native New Zealand. Ronnie Genz was not immediately available, having undergone an operation to the eye injury that troubled him throughout most of 1958. Happily, Howdy Byford had recovered from injury and returned to the side and the 'Champ' was made team captain for the year. Ken Adams moved in from Poole, with Reg Duval moving in the opposite direction to Dorset. The remainder of the early season side was made up with Gordon McGregor, Roy Bowers, Arthur Wright, plus the up-and-coming Colin Gooddy.

Above left: Blackheath-born Colin 'Joe' Gooddy scored 61 points for the Cheetahs during their National League programme in 1959.

Above right: Oxford made a wonderful signing in 1959, when reigning Danish Champion Arne Pander agreed to join. In his first term in the club's colours, he was to head the league scoring with 174 points.

There was an early change, though, when Arthur Wright disappeared from the Cowley scene having struggled to find form, but Nick Nicholls arrived from Coventry and was a more than adequate replacement. On the domestic front, the National League was now down to nine teams, with Ipswich pulling out after their disastrous 1958 campaign. The National Reserve League was introduced to give more interest in the second half of meetings, but its introduction was stormy, mainly because of the self-made muddle over the match format compared with that of the Britannia Shield. The Reserve League was a good idea in principle, but the idea bit the dust, with a number of matches not being run.

The Britannia Shield wasn't a very successful competition for the Cheetahs, who surprisingly competed in the northern section of the competition. Out of six matches ridden, Oxford won two (against Leicester and Belle Vue) and lost four, while they went out of the National Trophy to Southampton by 112 points to 104 on aggregate. In the league, the Cheetahs won seven matches and lost nine, the big problem being that the side relied far too heavily on Arne Pander. The Dane remained ever-present throughout the sixteen-match league programme to tally 174 points; this being a tremendous effort when one considers that he was riding on British tracks for the first time! Home victories over Belle Vue, Coventry, Leicester, Norwich, Southampton and Swindon cheered the Cowley supporters, but Poole sneaked a 1-point victory, and a powerful Wimbledon team inflicted a heavy 56-34 home defeat on 11 June.

The month of August brought home and away challenge matches against Poole. The Cheetahs won a thrilling home encounter 55-53 on 6 August, before going down 63-51 in a battling display at Wimborne Road a day later. The man of both meetings for Oxford was their Danish star Arne Pander, who recorded 14 points at Cowley and 16 at Poole. He shone like a beacon and the supporters of both sides cheered his efforts. Roy Bowers also enjoyed two excellent matches, scoring 9 points at home and a superb 13 down in Dorset.

Away from Cowley, the Cheetahs gave a fine performance at Belle Vue to win their league fixture 46-44 on 22 August, with Gordon McGregor scoring a maximum. Prior to that, the Cheetahs were desperately unlucky in the local derby at Swindon on 1 August, where they lost by a single point, 45-44, despite a quite brilliant 15-point maximum from the 'Great Dane' Arne Pander. The side were also unlucky at Leicester, where they went down by just 2 points. There was to be no further away success for Oxford and they lost heavily at Southampton, 74-34, which was their worst performance of the season. They were also hammered 70-38 at Wimbledon, who were to take the National League title by 9 clear points from their closest challengers, Leicester.

The Cheetahs finished the league campaign occupying seventh position from nine teams, which wasn't much of an improvement on their 1958 performance. After the immaculate Arne Pander, Oxford's best servant was Gordon McGregor, who yielded 153 points, but they were the only ones to top a century of points. Ronnie Genz was next in line, with 94 points, while Colin Gooddy made great progress to notch a creditable tally of 61. Meanwhile, in the incomplete National Reserve League, Oxford finished in sixth position having ridden twelve matches.

NATIONAL LEAGUE

Team	Mts	Won	Drn	Lst	For	Agn	Pts
Wimbledon	16	13	0	3	893	635	26
Leicester	16	8	1	7	759	768	17
Coventry	16	8	1	7	750	797	17
Norwich	16	8	0	8	784	762	16
Southampton	16	8	0	8	769	758	16
Poole	16	8	0	8	716	813	16
Oxford	**16**	**7**	**0**	**9**	**733**	**773**	**14**
Swindon	16	6	0	10	726	766	12
Belle Vue	16	5	0	11	735	793	10

1960

The 1960 season heralded a welcome upsurge in speedway's fortunes, with the formation of a brand new ten-team Provincial League. At last, there was welcome news, with tracks opening rather than closing, and there was further good news when it was announced that New Cross would be re-opening and joining the National League. Ipswich returned, after a season's absence, with the Poole promotion moving to Suffolk, while a new administration took over at Wimborne Road and entered the Pirates in the newly formed Provincial League.

Oxford were now members of a National League that comprised ten teams and everyone down at Cowley looked forward to an enjoyable season. And that is just what it turned out to be, with the Cheetahs making a real challenge for the silverware. Indeed, if they had had a little more strength at the lower end of the side, then they could easily have knocked Wimbledon off their perch at the top. With Arne Pander back for his second year at Oxford, things looked bright when Charlie New indicated he wanted to return to the side. Unfortunately, he had a last-minute change of heart and stayed at home, which became the second disappointment for the Cheetahs in their quest for team strength. The first had been the failure to land the

Danny Dunton makes some adjustments to his bike, having linked with the Cheetahs in 1960. Born in Cholesbury, Buckinghamshire, he was to net 50 league points for the side that year. Just a few years later, he was to become promoter at Oxford.

fast-starting Peter Moore, who had spent the latter part of 1959 on loan to Norwich. The Oxford management had agreed a transfer fee with Moore's parent club, Wimbledon; however, with Ipswich returning to the National League, the rider was keen to return to the scene of his former triumphs, and subsequently lined up with the Witches.

The Cheetahs began the campaign with much the same side as the previous season, with the exception of Nick Nicholls, who returned to Coventry. However, there was to be a marked contrast to the year before, and the most important factor was the return to form of Ronnie Genz. After two years of suffering with persistent eye trouble, it was a real treat to see Genno showing all his old form, and with Gordon McGregor maintaining remarkable consistency in his scoring, Oxford finally had two riders able to give Arne Pander the backing he so richly deserved.

In June, the Cheetahs' management pulled off a smart piece of business, which was to give them extra strength in depth, and provide further support for their top three. It came in the form of an exchange deal, with the promising Colin Gooddy going to Ipswich and the experienced Jack Biggs returning to Cowley. The Aussie hadn't had a very happy time at Ipswich and was unable to settle, but his return to Cowley proved to be a real tonic for him and he soon recaptured his form, giving the Cheetahs a really impressive top four. A further new face for the 1960 term was Danny Dunton, who was with Belle Vue in 1959. Dunton, of course, would return in later years to promote the fortunes of Oxford Speedway.

Eric Boothroyd returned after a short spell at Leicester. Regrettably, unlike Jack Biggs, the rider's return didn't mean a rekindling of form and Boothroyd struggled. Howdy Byford and Ken Adams were other riders to find it hard going, while it was Roy Bowers who was the best of the lower order, where the Cheetahs also gave opportunities to Dave Still, Cliff Cox and a young Bobby Dugard. At home, Oxford enjoyed plenty of success with a number of good, close matches. Both Leicester and Norwich were beaten by 8-point margins, with Swindon and Southampton being defeated by 6, while Wimbledon and New Cross were seen off by just 2 points in real nail-biting affairs. The biggest home victory was a 59-30 success over Coventry, with the next best being a 55-35 win against Ipswich. Meanwhile, Belle Vue were the only club to take points from Cowley, when, on 15 September, they won another tremendous meeting by 47 points to 43. Away from home, the Cheetahs enjoyed a decisive 51-39 win at Ipswich and a fine victory over Southampton, but the sweetest win of all was a 2-point success at Swindon on 1 October, when Arne Pander scorched to a 12-point maximum and Gordon McGregor weighed in with a 10+1 tally.

Nine days after the win at Swindon, and still with a hope of grabbing the League Championship, the Cheetahs visited Wimbledon, only to go down fighting by 8 points, 49-41. The worst away defeat was at Leicester, where Oxford lost 57-33, but they were desperately unlucky at Belle Vue, losing 47-43, an identical score to that at Cowley. All in all, it was a great season at Sandy Lane, with the Cheetahs providing good value for money and always being attractive visitors on their travels. Third position in the league was a fine effort, with only Champions Wimbledon and runners-up Belle Vue finishing higher, and a mere 4 points between all three sides.

NATIONAL LEAGUE

Team	Mts	Won	Drn	Lst	For	Agn	Pts
Wimbledon	17	13	0	4	838	691	26
Belle Vue	18	11	1	6	890	726	23
Oxford	**18**	**11**	**0**	**7**	**816**	**797**	**22**
Ipswich	18	10	0	8	751	863	20
Norwich	17	8	1	8	748.5	779.5	17
Leicester	18	7	2	9	793.5	825.5	16
Southampton	18	7	1	10	815	794	15
New Cross	18	7	1	10	770	840	15
Coventry	18	7	0	11	810	807	14
Swindon	18	5	0	13	754	863	10

NOTE: One match, Norwich *v.* Wimbledon, was not raced.

1961

Oxford Cheetahs had every reason to be optimistic when the 1961 season dawned, after their successful time the year before. The National League was as before, with the same ten teams, and although there were one or two Provincial League clubs that fell by the wayside, the new set-up was prospering and eventually healthily lined up with eleven competing sides. On the team front, Oxford had a few changes, with Eric Boothroyd and Ken Adams departing for the less demanding racing in the Provincial League, with Middlesbrough and Stoke respectively. Meanwhile, Reg Duval returned to Cowley following a year in the wilderness. With the same top four of Arne Pander, Ronnie Genz, Gordon McGregor and Jack Biggs, who had successfully done the business in 1960, plus Danny Dunton, Roy Bowers and Howdy Byford, things were really buzzing as the campaign dawned.

Things didn't go too badly to start with, and a storming league success over Coventry by 59 points to 19 suggested great things for the Cheetahs. But, as so often happens, it didn't work out and the hand of fate was to deliver a crushing blow to Oxford in July, when Arne

Pander suffered a fractured skull in a track accident at Coventry. This really knocked the club sideways and, in truth, they never really recovered from it. Pander, since his arrival in 1959, had been the cornerstone of the team, having taken on and beaten the best in the league, while his mere presence had inspired confidence amongst his teammates. They had come to rely on his regular double-figure scores and his absence was to have a demoralising effect on the rest of the side. The popular Howdy Byford, who had really found the pace of the National League a trifle hot over the previous couple of years, departed to join Exeter in the Provincial League. There, he linked up with another former Cheetah in Roy Bowers, who had lost form completely and had been granted a transfer. As if the Oxford promotion didn't have enough problems, Jack Biggs, who in 1960 had supplied vital backing to the Cheetahs' heat-leader trio, underwent an internal operation, which affected both his form and fitness.

With the Provincial League offering valuable opportunities to young riders to make good and a stimulus to veteran riders who wanted one last fling, there really became a shortage of riders in the top flight. The upshot of this was that team spots became too safe and, in particular at Oxford, no rider at the lower end of the side was seriously challenged for his place, resulting in complacency setting in. Despite the problems, the promotion did try to do something constructive. Jim Tebby was signed from Wimbledon, having previously appeared for the Cheetahs in 1956, but whilst he was young and promising, he needed to be in a team that could carry him for a spell whilst he learned the business. Indeed, had he been in the line-up the previous season, he could have been very useful, but in 1961, far too much was expected and he clearly wasn't the answer to the team's problems. Stylish Swede Bengt Brannefors had a short and unsuccessful time at Cowley. He was regarded as one of his country's up-and-coming riders, but was not of the Ove Fundin or Bjorn Knutsson class and proved most disappointing.

Roy Bowers was born in High Wycombe and had scored 59 league points for the Cheetahs in 1960. However, after losing form at the start of 1961, he was transferred to Exeter.

After the injury to Arne Pander, it was left to Ronnie Genz to lead the Cheetahs' challenge and he continued to give sterling service to the cause. Often, however, the team gave the impression that they were just going through the motions and that view was definitely held by the Oxford promoters. Towards the end of the season, Dickie Worth, the Cheetahs' boss, fed up with what he felt were some mediocre performances, threatened to put everyone in the squad (with the exception of Pander and Genz) on the transfer list. It put the final seal on a totally disappointing season.

Prior to Arne Pander's injury, in what was a welcome break from the pressure that goes with team fixtures, Oxford did at least have five representatives in the Midland Riders' Championship final at Swindon on 21 June, namely Danny Dunton, Ronnie Genz, Jack Biggs, Gordon McGregor and Pander himself. Pander quickly showed that he would be a force in the prestigious event by racing to a hat-trick of wins, and he made it four out of four by taking heat thirteen in blistering fashion. He then had to wait until heat twenty for his final outing and going into the race he needed just 1 point to go one better than he had in the 1960 final, when Coventry star Henryk Zyto had taken the title at Brandon Stadium. However, with the race in his pocket, the cruellest of luck hit Pander and he ground to a halt after his engine had blown to smithereens. This meant both Pander and Jack Geran had finished level on 12 points at the top of the tree, necessitating a title run-off. Things were different in those far off days and few riders had two bikes, so the popular Dane was stuck. It was then, in a wonderful display of sportsmanship, that Swindon's Neil Street offered his machine for Pander to use. Emphasising just how generous a gesture this was, for those who didn't know, Street was actually Geran's best mate within the sport! Anyway, Pander willingly accepted the offer and it would have been nice to have written a happy ending for the Oxford star, who was without doubt the best rider on view that night, but it Geran who went on to take the chequered flag in the showdown. For the record, the other Oxford riders scored thus: McGregor 10, Dunton 8, Genz 5 and Biggs 2.

The Cheetahs won only six league matches during the year, all at home, where they also drew once. Both Swindon and Wimbledon took the league points from Cowley, while away from home Oxford had no success at all, their best effort being a 2-point loss at Coventry. It was a troubled season for the fans, who saw their side slide down the league table to finish one place above bottom club Leicester.

NATIONAL LEAGUE

Team	Mts	Won	Drn	Lst	For	Agn	Pts
Wimbledon	18	15	0	3	830	573	30
Southampton	18	13	2	3	788	613	28
Coventry	18	10	1	7	676	728	21
Belle Vue	18	10	0	8	761	642	20
Swindon	18	8	0	10	683	719	16
Ipswich	18	7	1	10	681.5	720.5	15
Norwich	18	7	0	11	691.5	700.5	14
New Cross	18	7	0	11	626	774	14
Oxford	**18**	**6**	**1**	**11**	**665**	**727**	**13**
Leicester	18	4	1	13	599	804	9

1962

The 1962 season at Oxford saw an old familiar pattern, something that the supporters of the Cheetahs had often seen in the past, that of a weak team, with the poor results that accompanied it. Handicapped racing had been introduced, although unlucky Oxford had no rider of the class of the so-named 'Big Five', who were the top riders in the league, namely Barry Briggs, Peter Craven, Ove Fundin, Bjorn Knutsson and Ronnie Moore. The Cheetahs might have had a rider to join the illustrious group on the 20-yard handicap had Arne Pander been fit and able to ride, but the side's diminutive Dane was unfortunately missing due to the terrible injury he had suffered at Coventry the previous July. Much could be said for the quick thinking of Oxford boss Ted Flanaghan and the skill of neurosurgeon Dr. Joseph Pennybacker of the Radcliffe Infirmary, who took care of the rider. Thankfully, Pander made a wonderful recovery and was reported as being back on a speedway machine on the continental tracks prior to the end of the season. Regrettably for the Oxford public, the ace rider was never replaced and the team suffered. It was reported that the management made another approach to sign German star Josef Hofmeister, but nothing came to fruition as the rider found continental long-track racing more lucrative. With regard to the domestic set-up, New Cross closed down and Leicester opted to participate in the Provincial League, leaving the National League with just eight teams.

Oxford did at least sign two former Leicester riders in Alf Hagon and Australian Jack Geran. Meanwhile, John Bishop, a young rider from the High Wycombe area, was given trials and made the most of his opportunities. As for the rest of the side, despite the threat to transfer the whole of the 1961 team apart from Arne Pander and Ronnie Genz, most of the old guard did return. As the season progressed, any supporter of the Cheetahs could have been excused if they secretly thought that perhaps it might have been better if they had moved on. Jack Biggs, it was reported, was often in dispute with the management over first one thing, then another and, as was to be expected, it showed in his racing. Gordon McGregor also seemed to lose his zest for the sport as the campaign progressed, becoming gloriously inconsistent. Biggs and McGregor weren't alone, since many other members of the side appeared to lose their will to race on occasion. However, such criticism could not be levelled at Ronnie Genz, who, in a season not to be remembered fondly, was a shining light. Genno's attitude was exemplary and he was always willing to compete all the way to the chequered flag, irrespective of the opposition.

The season opened on Good Friday 20 April, with home and away challenge matches against near neighbours Swindon for the Hutchins Trophy. It wasn't a particularly good afternoon when the Cheetahs lined up for the first leg at Cowley. However, Jack Biggs gave one of his best performances to notch 10 points, while Danny Dunton looked sharp on his way to a tally of 9. Meanwhile, Ronnie Genz recorded 7 points despite a fall in the last heat. For Jack Geran, the meeting was a nightmare, as he suffered machine trouble all the way through, retiring in his first two outings and then failing to score from his other two rides. This clearly played a huge part in Oxford's 43-35 defeat, before the team journeyed to Blunsdon for the second leg in the evening. For the victorious Robins, Neil Street led the way with 11 points, while track specialist Ian Williams scored 9.

Unfortunately, at Swindon it was Ronnie Genz who couldn't get going, scoring just 2 points. On the other hand, Jack Geran seemed to have sorted out his mechanical gremlins to register a fine 8-point score. The big surprise was 10+1 points from Gordon McGregor, which the Oxford supporters hoped was a sign of things to come. Despite this, at the end of thirteen heats of competitive racing, it was the Robins who came out on top by 43 points to 34 to secure an aggregate success of 86-69. Neil Street went one better than he had at Cowley, romping to a fine 12-point maximum, with Mike Broadbank being the best of the supporting cast in scoring 9+2.

In an attempt to strengthen the Cheetahs' side, Per Tage Svensson, a Swedish international who had actually ridden in the past on the Cowley raceway, was signed. He made quite a stir on one particularly hot summer's evening, when he arrived wearing a pair of very trendy shorts, and he certainly made a bright start for Oxford with some good double-figure scores. Regrettably, a combination of the handicap system and his journeys home to Sweden took their toll and it wasn't long before he was struggling, just like many of his teammates.

Swede Per Tage Svensson
linked with the Cheetahs
during 1962 and recorded
77 points from the National
League programme.

Oxford again entertained their old enemies, Swindon, in a challenge match on 24 May. Jack Geran was the man of the match, showing blistering form and racing to a 12-point maximum, while Gordon McGregor also rode well to tally 10. Their efforts helped the Cheetahs to a comfortable 48-30 success, with the Robins' leading performer being Martin Ashby on the 7-point mark. Swindon visited once more on 28 June for a league encounter and Oxford were unable to repeat their performance in the challenge fixture, going down by 40 points to 37. Ronnie Genz was again in the wars, taking a tumble in only his second outing and missing the remainder of the meeting as a result. This was clearly a contributory factor in the Robins' success, although the visitors did possess two unbeaten riders in Neil Street (12) and Mike Broadbank (11+1). On what was a disappointing evening in the home camp, Jack Biggs headed the scorechart with 10+2 points, while Alf Hagon carded 10+1.

There was an unwanted happening in the National League, when Ipswich were forced to close down. This was a real blow since the league was now down to just seven teams, and any speedway fan could be excused for wondering just how long things could go on, especially as the Provincial League was flourishing. As a result of the Witches' closure, Colin Gooddy returned to Cowley and his all-action style was a welcome sight for the Oxford supporters. On the downside, with Ipswich's results being expunged from the records, the Cheetahs' 40-38 win at Foxhall Heath on 18 May was wiped out, as was a resounding 49-29 victory over the Suffolk side at Sandy Lane eight days previously on 10 May. Worse still for Oxford was the fact that this left them at the foot of the league standings and, unfortunately, that's where they stayed.

The National Trophy competition began well for the Cheetahs, with a 47-37 victory over Norwich in the first leg at Cowley on 14 June. The second leg also proved successful in a

Australian rider Jack Geran joined Oxford via Leicester in 1962. He was to top the Cheetahs' scoring that year, netting 154 points in the National League.

match full of controversy at The Firs on 16 June. To be fair, the racing strip was in poor shape and certainly caught out the home side, who seemed lost. The surprise for the Oxford fans was the riding of Jack Biggs, who wasn't known for great performances on 'dodgy' tracks. However, riding off scratch, he enjoyed a wonderful meeting and was his side's top scorer with 11 points. An on-track move, which left all the travelling supporters simply drooling, was when Ronnie Genz passed the great Ove Fundin, because not many visitors did that at Norwich. As the Oxford fans left for home, complete with a 51-33 success in the bag, the Norwich supporters were demonstrating about the state of the raceway. Cries of 'Bring back Aub, he wouldn't have put up with that track' could be heard, with reference to the club's former skipper Aub Lawson. However, it mattered not to the fans of Oxford, who had seen their team just get on with the job of racing.

Oxford visited Swindon for a league match on Saturday 4 August. Colin Gooddy was a member of the Cheetahs' side, riding in the number one spot. Meanwhile, the old Ipswich number one, Peter Moore, who in seasons past Oxford had tried to sign, was appearing for the Robins. The Aussie was quite superb for his new side too, scorching to a 12-point maximum as Swindon took victory by 42 points to 36; the win being clinched in the last heat with a 5-1. A lively Gordon McGregor scored 9 points for the Cheetahs, while Gooddy gained a hard-earned tally of 5+3. Ronnie Genz wasn't present for the match due to an injury and this was a shame since a normal score from him would surely have seen the Cheetahs take the points from their oldest rivals.

August also saw the staging of the National Trophy semi-final, when Oxford again met Swindon, who had been managed since the beginning of the season by Roger Wise, a former Cheetahs' rider from 1951. The first leg was at Blunsdon on 18 August, when Per Tage Svensson was unfortunately unavailable. Only Gordon McGregor with 9 points and Jack Biggs with 6+1 showed anything like worthwhile form as the Cheetahs were crushed 59-25. Aside from them, John Bishop could be excused; his 3 points from the reserve berth being the result of some wholehearted efforts. For the Robins, Neil Street registered a five-ride paid maximum (14+1) and Mike Broadbank scored 14. The second leg at Sandy Lane five days later saw the Oxford lads ride with considerably more spirit to win by 45 points to 39, although they were beaten 98-70 on aggregate. Jack Geran (13) and Colin Gooddy (11+1) were the leading lights for the Cheetahs, with Swindon best served by Peter Moore (11+1).

On 25 August, there was a shock for the Oxford supporters, although they had become accustomed to that kind of thing. This one seemed to come out of the blue, though, when promoter Ted Flanaghan parted company with the club to take charge of a petrol filling station situated close to Oxford Stadium. He had worked his fingers to the bone in his efforts to make a success of the club. Indeed, every supporter of the side would always be grateful to him for bringing Arne Pander to the Cheetahs' lair in 1959. After the departure of Flanaghan, it was left to Dickie Worth to continue as sole promoter of Oxford's fortunes.

In the National League, the competing teams faced each other four times, twice at home and twice away. It was very frustrating at the end of a troubled season to see that Oxford had won but four matches at Cowley. They recorded an excellent 47-31 win over Coventry on 19 July, having already defeated the Bees by 42 points to 36 on 17 May. Norwich were beaten 49-29 on 16 August and there was an oh-so-welcome win over Swindon on 13 September by 41 points to 37. That was the sum total of Oxford's successes for the season, with the win against the Robins being a triumph for Jack Geran, who finally showed his best form with a 12-point maximum.

There was another sign of Jack Geran's vintage form on 27 September, when he accrued 14 points to win the Double Diamond Trophy at Cowley. Meanwhile, Swindon's Mike Broadbank filled the runner-up position with 13 points. Prior to that, the other big individual meeting for the Kings of Oxford Trophy on 30 August had seen Belle Vue's Peter Craven take victory, with Bjorn Knutsson of Southampton in second spot. Craven's winning tally was 14 points and his only defeat came in heat twenty, when Barry Briggs took the chequered flag.

Oxford's away form was nothing short of dreadful as they were beaten in all twelve of their league matches on the road. Twice they were soundly beaten at Southampton, losing 60-18 on 5 June, before going down 59-19 on 28 August. Often the Cheetahs struggled to make the 30-point mark and it was the fixtures against Swindon that brought the best out of the side. Both matches at Blunsdon were close, with the Robins narrowly winning 40-38 and 42-36. With a bit of luck, Oxford could have won both meetings, but the non-arrival of Jack Biggs caused a problem on 26 May, when they went down by just 2 points. The Cheetahs could only field one rider in heat eight and this cost them dearly, since Brian Meredith and Neil Street posted a 5-1 for the Robins over John Bishop. Leading the Oxford scoring on this occasion was Gordon McGregor with 11 points, while Alf Hagon scored 10. For Swindon, Mike Broadbank went through the card for a 12-point maximum, with Street (9+1) and Ian Williams (8+1) supplying excellent backing. The second league match at Blunsdon was held on 4 August and although the Cheetahs only went down by 6 points, they provided just two race winners. Both Broadbank and Peter Moore notched four-ride maximums for Swindon, while Neil Street was also paid for the lot in scoring 11+1. With 9 points, McGregor again topped the Oxford scorechart, his total including a victory in heat eight. The only other visitor to take the flag was Per Tage Svensson in heat four, on his way to 7 points.

Regrettably, all the results added up to the Cheetahs claiming the cellar position, having finished 12 points adrift of Swindon in the final league standings. Jack Geran was the side's leading performer with 154 points from the National League programme, with Alf Hagon finishing second in the statistical rundown on 133. Next in line was Ronnie Genz on 116.5 points, while Gordon McGregor totalled 110.

NATIONAL LEAGUE

Team	Mts	Won	Drn	Lst	For	Agn	Pts
Southampton	24	18	0	6	1,084	785	36
Wimbledon	24	14	1	9	1,034	836	29
Coventry	24	13	0	11	992.5	875.5	26
Belle Vue	24	12	1	11	886	984	25
Norwich	24	12	0	12	909	962	24
Swindon	24	9	2	13	869	997	20
Oxford	**24**	**4**	**0**	**20**	**767.5**	**1,102.5**	**8**

NOTE: Ipswich withdrew from the league after completing fifteen matches, with their record expunged from the table.

1963

Oxford fans looked ahead to the 1963 season, believing that things could only improve after the dismal year before. After all, they had been cheered by the news that Arne Pander would be back following a year's absence, having fully recovered from the injuries he received during 1961. There were the usual changes before the off, and neither of the moves of riders away from Cowley were a surprise. Jack Biggs departed for Coventry, while Gordon McGregor left to join Belle Vue. Added to this, Per Tage Svensson remained in Sweden and Reg Duval retired. In their places came Pander, of course, and from Southampton came established Australian international Chum Taylor. The Aussie had missed the 1962 season and returned feeling confident that he'd be lining up with the Saints; however, the Control Board considered Southampton too strong and the rider was posted to Oxford. It would be fair to say that Taylor didn't welcome the move and made it clear that had he known of his move before the season began, he would have remained at home in Australia!

A pre-season shock, which in the event was almost beyond belief, was the announcement that the Oxford management would consider offers for Ronnie Genz. Such a statement was total nonsense, since Genno had been a great servant to the club and over the years had proved to be the most consistent rider in the Oxford camp. Thankfully, common sense prevailed and Genz stayed at Cowley, linking with Arne Pander, Jack Geran, Colin Gooddy, Alf Hagon and Chum Taylor, plus promising youngsters John Bishop and George Major to form a nicely balanced line-up.

On 9 May, Oxford raced in a challenge match against a team called Provincial Selected, which basically featured some of the top riders from what was effectively the lower sphere of British racing at the time. The Cheetahs registered a narrow win by 40 points to 38, with John Bishop really shining as he racked up a 12-point tally. Meanwhile, Ivor Brown of Cradley Heath was the leading performer for the opposition, with 10 points. It is fair to say that Oxford would have won more convincingly had Arne Pander not been hurt in a heat one accident, which also involved Wayne Briggs. The visitor was excluded from the re-run, but unfortunately Pander didn't ride again in the match. The real gem of the meeting was the added attraction of a *Sunday Mirror* British Golden Helmet Match-Race decider between Peter Craven of Belle Vue and Ove Fundin of Norwich. Craven was magnificent in the first race, rocketing around the Cowley circuit to set a new track record of 63.0 seconds. In his second ride, the diminutive rider wasn't quite as fast, but he still took victory in a time of 63.8 seconds. Seeing Craven in full flight was really something to savour, as all those lucky enough to see him in action would happily testify. As a measure of how fast Craven was going, his track record was to stand for just over seventeen years, until Dave Perks was clocked at 62.2 seconds on 19 June 1980.

Chum Taylor was born in Perth, Western Australia and had confidently expected to link with Southampton in 1963. However, the Control Board instead posted him to Oxford, for whom he was to score 105 league points that year. His full name was actually Edwin Vernon Taylor.

The National League continued with just seven sides, with the teams meeting each other twice. Handicap racing remained in place, with Arne Pander given a 10-yard handicap like most of the main body of the team. The handicap system, like other rules introduced, caused many problems over who started from where, with the result that match scores were often altered by officialdom due to riders starting from the wrong handicap. The Cheetahs were one of the sides to suffer, when, having beaten Belle Vue 40-38 on 6 June, the points scored by John Bishop were deducted as he had lined up at the gate, and not ten yards back. The result was subsequently amended to a 38-34 defeat. This was nonsense when you consider the experience of Bishop compared with Pander, Jack Geran or Ronnie Genz.

Happily, there was some evidence of increased enthusiasm from the team, although Oxford were to be badly hit by injuries. Chum Taylor broke a collarbone in a World Championship qualifying round at Poole on 12 June, and was hardly back in action when he suffered a fractured ankle at Swindon on 24 August. Alf Hagon was another rider to suffer a broken ankle, while Arne Pander sustained a broken thumb.

The injuries certainly took their toll and it was no surprise that the Cheetahs were unable to move up from their basement position of 1962, having won just six of their home matches, while drawing one other. There were no successes at all on the road, but Oxford did provide spirited opposition at a number of tracks. Most notably, they ran Coventry close in both matches at Brandon, losing by 2 points on the first occasion and 6 points in the second match.

Not for the first time, Ronnie Genz was a tower of strength and he ended the season as the highest points plunderer in the side, totalling 172 in league matches. Jack Geran had a much better year, and Colin Gooddy came on in leaps and bounds, making good progress. Quite understandably, Arne Pander was not back to his pre-injury form, although he still managed to top the 100-point mark.

NATIONAL LEAGUE

Team	Mts	Won	Drn	Lst	For	Agn	Pts
Belle Vue	24	17	0	7	989	875	34
Norwich	24	13	2	9	911	879	28
Wimbledon	24	12	1	11	934	920	25
Coventry	24	11	2	11	912	957	24
Swindon	24	10	2	12	907	875	22
Southampton	24	11	0	13	933	936	22
Oxford	**24**	**6**	**1**	**17**	**861**	**1,005**	**13**

1964

The 1964 season was the most troubled in the history of the sport, with the strong, thirteen-team Provincial League riding outside the jurisdiction of the Speedway Control Board. Things weren't so good in the National League, though, with Southampton closing down, having been a victim of the developers. That left the league with a mere six teams, although that was increased to seven when West Ham reopened.

There were storm clouds over Oxford too, as promoter Dickie Worth's lease had ceased early in the year. The new season was only weeks away, when two new promoters, namely Cyril Melville and Rodney Rycroft, took up the reins under the banner of Oxford Speedway Ltd. New boys they may have been, but they came in with one basic sensible idea, namely that the Cheetahs would no longer be the chopping block for the rest of the league and their subsequent signings proved they meant business. Ron How, an established international heat-leader, was signed from Wimbledon, and Jimmy Gooch was also recruited via Norwich. Eddie Reeves, who had enjoyed limited experience in the Provincial League with New Cross the previous year, also joined the Cheetahs' camp.

Ron How pictured with the winner's cheque after his triumph in the World Championship round at Cowley on 23 July 1964.

The 1964 Cheetahs celebrate their success in the Britannia Shield. From left to right: Eddie Reeves, Arne Pander, Cyril Melville (co-promoter), Jimmy Gooch, Jack Geran, John Bishop, Ron How, Colin Gooddy, Ronnie Genz.

With new eight-man teams and fourteen-heat matches being the order of the day, at last Oxford had a side strong in all departments: Arne Pander, Ronnie Genz, Jack Geran (captain), Colin Gooddy, Ron How, Jimmy Gooch, John Bishop and Eddie Reeves. Meanwhile, Chum Taylor from the 1963 outfit had returned to Australia, although he was later to appear for Provincial League Poole. George Major had a few meetings before the league campaign got underway, before he too opted for Provincial League action and linked with Cradley Heath.

Handicap racing, a thorny subject in pre-season wrangles, remained in National League racing, for part of the season anyway. In August, Barry Briggs, who had joined Swindon following the closure of Southampton, threatened to retire if the scheme wasn't abolished. Leading ACU referee Cecil Telling backed 'Briggo' all the way, with the result that handicapping ceased for the latter part of the season, thankfully never to return. With a limited number of teams in the National League, the promoters opted for a one home, one away league format, which was a surprise. The league, therefore, didn't begin until June, with the Easter Challenge Cup, Britannia Shield and National Trophy matches filling the early season fixtures. There is no doubt that the Cheetahs, who had changed their race jacket from the familiar blue with yellow sash to a cheetah's head on a blue background, were the team to beat. They were, in fact, awesome at home, and the most attractive of visitors on their travels, and it was strange after a number of mediocre seasons at Cowley to hear the cry from opponents that Oxford were too strong!

Yet, despite their success, support was not as forthcoming for the Cheetahs as their new promoters had hoped for. A hard core of loyal fans existed, but looking at the season as a whole, the successful 1964 Cheetahs did not really enjoy the sort of support their efforts deserved. As expected, Ron How proved to be the number one man at Cowley, and he and Jimmy Gooch formed as good a pairing as the entire league possessed. Arne Pander showed all of his old form, while Jack Geran was a fine skipper. Ronnie Genz and Colin Gooddy were consistent, and the reserves, John Bishop and Eddie Reeves, showed plenty of spirit. Reeves, in particular, despite his lack of experience, always battled for points, and his enthusiasm kept the top six on their toes.

Despite their general success, the Cheetahs had to wait for their final league match to be sure of becoming Champions. Coventry were breathing down their necks, but in the end it was Oxford who lifted the Championship by a single point, winning nine of their matches, and losing only three. Indeed, it was Coventry who inflicted one of those defeats, beating the Cheetahs at Brandon by 51 points to 33. Oxford's other two defeats were suffered at Norwich and Belle Vue, by scores of 45-39 and 46-38 respectively. At home, the team never tasted defeat, with their best success being a 54-30 victory over Wimbledon, and the closest they came to being beaten was when lowly Swindon visited on 17 September. Led by a brilliant 15-point maximum from Barry Briggs, the Robins pushed hard, but Oxford's strength in depth finally got them past the winning post by 45 points to 39.

The Britannia Shield competition resulted in another Oxford triumph, with the Cheetahs winning by a solitary point, again from rivals Coventry. In all, Oxford won eight matches, drew just once (at West Ham) and lost three times. Then, in the National Trophy, the Cheetahs defeated Norwich and Belle Vue on their way to facing West Ham in the final. The Hammers looked to be heading for victory after winning the first leg 52-32 at their Custom House raceway on 22 September. However, two evenings later, the Oxford lads produced a breathtaking performance to win 53-31, thereby securing a narrow 85-83 success on aggregate.

With so few teams operating in the National League, outside bookings were at a premium and envious glances were turned to the 'black' Provincial League. The Cheetahs' Ronnie Genz accepted a booking for Provincial League side Exeter under the assumed name of 'Reg Neal'. All things considered, Genno came off lightly when summoned before the Control Board, being fined only £5 for the offence. All this happened in September, when perhaps the ill feeling towards the Provincial League was easing a little.

To add to the happiness of Oxford fans in the remarkable season of 1964, Ron How, who had graced the individual World Final on seven occasions previously, again qualified for the big event in the speedway calendar. The meeting was held in Gothenburg, Sweden on 11 September, when How netted 10 points and became the first Cheetah to ride in the sport's premier event. It really was a season to cherish for the club's loyal fans, who had waited such a long time for their side to be successful, and in 1964 Oxford were undoubtedly the team of the year.

NATIONAL LEAGUE

Team	Mts	Won	Drn	Lst	For	Agn	Pts
Oxford	12	9	0	3	545	461	18
Coventry	12	8	1	3	528.5	479.5	17
Norwich	12	6	0	6	490.5	517.5	12
Belle Vue	12	5	1	6	496	511	11
Swindon	12	4	1	7	509	496	9
Wimbledon	12	4	1	7	475	532	9
West Ham	12	4	0	8	479	526	8

1965

The 1965 season heralded a new look to speedway, with an upsurge in the fortunes of the sport. Peace was declared after the problems that had prevailed in 1964 and a new eighteen-team British League was formed, following the amalgamation of the National and the Provincial Leagues. Norwich, of the old National League, fell to the developers, and Middlesbrough, formerly of the Provincial League, moved to Halifax, but everywhere else the sport was bubbling. The year also saw the formation of the BSPA, who took over the day-to-day administration of the sport.

John Hook, who incredibly went from being the tractor driver at Cowley to a member of the team during the early days of the 1965 season.

Despite the exciting happenings, it was, initially, another touch-and-go situation at Oxford. The 1964 management pulled out, and, yet again, the season had almost started before Danny Dunton and the returning Ted Flanaghan got the go-ahead to run the fortunes of the club, under the auspices of Cowley Speedway Promotions Ltd. The amalgamation of the two leagues saw the introduction of Rider Control; a system introduced to ensure equalisation of team strengths. The 1964 Cheetahs side was broken up, with long-serving Ronnie Genz moving to Poole, and Jack Geran going home to Exeter, together with Colin Gooddy. Nevertheless, Oxford still ended up with a strong heat-leader trio of Ron How, Arne Pander and Jimmy Gooch. Meanwhile, John Bishop and Eddie Reeves also remained onboard, and, in the beginning anyway, young and inexperienced riders were drafted into the side to make up the agreed seven-man line-up. Incidentally, matches were now decided over thirteen heats, and the competing teams raced each other once home and once away.

An interesting story around Oxford way in the early days of the season concerned tractor driver John Hook. It was claimed that he was driving the tractor one week, and drafted into the Oxford side the next. In truth, that did actually happen, but Hook wasn't without some speedway experience, having had rides at Aldershot in their Southern League days and second-half outings at Belle Vue, Swindon and Cradley Heath during the 1960s. Remarkably, he won what was only his second race in the Cheetahs' league match against Poole on 22 April, but couldn't find form thereafter and lost his team place. He was one of many riders introduced into the side at the lower end of the team. Other youngsters tried out included John Belcher, John Leader, Bill Finch and Wayne Barry.

The season began with a good 5-point home win over Sheffield, but this was followed by a shock the week after, when Poole (with Ronnie Genz) won by 10 points. Despite this setback, the Cheetahs continued to be quite a formidable combination at home, and the arrival of Ken Vale was a real boost to the second-string department. The wide-riding style of Vale around the Sandy Lane circuit was something that really got the pulses racing amongst the supporters and he soon became a great favourite. It looked as though Oxford had another winner when Glyn Chandler arrived and had a couple of useful meetings, but he lost form and soon disappeared from the Cowley scene. By June, the Cheetahs were climbing up the league table, and it was a good month with wins at Cradley Heath (42-36) and Glasgow (40-38). In addition to this, Jimmy Gooch won the World Championship qualifying round at Oxford, closely followed by another success at Halifax two days later. Ron How was also successful, winning a World Championship qualifying round at Hackney on 19 June.

However, on 5 July, the Cheetahs suffered a real body blow when Ron How suffered a shoulder injury in a Test match against Russia. The injury required surgery over a long period of time, with the result that the rider was out for the season, and, ultimately, the injury caused his premature retirement from the sport. To try and restore the balance of the side, Oxford drafted in Stan Stevens and Jimmy Heard. Both were lads with some experience, but in no way was either of them an adequate replacement for How, and it was left to Jimmy Gooch and Arne Pander to provide the Cheetahs' main source of points. July ended with a 2-point league victory at Swindon, and a visit from the Polish touring side, Gornik, with Oxford winning an interesting encounter by 46 points to 32.

As the season drew to its close, there came more triumph and further injury problems. The exciting Ken Vale badly injured his back, but Jimmy Gooch, having scored 10 points at West Ham in the British Final, thus qualified for the World Final at Wembley on 18 September, when he netted 4 points and became only the second Oxford rider to appear in the sport's biggest event. Arne Pander hit a purple patch, going through six successive league matches without defeat, and winning the Scottish Open Championship at Edinburgh, courtesy of a 15-point maximum. The inaugural British League Riders' Championship at Belle Vue on 16 October was won by Swindon's Barry Briggs, with that man Gooch a fine runner-up.

A speedway rider's lot is not always glamorous, as emphasised by Oxford's Ken Vale in 1965. The photograph shows him cleaning the shale from his boots in a flooded pits area. Vale unluckily suffered a bad back injury during this season.

Overall, it was a good season for the Cheetahs, who finished fourth in the league table, and one couldn't help thinking how different things might have been had Ron How and Ken Vale not been hurt. As it was, Oxford boasted three riders in the top ten of the British League averages, with How achieving a brilliant 10.16 figure from the eighteen matches he completed. Arne Pander remained ever-present over the thirty-four-match programme to score 353 points and yield a 10.01 average, while Jimmy Gooch supplied fantastic support, recording 326 points from 31 appearances for a 9.97 figure.

BRITISH LEAGUE

Team	Mts	Won	Drn	Lst	For	Agn	Pts
West Ham	34	23	1	10	1,430	1,215	47
Wimbledon	34	22	2	10	1,396	1,245	46
Coventry	34	20	0	14	1,384	1,258	40
Oxford	**34**	**19**	**2**	**13**	**1,308**	**1,340**	**40**
Halifax	33	18	3	12	1,322	1,240	39
Newport	34	19	0	15	1,360	1,288	38
Wolverhampton	34	18	1	15	1,429	1,216	37
Hackney	34	18	1	15	1,327.5	1,319.5	37
Exeter	34	18	0	16	1,325.5	1,323.5	36
Poole	34	17	1	16	1,378	1,266	35
Sheffield	34	16	2	16	1,300	1,346	34
Newcastle	34	16	1	17	1,363	1,282	33
Glasgow	34	15	1	18	1,315	1,329	31
Belle Vue	34	15	0	19	1,328	1,312	30
Swindon	34	13	2	19	1,345	1,300	28
Cradley Heath	33	11	1	21	1,132	1,438	23
Edinburgh	34	11	0	23	1,173	1,471	22
Long Eaton	34	7	0	27	1,107	1,534	14

NOTE: One match, Cradley Heath *v*. Halifax, was not raced.

1966

The British League now boasted nineteen teams, welcoming King's Lynn to the fold, after an open-licence season of racing at the Norfolk venue in 1965. Changes behind the scenes at Oxford saw Richard Austin replace Ted Flanaghan as co-promoter to administer the club's affairs alongside Danny Dunton. After their successful debut season in the British League, things looked to be on the up-and-up at Cowley, but it wasn't to be, with the Cheetahs dropping to fifteenth place in the final league table.

The problem was that the side lacked a third heat-leader, and they had never properly replaced the high-scoring Ron How. Aside from How, three other riders, Stan Stevens, Jimmy Heard and Ken Vale, were also missing from the 1965 team. Replacements came in the shape of Des Lukehurst (allocated from Exeter) and Tony Clarke (via West Ham), while Maury McDermott reappeared on the Cowley scene. Unfortunately, none of them filled a heat-leader berth, and they were terribly inconsistent in their scoring. Lukehurst, however, had two moments of triumph, scoring maximum points at Long Eaton in a Midland Cup fixture and producing a classic last-heat ride in the home match against Wimbledon on 7 July, when he came from behind to join Arne Pander on a 5-1, giving victory to the Cheetahs.

Apart from that, Lukehurst was only a good second string, as his final league average of 4.14 showed.

Some things in speedway never change – in particular, the weather – and the Cheetahs' start to the 1966 campaign was blighted by the elements. Following a challenge match against Coventry to open the season at Cowley on 8 April, the second home fixture of the season on 14 April against Wolverhampton was snowed off and five days later, an away match at West Ham succumbed to Jupiter Pluvias, as did the home fixture against Hackney on 12 May. To add to their problems, Jimmy Gooch suffered a slipped disc, and John Bishop was absent for a spell with glandular fever. However, one thing did cheer Cowley supporters, namely the form of the Great Dane Arne Pander. He was back to his brilliant best, and double-figure scores just flowed from his wheels.

The Cheetahs won their first home league fixture on 21 April, against Belle Vue, and it wasn't until 28 July, when Poole forced a draw, that they dropped a home point. During that time, Arne Pander registered double-figure scores in all nine of their league matches at Cowley. Halifax visited Sandy Lane the following week, with Pander having, for him, an off night with just 7 points, and bang went the Cheetahs' home record, as the West Yorkshire outfit claimed a 42-35 success. Jimmy Gooch, upon his return from a back injury, gave Pander the backing he deserved and, in fact, as the season progressed, it was Gooch who more often led his side's scoring.

Amersham-born John Bishop was unfortunate to suffer a bout of glandular fever during the 1966 campaign with Oxford.

There was an occurrence of note on 1 October, when Oxford made the long journey to Belle Vue for a league fixture. Maury McDermott was late in arriving at Hyde Road, so to make up their side the Cheetahs borrowed Belle Vue junior Taffy Owen. The Welshman took an outing in heat two, before McDermott arrived to take his three remaining rides – all with the approval of the meeting referee. Thus, Oxford created their own little piece of history by becoming the first British League side to use eight riders in a match. Even with eight riders, the Cheetahs didn't do very well. The Aces were in a mean mood and won the match by 51 points to 27.

Mulling over the campaign, Eddie Reeves made good progress and his end-of-season league average of 6.06 looked good for the future, and John Bishop, whilst not coming on as fast as Reeves, still looked a useful prospect. At home, Oxford were always good value, and it was only as the season drew to a close that their form slipped. The main problem was the side's lack of success away from Cowley, with a 3-point triumph at King's Lynn on 16 August being their sole win in the league. They did beat Long Eaton in a Midland Cup encounter, 46-32, thanks to Des Lukehurst's maximum, but apart from these two successes, nothing else came the Cheetahs' way on their opponents' tracks. At Cowley, thirteen matches were won, with two draws and three defeats, which wasn't a bad record, but the seventeen away losses proved disastrous.

Tony Clarke, from whom much was expected, did not prove himself at Cowley, and it was no surprise when he asked for a move at the end of the campaign. He wasn't the only one to request a transfer, and the club was rocked when Arne Pander indicated that he wanted away from Oxford. This was a real shock, but Pander, who'd enjoyed a fine season – netting 333 points from 35 matches for a 9.51 British League average – claimed he was at loggerheads with the Cowley promoters and would be seeking pastures new in 1967.

As if this wasn't bad enough, the promoters indicated that the season had been poor financially, with crowds down on average. So 1966, which had produced so much thrilling racing at Cowley, ended on a note of uncertainty. As Robin Major, the *Oxford Mail* reporter, put it, '1967 could be decisive at Oxford, one way or the other.'

BRITISH LEAGUE

Team	Mts	Won	Drn	Lst	For	Agn	Pts
Halifax	36	27	0	9	1,574	1,229	54
Coventry	36	25	1	10	1,548	1,255	51
Swindon	36	23	0	13	1,553	1,248	46
Wimbledon	36	22	0	14	1,485	1,314	44
Newcastle	36	20	0	16	1,491.5	1,304.5	40
Poole	36	19	2	15	1,443	1,356	40
West Ham	36	19	1	16	1,499.5	1,304.5	39
Glasgow	36	18	0	18	1,395	1,394	36
Wolverhampton	36	17	2	17	1,340.5	1,461.5	36
Exeter	36	17	1	18	1,392.5	1,403.5	35
Sheffield	36	17	0	19	1,410	1,394	34
Edinburgh	35	17	0	18	1,310.5	1,413.5	34
Belle Vue	36	16	0	20	1,362	1443	32
Hackney	36	15	1	20	1,347.5	1,456.5	31
Oxford	**36**	**14**	**2**	**20**	**1,291**	**1,510**	**30**
King's Lynn	36	15	0	21	1,275	1,524	30
Newport	36	12	1	23	1,319	1,486	25
Long Eaton	36	12	1	23	1,286	1,516	25
Cradley Heath	35	10	0	25	1,196	1,506	20

NOTE: One match, Cradley Heath *v.* Edinburgh, was not raced.

1967

Thankfully, the 1967 season saw an upsurge in Oxford's attendances, with the Cowley turnstiles clicking away healthily to the joy of the promoters, Danny Dunton and Richard Austin. Before the season began, there was the familiar movement of riders, with the popular Jimmy Gooch and the promising John Bishop both moving on to Newport, while Tony Clarke returned to West Ham. The good news was that Arne Pander decided that he wanted to stay after all. Meanwhile, Roy Trigg was allocated to Oxford from Hackney, while the Cheetahs also signed Leo McAuliffe upon his return to speedway. Another incoming rider was a highly promising first-timer from New Zealand, who went by the name of Frederick Timmo, although he quickly became known as Rick. So, with Des Lukehurst, Eddie Reeves and Maury McDermott, the Cheetahs looked to have a well-balanced side, and one that was capable of challenging for league title honours.

At home, Oxford made a bright start with victories over Belle Vue, Edinburgh and Cradley Heath, followed by a thrilling draw against Poole and a win versus Exeter. Away from Cowley in the early weeks of the season, the side took time to settle, and apart from a 2-point defeat at Hackney on 14 April, they were generally soundly beaten on their travels. However, the Cowley faithful believed it was only a question of time, as the potential was obviously there. Regrettably, the cruel hand of fate was to strike on 11 May in a home league fixture against near neighbours Swindon. From that moment on, the Cheetahs seemed destined to struggle near the foot of the league table. What was to be the pivotal moment of the campaign occurred in heat seven, when Arne Pander suffered a broken leg in a nasty-looking crash, which was to rule him out of action for the remainder of the season. There was no doubt it was a major blow, as the speedy little Dane was riding with all his old fire and this was fully emphasised by his 9.57 league average.

Eddie Reeves took over the captaincy of the Cheetahs following Arne Pander's accident and promptly became the youngest skipper in the British League. Indeed, the youthful rider seemed to enjoy the extra responsibility and was always good for at least half-a-dozen points a match. The search to replace Pander saw the return to Cowley of the hard-riding Colin Gooddy, who had been a member of their 1964 National League title-winning side. Gooddy, who had moved to Exeter in the 1965 Rider Control allocations, welcomed a return to Oxford, and soon thrilled the Cowley faithful with a series of fighting displays. Despite the loss of Pander, and their general inability to win away from Cowley – their sole success being a win over Cradley Heath by just 1 point – there was much to cheer and interest the Oxford public in 1967. Rick Timmo was proving a most useful signing and showed his battling qualities when forcing his way back into the side following a period of mid-season blues, which had seen him briefly forfeit his team place.

Roy Trigg took over the mantle of the Cheetahs' number one, as he averaged 9.38 points from a full quota of thirty-six league matches, and also won the qualifying rounds for the Midland Riders' Championship and the World Championship at Cowley with fine 15-point maximums. Des Lukehurst proved a reliable second string and was always good for a few points, but the form of Maury McDermott was patchy, as was that of Leo McAuliffe, who never really raced to his true potential. The Cheetahs ended up occupying fourteenth position in the nineteen-team league, based almost entirely on a good home record. Only Wimbledon and Coventry took points away from Oxford, with the Bees winning a thriller by just a single point, 39-38, on 20 July. Poole also gleaned a point from Cowley on 20 April, but all the same, fifteen home wins was a fine effort. Away from home, there was only the one success at Cradley Heath on 3 June, when they triumphed 39-38, so there wasn't much for the supporters to cheer about on the road.

The season provided much in the way of fine close racing, which was enjoyed by the improved Oxford gates. Frustratingly, it was a case of what might have been, though, had Arne Pander not been injured. Indeed, with the Danish ace available, the Cheetahs could well have been British League Champions, an honour that instead went just down the road to arch rivals Swindon.

Maury McDermott hailed from Battersea in London and had a patchy season for the Cheetahs in 1967.

BRITISH LEAGUE

Team	Mts	Won	Drn	Lst	For	Agn	Pts
Swindon	36	24	0	12	1,536	1,266	48
Coventry	36	22	2	12	1,524	1,275	46
West Ham	36	21	3	12	1,514	1,288	45
Edinburgh	36	20	2	14	1,485	1,318	42
Hackney	36	20	1	15	1,402	1,400	41
Poole	36	17	3	16	1,462	1,339	37
Halifax	36	18	1	17	1,456	1,349	37
Wolverhampton	36	18	1	17	1,423	1,376	37
Sheffield	36	18	1	17	1,333.5	1,470.5	37
Newcastle	36	18	0	18	1,386	1,417	36
Wimbledon	36	16	3	17	1,392	1,409	35
Newport	36	17	1	18	1,387	1,413	35
Glasgow	36	16	2	18	1,343	1,457	34
Oxford	**36**	**16**	**1**	**19**	**1,368.5**	**1,432.5**	**33**
Exeter	36	16	0	20	1,384.5	1,418.5	32
Belle Vue	36	16	0	20	1,333.5	1,463.5	32
Long Eaton	36	14	3	19	1,322	1,481	31
Cradley Heath	36	12	0	24	1,262	1,533	24
King's Lynn	36	11	0	25	1,297	1,505	22

1968

Before the 1968 season began, there was the usual rider moves, courtesy of the Rider Control Committee, which posted Roy Trigg to Cradley Heath after just one year at Cowley, while the steady Des Lukehurst found himself Hackney-bound. To replace them, John Bishop returned after a season at Newport, and Ronnie Genz came back after three years with Poole. At least the popular Genno knew every inch of the Cowley circuit and was riding well, so Cowley fans knew that there was a ready-made replacement for the departed Trigg. However, the news that gladdened everyone was that Arne Pander was now fit, and with Colin Gooddy, Eddie Reeves, Leo McAuliffe and the promising Rick Timmo, the 1968 Cheetahs looked capable of making a real challenge for silverware. Off track, Richard Austin became company secretary, leaving Danny Dunton in the head role of promoter at Sandy Lane, still under the auspices of Cowley Speedway Promotions Ltd. Going into the campaign, Mr Dunton predicted with confidence that his team would finish in the top three of the British League Division One.

Regrettably, though, Oxford were to witness an old familiar pattern, since the injury bug struck with a vengeance before the tapes had even risen at Cowley. Again, it struck the unfortunate Arne Pander, who broke his collarbone in an individual meeting for the Crossroads Trophy at Wolverhampton on 29 March, a week before the Oxford opener. Fortunately, the plucky Dane made a swift recovery, but his absence caused the Cheetahs to make an indifferent start to the campaign. Swindon beat them in an opening challenge, and they were held to a home draw by King's Lynn in the Easter Egg Trophy, losing on aggregate. The match against West Ham fell victim to the weather, and their first home success came on 25 April, when they defeated Belle Vue 43-35 in a league fixture.

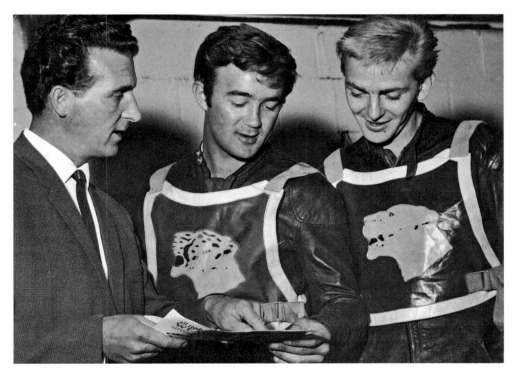

Danny Dunton discusses tactics with Kiwi Rick Timmo and Dane Godtfred Andreasen during the 1968 season at Cowley.

Eddie Reeves leads the way from teammate Ronnie Genz at Sandy Lane in 1968.

Cradley Heath won 47-30 at Cowley on 2 May, but the following evening disaster struck yet again for Arne Pander, who crashed in a match at Hackney and fractured his shin, an injury that was to rule him out of the side for at least three months. Pander's run of bad luck was almost unbelievable and Danny Dunton was forced to look around for a replacement. However, no adequate replacement was available in the British League, so Mr Dunton turned his attention abroad, and after a month-long search came up with promising Danish youngster Godtfred Andreasen. It was obvious that the newcomer would take time to settle, and everyone was prepared to be patient, but fortune refused to smile on the Cheetahs. In an away fixture at Newcastle, Andreasen unluckily hit the Brough Park safety fence and was carried off with a broken leg.

Despite the setbacks, the Cheetahs battled on and the month of May proved to be a turning point in the fortunes of Leo McAuliffe, who had achieved very little in the early matches. A large investment in new equipment began to pay dividends and it was a very different McAuliffe during the second half of the season.

By the time both Godtfred Andreasen and Arne Pander were fit again, the Rider Control Committee, who had done precious little to help Oxford find a replacement when Pander was injured, ruled that the Cheetahs couldn't keep both Danes. This resulted in Pander finally breaking his Cowley connections to go on loan to Poole. No sooner had this happened, than Andreasen decided he was homesick and promptly upped and returned to Denmark! The last day of August saw the Cheetahs in a British League match at Cradley Heath, and there was more misfortune when linchpin Ronnie Genz crashed and was forced to miss the remainder of the season due to a severe bout of concussion. Still the Cheetahs fought on, and September saw two excellent home league successes over Exeter and King's Lynn, while October proved a good month, with the Cheetahs winning their final three home league engagements, despite losing skipper Eddie Reeves with a blood infection.

With so many injury problems, it was hardly surprising that the Cheetahs finished in fifteenth position in the nineteen-strong British League table. They still managed sixteen home victories, with only Cradley Heath and Swindon taking league points from Cowley. Meanwhile, on the road, Oxford had but one success, a fine 41-37 win at Wimbledon on 16 May. Ronnie Genz was the side's most productive rider until his unfortunate accident, while Eddie Reeves was steady and averaged nearly 8 points a match. Leo McAuliffe was a revelation in the post-May period, and a young novice called Mick Bell looked a fine prospect for the future. However, not for the first time Oxford supporters were left wondering just what might have been.

BRITISH LEAGUE DIVISION ONE

Team	Mts	Won	Drn	Lst	For	Agn	Pts
Coventry	36	22	0	14	1,436	1,369	44
Hackney	36	21	2	13	1,421	1,383	44
Exeter	36	20	1	15	1,556.5	1,248.5	41
Sheffield	36	20	1	15	1,463.5	1,337.5	41
Newcastle	36	20	0	16	1,454	1,350	40
West Ham	36	19	1	16	1,454	1,348	39
Halifax	36	19	1	16	1,424	1,379	39
Coatbridge	36	18	1	17	1,404	1,397	37
Wimbledon	36	18	0	18	1,411	1,384	36
Belle Vue	36	18	0	18	1,387	1,417	36
Swindon	36	17	1	18	1,448	1,353	35
Leicester	36	17	1	18	1,373	1,430	35
Newport	36	17	1	18	1,348	1,457	35
Cradley Heath	36	15	4	17	1,373	1,430	34
Oxford	**36**	**17**	**0**	**19**	**1,319**	**1,487**	**34**
Wolverhampton	36	16	0	20	1,388	1,413	32
Poole	36	13	2	21	1,327	1,478	28
King's Lynn	36	13	1	22	1,330	1,473	27
Glasgow	36	13	1	22	1,312	1,495	27

1969

The 1969 season at Oxford was very much the same mixture as before, with the injury bug showing no sign of letting up. Despite this, the Cowley fans enjoyed some good racing, with the Cheetahs continuing to ride very well at home. Problems started before the season really got underway, when Ronnie Genz attempted to make a comeback, but it was obvious that the brave speedster wasn't going to make it. Meanwhile, Arne Pander was posted to Halifax, so at the start of the season, Oxford were down to just six riders. As a result, they had to use Swindon's Mike Broadbank as a guest for their opening challenge match against Hackney on 27 March. It was obvious that this situation couldn't go on, and to bring the side up to strength Pete Jarman was signed from Wolverhampton. That gave the Cheetahs a full side, and although there were no recognised top stars, every rider was a potential 7-point man. Eddie Reeves was skipper again, supported by Colin Gooddy, Leo McAuliffe, Rick Timmo, Pete Jarman and John Bishop, with the highly promising Mick Bell, and other youngsters, Pete Saunders and Pete Seaton, waiting in the wings.

Oxford Cheetahs 1969. From left to right, back row: Sid Knibbs (team manager), Pete Jarman, Mick Bell, John Bishop, Conny Samuelsson, Colin Gooddy, Rick Timmo. Front, on bike: Eddie Reeves, Ronnie Genz.

Misfortune, however, was just around the corner and struck again on 17 May, when Leo McAuliffe was badly injured in a track crash at Halifax whilst competing in a World Championship qualifying round. Regrettably, McAuliffe, who was averaging over 7 points a match, was out for the remainder of the season. As in 1968, Oxford were left to find their own replacements, since Rider Control couldn't assist, which was hardly surprising as they had solved a problem at Newcastle by giving permission for the Diamonds to use a permanent guest rider!

Oxford looked abroad again, and secured the services of a rider from Sweden by the name of Conny Samuelsson. The incoming youngster had a fine reputation in the land of the lakes and was being described as the new Olle Nygren or Ove Fundin. Oxford promoter Danny Dunton was clearly on cloud nine, but, unfortunately for both him and the club, Samuelsson just couldn't come to terms with the Cowley circuit. With his confidence affected badly, he left for home after two months, never to return to the British racing scene.

The story of Conny Samuelsson was simply a case of a young rider being at the wrong club, as was emphasised at larger circuits, such as Coventry and Swindon. The young Swede was so happy on the sweeping Coventry bends that not only did he score well, but he also set a new track record. It was a similar situation in the league match at Swindon on 12 July. Riding from the number seven position, Samuelsson started the local derby on good form by running a second to Mike Broadbank in heat two. Two races later, he again met Broadbank, while the other home rider was the fast-starting Bob Kilby. Undaunted, he thrilled the travelling supporters and dashed to a brilliant victory. Next time out, he came down to earth with a bump, finishing behind the home duo of Barry Briggs and Clive Hitch in heat six. However, he recovered quickly to post a second win in heat eight, this time showing a clean pair of heels to Hitch. In heat twelve, the Oxford reserve was again on the wrong end of a 5-1, behind Barry Briggs and Broadbank. Having scored 10 points, team manager Sid Knibbs put him in

Swede Conny Samuelsson had a fine reputation in his home country, but just couldn't get to grips with the Oxford raceway during his short stint with the club in 1969.

heat thirteen as a reserve replacement for Rick Timmo and, although he failed to add to his tally, he still ended the match as the Cheetahs' top scorer. Many Oxford supporters were both surprised and pleased, since, on the night, Samuelsson looked a completely different rider than the one who had struggled around his own home circuit.

Replacement riders were urgently needed, and they arrived in the form of George Major, a former Cheetah who wasn't enjoying the best of luck at Leicester, and David Crane, via King's Lynn. The move did Major the world of good and in sixteen league matches he averaged 5.27 points a match, and was riding exceptionally well as the season drew to a close. Crane wasn't quite so successful, but still averaged around 4 points a match, which wasn't bad going all things considered. Indeed, in his early meetings Crane looked as though he could do a useful job, however, he was injured in a bad crash at Leicester and, with his confidence badly affected, was never the same rider again.

Eddie Reeves and Colin Gooddy proved to be the mainstays of the side, with consistent scoring. Reeves was rapidly becoming unbeatable at Cowley, while Gooddy (or 'Joe' as he was known) was always battling away in the thick of things. Pete Jarman came good after an indifferent start and began to give the top two vital backing, while a mid-season switch of machinery worked wonders for Rick Timmo, who began to make real progress.

Over at Reading in the Second Division, Mick Bell, who was on loan to the Berkshire club, was having the time of his life topping the Racers' scorechart with the utmost regularity and ending the season with 254 points and a 9.03 average from 29 league appearances. He was also runner-up in the Second Division Riders' Championship, and when called upon to assist the Cheetahs in the top flight, he scored many useful points.

The Cheetahs' final position was again fifteenth in the British League Division One, and once more they enjoyed a reasonably good home record, winning thirteen matches, while losing four and drawing just once. There was, as usual, not much luck on opponents' tracks, but they did come away with the league points from both West Ham and Wolverhampton. The worst away performance occurred at Coventry on 12 April, when the Bees ran riot and thrashed Oxford by 60 points to 18.

BRITISH LEAGUE DIVISION ONE

Team	Mts	Won	Drn	Lst	For	Agn	Pts
Poole	36	26	1	9	1,518.5	1,284.5	53
Belle Vue	36	23	1	12	1,533	1,268	47
Wimbledon	36	22	2	12	1,555.5	1,248.5	46
Halifax	36	22	2	12	1,483	1,244	46
Leicester	36	21	2	13	1,493	1,312	44
Sheffield	36	19	1	16	1,467.5	1,336.5	39
Cradley Heath	36	18	2	16	1,376	1,426	38
Glasgow	36	17	3	16	1,423	1,380	37
King's Lynn	36	18	0	18	1,413	1,390	36
Swindon	36	18	0	18	1,390	1,408	36
Coatbridge	36	17	1	18	1,390	1,418	35
Exeter	36	16	0	20	1,378	1,425	32
Newcastle	36	15	2	19	1,348	1,450	32
Coventry	36	14	3	19	1,419.5	1,383.5	31
Oxford	**36**	**15**	**1**	**20**	**1,290**	**1,436**	**31**
Wolverhampton	36	13	1	22	1,311	1,494	27
Newport	36	13	1	22	1,256	1,546	27
West Ham	36	11	3	22	1,276	1,527	25
Hackney	36	10	2	24	1,229	1,573	22

1970

The 1970 season dawned with good news for the Oxford Cheetahs. Firstly, Ronnie Genz, who had missed the 1969 season through injury, declared himself fit and prepared to make a comeback, and secondly, promoter Danny Dunton was able to persuade Swedish star Hasse Holmqvist to become an Oxford rider. In addition to this, Mick Bell, after a successful season on loan to Second Division Reading, became a full-time Cheetah, so along with Colin Gooddy, Eddie Reeves, Rick Timmo, Pete Jarman and George Major, the squad had a pleasing look about it. Rider Control moved John Bishop, who had had a torrid time at Cowley during 1969, down the road to Swindon, while David Crane was allowed to seek pastures new.

As things turned out, George Major had a poor start to the campaign and eventually left to link with Second Division Doncaster. However, the signing of Hasse Holmqvist was a real feather in the cap of Danny Dunton, since it gave Oxford a proven heat-leader, capable of scoring points on any track. In addition, he was a real personality and an exciting rider to watch in action. The Swede had already proved his worth a few seasons earlier when, in 1967, he had signed for Wolverhampton and shown that he was capable of taking on and beating the best riders in the British League. He had returned to Wolverhampton in 1968, but had failed to agree terms with them in 1969, preferring to remain in his homeland.

The Cheetahs had started the campaign at Wimbledon on 26 March with high hopes, but found the Dons in a determined mood, and crashed to a 49-29 defeat. Nevertheless, Hasse Holmqvist showed his class with 12 points and if Mick Bell had not blown an engine,

Oxford Cheetahs 1970. From left to right: Danny Dunton (promoter), Rick Timmo, Colin Gooddy, Hasse Holmqvist, Mick Bell, Pete Jarman, Ronnie Genz, George Major. Front, on bike: Eddie Reeves.

the result could have been much closer. The following day saw the season open at Cowley, with the Dons again supplying the opposition, and again they ran out winners, this time by 46 points to the Cheetahs' 35. Holmqvist quickly settled down to his new home track with a well-taken 10 points, and only machine problems prevented him from scoring a maximum. Meanwhile, Ronnie Genz scored 6 points, but wisely, as at Wimbledon, where he'd tallied 2 points, he took things steadily.

Rick Timmo had been awaiting the arrival of his machine and missed the two opening matches as a result, but he was back for the visit to Newcastle on Monday 30 March, when he made use of the track spare as the Cheetahs raced to their first league success of the season, winning 41-37. King's Lynn visited for the Easter Egg Trophy on 2 April, with Oxford recording a narrow 41-37 victory, but they were beaten 80-76 on aggregate after losing the second leg 43-35 at Saddlebow Road on 4 April. The home fixture against Belle Vue on 9 April fell victim to the weather, and the Cheetahs lost by 10 points at Glasgow the following day. Leicester came to Cowley on 16 April and the Cheetahs registered a resounding victory and followed it up with a 45-33 success over Wembley in a special challenge match to mark the twenty-first anniversary of post-war speedway at Oxford Stadium. This was followed by a home defeat by Cradley Heath and an away thrashing at Coventry, but the Cheetahs sprang a real surprise by journeying to Exeter on 11 May, and coming away with a 4-point victory.

Another night to remember occurred on 18 June, when Swindon visited for a Midland Cup fixture. Pete Jarman was injured in heat four and ruled out of the remainder of the meeting, which had begun in tremendous style for Oxford, with Rick Timmo defeating Barry Briggs and bettering the season's best time of 66.4 seconds, as set by Hasse Holmqvist. Not to be outdone, Holmqvist equalled the new time in heat three. Just for good measure, Colin Gooddy then defeated Briggo in heat eleven, although the four-times World Champion subsequently gained his revenge in heat thirteen. The loss of Jarman cost the Cheetahs dear in the end, though, and the Robins ran out winners by 4 points. At Swindon on 24 June, the Cheetahs lost the second leg 46-32, with Richard May, of Second Division Reading, guesting for the absent Jarman.

Perhaps the match most enjoyed by Oxford supporters came as the season drew to its close on 1 October, when Poole visited Cowley for a league fixture. The 1969 British League Division One Champions had previously beaten the Cheetahs in the Knock-Out Cup on 28 May by just 2 points. The match had been littered with controversy, and the final result had left the Cheetahs' management somewhat angry. However, this time there was to be no mistake as Oxford went on the rampage to win by 22 points, with Ronnie Genz recording a maximum, while Hasse Holmqvist and Rick Timmo each contributed tallies of a paid dozen.

Oxford finished the campaign in thirteenth position, which spelt a slight improvement on the previous year. As in the past, they were good value at home, winning fourteen matches and losing four, but it was the same old story away from Cowley, and after their early wins at Newcastle and Exeter, there was no further away success. All in all, it wasn't a bad season, with Hasse Holmqvist proving a great success in achieving a final average of 9.10, having yielded 212 points from 23 league appearances. Meanwhile, Ronnie Genz made a successful return to action, and Colin Gooddy had his moments. The rest of the team were inclined to be patchy, being just as likely to score double figures one week and nothing the next.

BRITISH LEAGUE DIVISION ONE

Team	Mts	Won	Drn	Lst	For	Agn	Pts
Belle Vue	36	27	2	7	1,595.5	1,205.5	56
Wimbledon	36	22	2	12	1,506	1,297	46
Coventry	36	22	1	13	1,517.5	1,287.5	45
Leicester	36	21	0	15	1,423	1,381	42
Poole	36	20	0	16	1,392	1,409	40
Halifax	36	19	1	16	1,492.5	1,313.5	39
Sheffield	36	18	3	15	1,414.5	1,391.5	39
Glasgow	36	18	1	17	1,438	1,367	37
Wolverhampton	36	16	2	18	1,371	1,433	34
Exeter	36	16	1	19	1,369.5	1,434.5	33
Hackney	36	15	2	19	1,369.5	1,435.5	32
King's Lynn	36	16	0	20	1,359	1,443	32
Oxford	**36**	**16**	**0**	**20**	**1,360.5**	**1,445.5**	**32**
Wembley	36	15	2	19	1,327.5	1,474.5	32
Cradley Heath	36	15	1	20	1,351.5	1,445.5	31
Swindon	36	14	2	20	1,386	1,418	30
Newcastle	36	15	0	21	1,364	1,444	30
West Ham	36	14	2	20	1,341.5	1,463.5	30
Newport	36	12	0	24	1,258	1,548	24

1971

The 1971 season was one of problems for Oxford, and from day one they struggled with what was a mediocre side. Promoter Danny Dunton's difficulties began when Hasse Holmqvist informed him that he would not be available until May, and even then he would still have to be free for his Swedish commitments. This, following the posting of Eddie Reeves to Hackney, Pete Jarman to Cradley Heath, and Mick Bell to Reading (who had replaced Newcastle in the British League Division One) by the Rider Control Committee, really was the last straw for the Oxford boss. After working morning, noon and night to put a side together, Dunton finally decided to manage without Holmqvist's services.

The Rider Control Committee allocated Oyvind Berg to Oxford via Glasgow in 1971 and the Norwegian had a good year to head the club's league averages on a 7.52 figure.

The Rider Control Committee had allocated replacements to Oxford in the shape of Norwegian Oyvind Berg, who arrived via Glasgow, while Ted Laessing and Mike Gardner were also posted to the club from King's Lynn and Cradley Heath respectively. The hard-riding Berg was happy to join the Cheetahs' camp, but both Laessing and Gardner said 'Thanks, but no thanks,' and refused to come to Sandy Lane. Rider Control did nothing to ease the Cheetahs' problems, so Mr Dunton turned his attention to Ken McKinlay of West Ham. 'Hurri-Ken' was rapidly approaching the veteran stage of his riding career and was initially posted to Wembley, but didn't fancy the move. Although he could not be described as a replacement for the absent Holmqvist, at least the Scot was prepared to ride for Oxford, which was something.

As the first match approached, Oxford had just four riders on their books, namely Oyvind Berg, Colin Gooddy, Rick Timmo and Ronnie Genz. So Ray Wilson of Leicester guested for the Cheetahs in their opening fixture against King's Lynn in the annual Easter Egg Cup, and Richard Greer from Mr Dunton's Second Division track, Peterborough, rode at reserve, with Pete Saunders filling the other reserve berth. To add to Oxford's problems, Berg wasn't available for the match, so the Cheetahs used the rider replacement rule. All things considered, the patched-up side did very well to only lose by 4 points, with the ever-reliable Genz and Gooddy being joint top scorers with 11 points apiece from five starts.

Ken McKinlay finally arrived at the Cheetahs' camp, but they still went down by 2 points in their next home match, a challenge against Coventry. The following week saw the Cheetahs win their first British League match of the season, against Wimbledon, by a single point, with Oxford denying the visitors the use of rider replacement for the absent Cyril Maidment, on the grounds that they had no number eight rider present! Still, the Cheetahs did not have a proper seven-man side, with both Richard Geer (again) and Arthur Price from Second Division Boston filling in. This was a situation that really couldn't continue and subsequently Col Cottrell, who was having a tough time at Coventry, joined the Cheetahs, while from Newport came Norman Strachan. Neither signing could be regarded as the answer to Oxford's need for heat-leaders, but at least the Cheetahs now had seven riders and on 6 May in a Knock-Out Cup match against Poole, they were able to finally track a side of their own. Oxford celebrated in fine style too, defeating the Pirates by 46 points to 32, with Ronnie Genz, Oyvind Berg and Colin Gooddy all recording double-figure tallies.

Scot Ken McKinlay is pictured with legendary Swindon ace Barry Briggs in 1971. McKinlay was initially posted to Wembley, but wasn't keen on the move and eventually joined Oxford.

After some indifferent results, the Cheetahs scored a 1-point victory over Exeter in the Knock-Out Cup on 17 June, and the winning form returned for the visit of Wolverhampton on 1 July, when the Cheetahs recorded a fine 53-24 success. As the season progressed, Danny Dunton continued to canvass the Rider Control Committee for additional strength, and the news that Belle Vue's Tommy Roper was available prompted a request from Oxford for his services. Dunton had pursued Arthur Price as well, regularly making offers for the young Boston rider. By the end of July, Dunton had got his man with the signing of Roper, but lost out on Price, who was bound for King's Lynn. Despite the plight of Oxford, the Rider Control Committee ordered the posting of Ronnie Genz to Newport upon Roper's arrival, so the Cheetahs' situation was largely unchanged. This was a truly unbelievable state of affairs.

Tommy Roper made his Oxford debut on 5 August, and top scored with 12 points in the Cheetahs' 45-31 win over Halifax. Two weeks later on 19 August, however, Oxford entertained Exeter and Rick Timmo was involved in a frightening spill. The accident happened in heat six, when, leaving the fourth turn, the youngster came down. Behind, the closely following Roper made a tremendous attempt to avoid his stricken teammate. It was impossible to lay down his machine, so Roper tried to go around Timmo, only for his footrest to go right across the young New Zealander's throat. For a brief moment Timmo stopped breathing and actually 'died' on the track. Fortunately, track doctor Tim Faulkner was on hand and his skills quickly brought the rider back. It had been a bad moment and for a while the stadium fell silent. Thankfully, Timmo's injuries amounted to nothing more than a broken collarbone and everyone was mighty relieved, since it could have been so much worse. Adding insult to injury, Exeter, with Bob Kilby scorching to a fine 15-point maximum, took the league points, winning the match 41-37.

To add to Oxford's problems, by the end of August, Col Cottrell had retired and for the rest of the season Mr Dunton placed his faith in the up-and-coming youngsters from the Second Division. John Jackson from Crewe, Laurie Sims of Eastbourne and Peterborough's John Davis were drafted into the side as and when required, with Jackson looking particularly useful.

Rick Timmo was back in action by mid-September and the month ended with Oxford picking up four valuable league points in a double-header against King's Lynn and Cradley Heath. Then, on 7 October, the season ended with a fine home win by 41 points to 37 over Hackney. So, a disappointing and frustrating campaign finished with the Cheetahs dropping down the British League Division One table and ending up in seventeenth position. At home, they won a dozen matches and suffered defeat on six occasions, with a draw at Cradley Heath on 24 July representing their sole point gained on the road. Oyvind Berg topped the Cheetahs' averages with a 7.52 figure, and Ken McKinlay also made the 7-point mark, whilst Colin Gooddy, Timmo and Tommy Roper all hovered around 6 points per match.

BRITISH LEAGUE DIVISION ONE

Team	Mts	Won	Drn	Lst	For	Agn	Pts
Belle Vue	36	25	1	10	1,583	1,217	51
Leicester	36	22	3	11	1,490	1,309	47
Coventry	36	23	0	13	1,495	1,310	46
Sheffield	36	21	1	14	1,450	1,357	43
Swindon	36	19	3	14	1,413	1,392	41
Reading	36	18	4	14	1,438	1,361	40
Hackney	36	17	4	15	1,410	1,393	38
Newport	36	19	0	17	1,390	1,416	38
Wembley	36	17	3	16	1,433	1,372	37
Wimbledon	36	18	1	17	1,389	1,415	37
Poole	36	17	2	17	1,407	1,399	36
Wolverhampton	36	17	1	18	1,382	1,412	35
King's Lynn	36	16	2	18	1,396.5	1,406.5	34
Halifax	36	16	2	18	1,374	1,430	34
Exeter	36	16	0	20	1,379	1,424	32
Glasgow	36	15	1	20	1,403	1,401	31
Oxford	**36**	**12**	**1**	**23**	**1,263.5**	**1,537.5**	**25**
Cradley Heath	36	8	4	24	1,298	1,507	20
West Ham	36	9	1	26	1,236	1,571	19

1972

It was all change in 1972, as Bob Dugard (from Eastbourne) joined Danny Dunton in a new company, Oxspeed Ltd, to run the shale sport at Cowley. Showbusiness also arrived with Acker Bilk becoming a director of the company, while Dave Lanning came on board to supervise the whole thing. The nickname of Cheetahs was dropped and Oxford became known as the Rebels, with the confederate flag of the American Civil War being used as the side's body colour.

It looked as though the Rider Control Committee had done the Oxford promotion proud, when Neil Street, the vastly experienced Australian, was allocated to the club. Street had always enjoyed his visits to Cowley and his engineering experience would have been invaluable, but no sooner had he received notice of his allocation than it was changed. He was sent instead to Newport, a track that Street was the first to admit he couldn't ride at all. Anyway, Oxford's loss was the Welsh club's gain and the wily Aussie brought all his experience and know how into play as he strove to master the Somerton Park circuit. And master it he did, but anyone who was an established Oxford fan would have realised just what the club had missed out on due to the last-minute change of heart by Rider Control.

Norwegian Svein Kaasa was signed by Oxford in 1972, but was released to Glasgow after struggling for form. Regrettably, he lost his life later that season on 29 September, following a heat-eleven crash at Hampden Park while representing the Scottish side in a league encounter versus Swindon.

A change that did occur saw the departure of Tommy Roper, and the publicity-conscious management replaced him with Australian fireball Garry Middleton, who wanted away from Hackney. Middleton was a real personality, being an all-action racer who had a habit of getting into all sorts of scrapes and often incurring the wrath of his fellow riders. Colin Gooddy, Ken McKinlay, the gutsy Oyvind Berg, Rick Timmo and Norman Strachan were back, and to complete the side, the management signed young Norwegian Svein Kaasa, who had been showing a great deal of promise in his homeland and looked to be a fine prospect.

There was no doubt that Oxford was buzzing speedway-wise, and the fans eagerly looked forward to the team's initial meeting of the season on 25 March. It wasn't a dream debut for the new Rebels, though, for they went down to a heavy defeat, losing 59-19 at Coventry in a British League Division One encounter. Oxford subsequently took to the track at Cowley for their opening home fixture on the morning of 31 March, with Wimbledon providing the opposition for a league fixture. Ken McKinlay was missing, having still not returned from a winter of racing in Australia, so the Rebels utilised the rider replacement facility to cover for him, with Laurie Sims coming in as the number eight man. The meeting began in the best possible way, with new skipper Garry Middleton defeating Ronnie Moore in a sensational opening heat. It went on to be a fine home start, for in an exciting contest, Oxford ran out winners by 43 points to 35. Unfortunately, the good beginning didn't last, and the Rebels lost their next two home matches against King's Lynn and Coventry, while they also had no luck on their away trips to Wimbledon and Halifax.

Wolverhampton visited Cowley on 20 April, and the Rebels' winning form returned with a 41-37 victory, although Rick Timmo suffered a shoulder injury which sidelined him for a while. After a reasonable start in the Cowley opener, Svein Kaasa had struggled and was released (he was later to link up with Glasgow), and the match against Wolverhampton saw him replaced with young Danish rider Preben Rosenkilde, formerly of Halifax. Rosenkilde looked a tad unconvincing in his early races, but showed plenty of promise and the following week lined up in the Midland Riders' Championship qualifying round, where he scored a creditable 5 points. Barry Briggs won the meeting with a 15-point maximum, with home star Garry Middleton finishing as runner-up on a tally of 13.

May was a good month for the Rebels, with home wins over Hackney, Exeter and Halifax; however, Poole visited Cowley on 1 June and left with the league points. Bad luck hit the Rebels a week later in a challenge match against local rivals Reading, when the hard-riding Oyvind Berg crashed and hurt his shoulder and ribs, ruling him out of the side for a month. Dave Lanning described the problems in his programme editorial as a 'Midsummer Nightmare', which was apt indeed.

Going through the side, Garry Middleton was doing a good job, as was the popular Berg, while Rick Timmo was a useful second string, but Ken McKinlay, Norman Strachan and Preben Rosenklide were struggling, and Colin Gooddy was terribly inconsistent. The Rebels were in desperate need of strengthening, as they were struggling to keep away from the cellar position in the British League. On 15 June, they were confident they had got their man when spectacular Swede Torbjorn Harrysson agreed terms, but in the event he couldn't get released from his work. Hasse Holmqvist was contacted, but Swedish commitments meant it was a no go, so another Swede, Gote Nordin, was sounded out, but he ended up helping out at Halifax.

There were further problems for the Rebels when Sheffield visited Cowley on 22 June, though. Garry Middleton withdrew from the meeting, complaining of being unfit to compete, with the result that the under-strength Oxford team went down to a 42-36 defeat. Winning form returned a week later when the Rebels, with youngsters Roger Johns and Malcolm Ballard from Eastbourne in the side, walloped Newport 51-27. Middleton recorded a 12-point maximum, and Ken McKinlay came back to form with 11 points from the reserve berth.

A league success against Swindon was followed by defeats against Belle Vue and Leicester. Then came a creditable aggregate draw against Swindon in the Midland Cup and in the replay at Blunsdon, the Rebels raced to a marvellous 39-39 draw, before winning the second leg at Cowley 41-36 (or so they thought) to become overall victors, but it wasn't to be. The match was full of controversy and ended with the Robins putting in an official protest over a starting malfunction in heat eleven. The result was amended by the Control Board to read Oxford 38 Swindon 40, which typified the sort of luck the Rebels had been experiencing.

Reading came to Cowley for a league match on 14 September, and in a real nail-biter of a match, the Rebels held a 2-point advantage going into heat eleven, but two Racers' 5-1s in heats twelve and thirteen meant that the visiting side left with the league points. So, the campaign drew to a close with the Rebels just avoiding the basement position. It was a season of exciting racing, with Oxford at least high in the publicity stakes. Garry Middleton was their best rider courtesy of a superb 9.21 average, having gleaned 300.5 points from his 29 league matches, while Oyvind Berg always gave good support. If only the Rebels had been able to secure the services of a third heat-leader, they could well have scaled the heights. Things were, however, looking up, with a marvellous array of young talent from Eastbourne and Peterborough frequenting the Oxford second halves. It may have been a disappointing year in terms of results, but the future was beginning to look rosy.

BRITISH LEAGUE DIVISION ONE

Team	Mts	Won	Drn	Lst	For	Agn	Pts
Belle Vue	34	31	1	2	1,592.5	1,051.5	63
Reading	34	25	1	8	1,454	1,194	51
King's Lynn	34	24	3	7	1,432	1,219	51
Sheffield	34	23	3	8	1,488	1,163	49
Leicester	34	17	5	12	1,365	1,287	39
Ipswich	34	17	1	16	1,332	1,313	35
Poole	34	15	2	17	1,307	1,342	32
Hackney	34	16	0	18	1,306	1,341	32
Wolverhampton	34	16	0	18	1,302	1,348	32
Coventry	34	14	2	18	1,327	1,317	30
Exeter	34	13	2	19	1,291.5	1,357.5	28
Halifax	34	13	2	19	1,261	1,388	28
Wimbledon	34	14	0	20	1,225	1,421	28
Glasgow	34	12	2	20	1,263	1,385	26
Swindon	34	12	1	21	1,314	1,337	25
Cradley Heath	34	11	3	20	1,234.5	1,416.5	25
Oxford	**34**	**10**	**0**	**24**	**1,200.5**	**1,443.5**	**20**
Newport	34	9	0	25	1,139	1,510	18

1973

There were changes again as Dave Lanning departed, while on the team front, there were the normal comings and goings. From the previous season's line-up, Colin Gooddy moved on to Cradley Heath, with Ken McKinlay and Norman Strachan moving to Second Division Scunthorpe and Long Eaton respectively. Regrettably, the popular Oyvind Berg retired from British racing, while Garry Middleton decided he wanted away from Oxford. The Rebels welcomed Hasse Holmqvist back to Cowley, thanks to some sweet-talking on the part of Danny Dunton, and another returnee was Eddie Reeves, who was back after a year at Hackney. Meanwhile, Malcolm Ballard and Gordon Kennett became permanent Rebels, while Rick Timmo returned and was made skipper of the side. Some things, however, did not change and, not for the first time, the allocations made by Rider Control came to nothing. Dave Hemus wasn't interested in furthering his racing career at Oxford, and nothing was done to replace Middleton, who was determined to sit on the fence until he got a move. As a result, Oxford again began the season with guest riders, although the steady John Dews moved in from Wimbledon in place of Hemus.

The season was a month old before the Oxford team problems were settled, when Tony Lomas, who wanted a move from Coventry, came to Cowley, with Middleton going in the opposite direction to Brandon. To be fair, Lomas didn't really want to ride for the Rebels, for he had his sights set on a move to Exeter, but on 12 April he made his home debut for Oxford sporting the number one race jacket. It was a nightmare debut too, as his style just wasn't suited to the Oxford track and he looked most uncomfortable. Two days later, the Rebels journeyed to Halifax, where Lomas was much happier on the wide sweeping bends of The Shay. The Rebels went down by 14 points, but Lomas' 7-point return was well taken. A group of Oxford supporters certainly appreciated his efforts and organised a whip-round. They managed to collect £1.30, so that the club's latest signing could buy himself a pint (or two)!

News that Ivan Mauger was available from Belle Vue prompted an enquiry from Oxford, but despite a great deal of interest in the offer, the legendary New Zealander moved to Exeter, so the team position remained the same at Cowley. On Good Friday morning, the Rebels entertained Reading in a challenge match, and lost by 8 points. Tony Lomas recorded a second place in his opening ride, but still couldn't come to terms with the Oxford track, and was actually replaced by Hasse Holmqvist in his final race. It wasn't until 17 May that Oxford picked up their first league success of the season, a 44-34 victory over Leicester, thanks to a fine maximum from guest rider Terry Betts of King's Lynn. Constructive things were now happening on the team front, and finally, in mid-May, the Rebels solved their team problems when Bob Kilby, the Exeter skipper, came to Cowley, with Lomas moving to Exeter in return. Kilby had been recovering from a leg injury, and the arrival of Mauger left him unsettled down in Devon, so a move that suited everyone finally came to pass. On 24 May, in a World Championship qualifying round at Oxford, 'Kilb' made his debut as a Rebel, and it was a sensational start too, as he raced to a superb 14-point tally to win the meeting.

Oxford's joy in finally finding an established British League heat-leader was unfortunately destined to be short-lived. A track accident at Exeter had resulted in a badly torn cartilage for Bob Kilby and although he had bravely soldiered on, he was forced to pull out during a match versus Swindon on 7 June. Not long afterwards, on 20 June, he entered hospital for an operation, so it was back to guest riders for the unfortunate Rebels.

Fast-starting Bob Kilby joined Oxford from Exeter in May 1973 after becoming unsettled at the Devon club.

Popular Norwegian Oyvind Berg was in Britain for the *Daily Mirror* International Tournament, and he returned to the Oxford side for a challenge match against Reading on 5 July. It was, however, to be a one-off appearance, as the rider wasn't interested in a permanent return to Cowley. A change in the team saw Eddie Reeves, who had been unable to find form at Oxford, leave for King's Lynn and a dispensation was obtained to use the promising John Davis of Peterborough for the remainder of the season.

Despite their problems, Oxford continued to serve up exciting speedway racing. Both Gordon Kennett and Malcolm Ballard had settled down to the cut and thrust of British League racing beautifully. Hasse Holmqvist was a tower of strength, while John Davis and Rick Timmo were steady. If only the Rebels had been able to track a settled side from the beginning of the year, they could well have challenged Reading for league honours. August saw four home wins out of five, but the Rebels still couldn't beat Reading, who stole a 2-point win halfway through the month. Thankfully, there was some good news when Bob Kilby returned to the saddle for a 45-33 win over Exeter a week later.

On 4 October, a double-header was staged against Cradley United and Reading, with the fixture versus the Racers being a challenge for the Twelfth Night Trophy. Hasse Holmqvist was absent, since he had to enter hospital for surgery on a knee injury, so Swindon's Norman Hunter deputised. In the first match, the Rebels really went on the rampage to thrash Cradley United by 59 points to 19, with John Davis romping to a fine maximum. In the match that followed, the Rebels still couldn't break the Reading bogey, though, losing 42-36, despite a fine 11 points from Bob Kilby.

The season closed at Oxford on the evening of Sunday 7 October, with a rearranged league fixture against Wimbledon. The Rebels finished with a 47-30 success, helped no end by a superb 12-point maximum from Bob Kilby. That enabled the Cheetahs to finish the year in eleventh position, with Hasse Holmqvist and Kilby topping the averages on 7-plus figures, while Gordon Kennett, John Davis and Malcolm Ballard all did exceptionally well to achieve averages in excess of 6.

BRITISH LEAGUE DIVISION ONE

Team	Mts	Won	Drn	Lst	For	Agn	Pts
Reading	34	25	1	8	1,494	1,156	51
Sheffield	34	22	3	9	1,489	1,157	47
King's Lynn	34	20	3	11	1,395	1,253	43
Leicester	34	21	0	13	1,394	1,254	42
Ipswich	34	19	3	12	1,393	1,255	41
Belle Vue	34	19	1	14	1,451	1,188	39
Wolverhampton	34	18	1	15	1,319	1,331	37
Exeter	34	16	3	15	1,344.5	1,303.5	35
Halifax	34	16	2	16	1,255	1,394	34
Newport	34	16	0	18	1,350.5	1,295.5	32
Oxford	**34**	**14**	**2**	**18**	**1,267**	**1,381**	**30**
Wimbledon	34	14	1	19	1,263	1,383	29
Swindon	34	13	3	18	1,244	1,407	29
Poole	34	13	2	19	1,300	1,351	28
Coventry	34	13	0	21	1,233	1,415	26
Hackney	34	11	4	19	1,227	1,421	26
Coatbridge	34	12	1	21	1,219	1,421	25
Cradley United	34	7	4	23	1,187	1,459	18

1974

The 1974 season dawned with the Oxford Rebels tracking a useful-looking team, featuring a fine blend of youth and experience. From the previous year's line-up, Hasse Holmqvist was missing, and the sometimes controversial Malcolm Ballard was transferred to Poole, but Bob Kilby, John Dews, Gordon Kennett and Rick Timmo were all back. John Davis became a full-time Rebel, as did Richard Greer, who was transferred to Oxford from Peterborough. To replace Holmqvist, the Rebels' management obtained the services of Norwegian Ulf Lovaas, who had ridden for Cradley United towards the end of the 1973 season, and had shown a great deal of promise. Certainly there was much to interest Oxford fans, because the youth and enthusiasm of youngsters Kennett, Davis, Greer and Lovaas was backed by the experience of Kilby, Dews and Timmo.

Off track, one change saw Bob Radford arrive at Cowley as both general manager and team manager, having filled the latter role at Reading the year before, when he guided the Racers to the League Championship. He had been influential in bringing Norwegian Ulf Lovaas to the club, but was to resign in August. Roger Jones subsequently took over as team manager, whilst Danny Dunton resumed all his former duties.

Going back to the beginning of the season, the opening fixture on 21 March was a Knock-Out Cup tie against Ipswich and this provided some excellent racing, with the Rebels taking a 40-37 victory. Bob Kilby, who had been appointed skipper for the season, led the scoring with 10 points, and Richard Greer had a fine match, also notching 10. Exeter were the visitors the following week in a Spring Gold Cup match, and the Rebels enjoyed more success, winning 49-29. The next day, however, they came back down with a bump when, on a visit to Newport, they were beaten 54-24, with only John Davis making an impression on the tricky circuit courtesy of a 10-point return.

Oxford Rebels 1974. From left to right, back row: Ulf Lovaas, Rick Timmo, Bob Webb (mechanic), John Davis, Bob Radford (team manager), Bobby McNeil, Richard Greer. Front row: John Dews, Bob Kilby (on bike), Gordon Kennett.

Home victories throughout April against Newport (Spring Gold Cup), Wimbledon (British League) and Swindon (Midland Cup) showed that the Rebels were quite a force at Cowley, although away they found success hard to come by. However, on 25 April, Belle Vue visited Oxford and left with the league points, with Bob Kilby having a terrible time. Thankfully, Kilby didn't take long to put things right, as he romped to victory in a World Championship qualifying round at Sandy Lane a week later.

On 8 May, the Rebels travelled to Hull and gave their best performance away from Oxford to date, losing by just 2 points. On the downside, Rick Timmo, who was having a tough time, requested that he be rested from the side and for the match against Halifax on 16 May, Trevor Geer, a talented youngster from the Eastbourne stable, came into the side as a replacement. This match also saw the return of Pete Jarman, now a member of the Eastbourne side as well, filling in for the injured John Dews. It was a successful night for the Rebels too, as they secured a 41-37 victory. Bob Kilby and Richard Greer led the scoring with 10 points apiece, but it was young Geer who was the match-winner with a fine 8 points. Two days later, Oxford travelled to Belle Vue and lost a thriller of a meeting by just 6 points. Kilby played a real captain's part, with a 14-point tally, while Ulf Lovaas also showed good form to yield 9 points.

Sheffield visited Oxford on 23 May and left with the league points, winning 43-35, thanks to Gordon Kennett having to compete in a World Championship qualifying round, ironically at Sheffield, which, in the event, was rained off! May ended with the Radio Oxford Best Pairs, which John Dews and Richard Greer won in fine style. June saw Kennett suffer a foot injury in a four-team tournament at Eastbourne, which caused him to miss a few matches, and then Dews was injured in a spill against Newport. With Bob Kilby also on the injured list, it was somewhat surprising when the Rebels defeated Coventry on 27 June, with Greer recording an excellent maximum and Ulf Lovaas displaying good form for 10 points. Rick Timmo, who had been absent for a month, now returned to racing, but suffered a broken thigh in an off-track accident, which meant he was out for the rest of the season. There was still no luck on opponents' tracks, although the Rebels managed a draw at Cradley United in a challenge fixture on 8 June. The meeting had begun as a league fixture, but was later changed to a challenge by officialdom.

July provided a month of mixed fortunes, with home wins against Wolverhampton and Leicester, but defeats at the hands of Ipswich and Cradley United. Away from Cowley, the Rebels won a challenge fixture at Swindon, and on 27 July they claimed a first away league success at Cradley United, with the 2-point victory ensuring that justice had been done following what had happened on 8 June. The month of August opened well, as Belle Vue were beaten 40-38 in a challenge match, but a much-anticipated Test match between England and Russia was unfortunately lost to inclement weather. Poole were thrashed 52-26, with Gordon Kennett and Bob Kilby scoring maximums, and on Bank Holiday Monday, 26 August, Dutchman Henk Steman made his British debut as a Rebel against Swindon. His presence couldn't stop a Swindon victory, however, with the Robins winning 42-36. The Rebels quickly avenged that defeat to their local rivals, when they made the trip to Blunsdon on 28 September and shocked everyone by securing a brilliant 46-32 win. Their scoring was solid on the night, headed by John Davis (9+1), Ulf Lovaas (9), Kennett (8+2) and Kilby (8).

The home league programme finished with a storming 50-28 win over Hull on 26 September, and the next week, Oxford walloped Swindon in a challenge match by the same score. The final meeting of the season was to have been a speedway bonanza featuring thirty heats of racing, including the Autumn Stakes and a ten-heat challenge match between Birmingham and Eastbourne, but the weather intervened and stopped the attractive-looking event from taking place. Oxford finished the season by filling the bottom position in the final British League Division One table. The side's leading rider was skipper Bob Kilby, who achieved an 8.28 average, having totalled 260 points from his 31 league appearances.

BRITISH LEAGUE DIVISION ONE

Team	Mts	Won	Drn	Lst	For	Agn	Pts
Exeter	32	25	1	6	1,375	1,117	51
Belle Vue	32	23	0	9	1,380	1,106	46
Ipswich	32	22	1	9	1,364	1,128	45
Sheffield	32	21	0	11	1,426	1,067	42
King's Lynn	32	20	1	11	1,281	1,210	41
Newport	32	17	3	12	1,299	1,197	37
Halifax	32	14	3	15	1,209	1,286	31
Wimbledon	32	14	1	17	1,200	1,287	29
Hackney	32	13	2	17	1,218	1,273	28
Leicester	32	13	1	18	1,210	1,282	27
Wolverhampton	32	13	1	18	1,157.5	1,332.5	27
Swindon	32	12	2	18	1,179	1,316	26
Cradley United	32	12	1	19	1,171	1,322	25
Poole	32	12	1	19	1,147	1,344	25
Coventry	32	12	0	20	1,147	1,342	24
Hull	32	10	0	22	1,212	1,269	20
Oxford	**32**	**10**	**0**	**22**	**1,196.5**	**1,293.5**	**20**

1975

The 1975 season began at Oxford, as in past years, with a number of team changes. Both Bob Kilby and John Davis requested transfers, while family commitments prevented Ulf Lovaas from returning to further his career in British racing. Kilby returned to his old home base at Swindon, and a real buzz went around Oxford when it was announced that Ole Olsen had been allocated to the Rebels from Wolverhampton. The enthusiasm amongst the Oxford supporters was further heightened when it was also announced that popular Swede Hasse Holmqvist would be returning.

Dag Lovaas joined Oxford in 1975 and the Norwegian enjoyed a wonderful campaign to finish at the top of the Rebels' averages on a 10.22 figure, having plundered 354 points from 31 league appearances.

The proposed Ole Olsen move was quickly dashed, however, when the Control Board met on 21 March to hear an appeal by Wolverhampton over his allocation to Oxford. The result was that Olsen was allocated back to Wolverhampton, with Dag Lovaas, the younger brother of Ulf, joining the Rebels instead. Lovaas arrived via Reading, but part of the deal meant John Davis moved in the opposite direction to link with the Berkshire club. Nobody connected with Oxford minded this move, though, for Lovaas had made it clear that he wanted to race for the club, whereas Olsen didn't. The move that the brilliant Dane really yearned for, of course, was to join Coventry. To complete the Rebels' side, which included new skipper Gordon Kennett, Richard Greer, Hasse Holmqvist, Trevor Geer and John Dews, the promotion signed Swede Richard Hellsen, who had ridden a handful of matches for King's Lynn in 1973.

The Rebels began the campaign with two away defeats on successive evenings in a challenge match at Newport and a league fixture at Coventry. Bizarrely, John Davis appeared in the latter meeting at Coventry as a guest for himself, since the teams were still not finalised! The Rebels opened at Cowley on 28 March, with a challenge match against Coventry, and romped to a 48-29 victory. Hasse Holmqvist was an absentee and was reported to be having trouble getting released from his work, so Paul Gachet, another product of the Eastbourne school, deputised and scored a creditable 4 points. Meanwhile, new boy Dag Lovaas made a highly satisfactory home debut in a Rebels race jacket to lead the Oxford scoring with 10 points. The following week saw a truly incredible meeting, when, following a snowstorm, Cradley United withdrew from the match after heat seven, despite the fact that the referee had ruled the track rideable. The Rebels continued on regardless to chalk up six successive 5-0 victories and win 58-14. Holmqvist was still absent for this meeting, so the rider replacement facility was used to cover his programmed outings.

Swindon raced to a 39-39 draw in the Midland Cup on 17 April, and the Rebels returned the compliment at Blunsdon on 10 May, so the tie had to be raced all over again. In the meantime, the Rebels had lost away at Ipswich, Halifax and Cradley United, but they beat Ipswich at Cowley by the smallest of margins, 40-38. Phil Crump won the Champions Trophy on 24 April, and Ray Wilson was the victor in the Midland Riders' Championship qualifying round on 8 May. Swindon returned on 15 May for the Midland Cup replay, and this time the Rebels made no mistake, emphatically winning 53-25. Belle Vue visited Cowley the following week, when Dag Lovaas was absent. The popular Norwegian was replaced by guest Terry Betts, but despite a brilliant 14 points from skipper Gordon Kennett, the Rebels went down to a 10-point defeat, with Betts, who usually flew around Cowley, managing just 2 points. Things were better the following day, though, when the Rebels produced a spectacular 41-37 victory at Hackney.

Having beaten Swindon on aggregate, Oxford welcomed Leicester for the second round of the Midland Cup on 12 June. The Rebels took a 46-32 victory, but there was no Hasse Holmqvist, and the following week he was still absent, as was Richard Hellsen, who had the misfortune to suffer a broken leg at Leicester. However, this didn't stop Oxford from winning 60-18 against Coventry in the first round of the Knock-Out Cup. Following this match, it was announced that Holmqvist was no longer available to ride for the Rebels and on 26 June, new rider Eddie Davidsson was introduced into the team. It was an inauspicious debut for the new Swede, though, as he failed to register a single point.

Hackney were beaten 44-34 on 3 July, but the Rebels went down at home the following week, losing 43-35 to a powerful Exeter side, for whom Ivan Mauger raced to a fine maximum. Had Dag Lovaas not been badly shaken in a heat seven pile-up, the result could well have been different. Following a challenge match victory over Reading on 17 July, the Rebels suffered a surprise loss to Newport, going down 42-36. Despite putting in plenty of effort, Eddie Davidsson was having a tough time, and prior to the Knock-Out Cup match against Belle Vue on 7 August, he was released. The Swede was replaced by Norwegian Hilge Langli, who had previously ridden for Newcastle in 1969. Regrettably, the incoming rider failed to score in the match and the Rebels went down to a 42-36 defeat. Leicester were beaten in the last heat the following week, with Langli showing promising form, which continued when he recorded 5 points in a 49-29 win over Halifax on 21 August.

Wimbledon were beaten on Bank Holiday Monday, 25 August, with Dag Lovaas racing to a superb 15-point maximum. This was followed by a victory over Poole, and on 14 September there came a really sweet 46-32 success over Reading, with Lovaas racing to another 15-point full-house, this time against his former club. Wolverhampton came to Cowley on 11 September, and Langli was now an absentee, having suffered an injury. With Richard Hellsen also still missing, use of the rider replacement rule for the absent Hasse Holmqvist ensured excellent cover and the result was a Rebels win by 43 points to 35. With Holmqvist unavailable to ride, it was something of a strange situation that allowed Oxford to employ the rider replacement facility for him, as and when the position allowed!

Richard Hellsen returned for the match against Swindon on 18 September, when the Rebels dispensed with the rider replacement rule and ran out winners by 44 points to 34. A double-header against Coventry and King's Lynn on 2 October saw more success with 58-20 and 49-29 victories respectively. Then came the final match of the season on the afternoon of the 5 October, namely the first leg of the Midland Cup final against Wolverhampton. Although the Rebels achieved only a slender 2-point victory, they then went on to win the trophy. Their success however, was overshadowed by the tragic death of Wolverhampton rider Gary Peterson, in a track accident during the second leg at Monmore Green on 17 October.

The final league table saw Oxford perched in a satisfactory seventh place, having jumped ten places from the previous season's wooden spoon position. There was a greater solidity about the team, with Dag Lovaas adding much needed top-end strength, scoring 354 points to finish with a tremendous 10.22 average from 31 league appearances. As the season ended, storm clouds were gathering with the news of the impending sale of the stadium to Oxford City Council for £230,000, and the move of the Rebels to White City in London. It appeared to be the end of an era, with Oxford Stadium looking likely to fall to the developers. The winter break was to be full of drama, as a hardcore of fans formed the 'Save Our Speedway' committee. They were determined that Oxford Speedway would live on, and for the first time, Cowley supporters were to hear the name of Bernard Crapper, who, together with other enthusiasts, began the fight to save the track.

BRITISH LEAGUE

Team	Mts	Won	Drn	Lst	For	Agn	Pts
Ipswich	34	26	1	7	1,458	1,192	53
Belle Vue	34	25	2	7	1,488	1,164	52
Newport	34	24	1	9	1,538	1,112	49
Exeter	34	20	3	11	1,410	1,240	43
Sheffield	34	21	0	13	1,368	1,281	42
Reading	34	21	0	13	1,342	1,308	42
Oxford	**34**	**18**	**0**	**16**	**1,370**	**1,274**	**36**
Leicester	34	16	4	14	1,348	1,303	36
Wimbledon	34	16	2	16	1,317	1,331	34
Halifax	34	15	3	16	1,289	1,362	33
Cradley United	34	15	2	17	1,288	1,356	32
King's Lynn	34	14	3	17	1,295	1,355	31
Wolverhampton	34	13	1	20	1,237	1,414	27
Hull	34	10	4	20	1,258	1,393	24
Poole	34	10	3	21	1,240	1,411	23
Coventry	34	9	2	23	1,176.5	1,473.5	20
Hackney	34	9	1	24	1,221.5	1,429.5	19
Swindon	34	8	0	26	1,202	1,447	16

1976

The fact that there was racing at Cowley in 1976 was due entirely to the efforts of the Save Our Speedway committee, who had campaigned vigorously throughout the winter months. Their success in finally saving the stadium is a tribute to their hard work and the fact that they refused to give in, even though at times the odds appeared to be stacked heavily against them. However, having saved the stadium, there then came the task of re-establishing speedway racing at Sandy Lane, and here they were in luck. Tony Allsopp and Harry Bastable had promoted in the New National League at Stoke and were now looking for another venue. They had a team, or at least a number of riders, so it seemed sensible that they should come together with Oxford, who now had a venue but no team. So, negotiations started and happily reached a satisfactory conclusion, with Stoke riders Mick Handley and Phil Bass, together with juniors Kevin Young, Harry MacLean and Steve Holden, joining their former bosses to begin a new era of racing.

There is no doubt that Messrs Allsopp and Bastable, who traded as Five Star (Speedway) Promotions, had taken a huge gamble, as the 1975 Rebels had been a British League team, but now the public would be watching lower tier racing and a team of new riders that they had not previously seen. So, there was always the chance that the Cowley public would not respond favourably to the venture. However, the hard core of fans were cheered by the fact that there was speedway at Oxford and they did come along to support the new Cheetahs. Reverting to their old nickname was an astute move, as Oxford had always been the Cheetahs and the change to Rebels had never felt comfortable. Another move in the right direction was the appointment of Roger Jones to look after things on the team front. His persuasive tongue soon brought new signings to Sandy Lane in the form of Carl Askew, via Birmingham, and Malcolm Corradine, from Stoke. Meanwhile, another rider to come on board was Brian Leonard, who had assisted Leicester during 1975.

The new-look Cheetahs took to the track on the 18 March in a challenge match against Eastbourne, with Mick Handley skippering the side. Other team members for the start of a new era at Oxford were Aussie Carl Askew, who top scored and instantly became the darling of the Cowley crowd, together with Kevin Young, Steve Holden, Mal Corradine, Harry MacLean and Roy Sizmore. The Cheetahs lost this opening fixture by just 2 points, but the fans went home happy, having enjoyed a good evening's racing – it was different from what they had been used to, but exciting, nonetheless. The following week saw an impressive Oxford win over Swedish tourists Vetlanda, with Phil Bass and Brian Leonard now in the Cheetahs team. Peterborough won a challenge match at Cowley on 1 April, but Oxford then secured their first league points when defeating Boston 42-36 a week later. Unfortunately, though, Edinburgh-born MacLean, who had begun the season well, was injured at Teesside on 15 April and didn't ride again all year.

In the early weeks of the season, both Workington and Newcastle took points from Oxford, but after a 39-39 draw against Rye House on 10 June, the Cheetahs really found their form at Cowley and put together an impressive series of twelve successive home wins. Oxford also reached the quarter-finals of the Knock-Out Cup, beating Weymouth and Eastbourne before going down to Berwick.

There was no doubt that the 1976 Cheetahs had settled down well and had become a real force at home. Away from Cowley, however, it was the same old story with victories non-existent. The Cheetahs' best efforts occurred at Coatbridge on 30 April, when they lost by 2 points, and at Boston on 30 May, when they went down by 3 points. The side's worst away performance was the match that never was on 10 September, when they refused to ride on a wet track at Peterborough. The end result was that the home riders rode eight heats, scored 40 points, claimed the league points and went home. The Oxford riders were fined for their failure to race and, surprisingly, the result was allowed to stand as Peterborough 40 Oxford 0.

Mick Handley arrived at Oxford via Stoke in 1976 and showed steady form to score 160 league points, yielding a 6.95 average.

As the season progressed, riders came and went, with New Zealander Jim Wells making his debut as a Cheetah against Newcastle on 6 May. By the end of June, Mal Corradine had retired, while Colin Meredith was signed from Stoke in mid-August. Pip Lamb, a young man with a fine record on the grass-track scene, made his home debut on 16 September, scoring a paid 6 points in Oxford's 41-37 victory over Scunthorpe.

The Cheetahs finished fourteenth in the eighteen-team National League, with their home record of fourteen wins, a single draw and two defeats being a very fine effort. It was their away form that let them down, as they didn't glean a single point from seventeen matches. Carl Askew was the team's best rider, weighing in with 236 points from 33 league matches for an average of 7.79. Meanwhile, Brian Leonard, Phil Bass and Mick Handley were steady enough, while Kevin Young looked a marvellous prospect for the future. Pip Lamb also impressed, although he was restricted to just a couple of league appearances for the side.

NEW NATIONAL LEAGUE

Team	Mts	Won	Drn	Lst	For	Agn	Pts
Newcastle	34	30	1	3	1,642	1,007	61
Ellesmere Port	34	24	1	9	1,446.5	1,196.5	49
Workington	34	20	1	13	1,405.5	1,235.5	41
Canterbury	34	20	0	14	1,344	1,302	40
Rye House	34	17	2	15	1,357.5	1,205.5	36
Crayford	34	17	1	16	1,354	1,286	35

Coatbridge	34	17	1	16	1,316	1,320	35
Eastbourne	34	17	0	17	1,361	1,281	34
Peterborough	34	16	2	16	1,351	1,260	34
Berwick	34	17	0	17	1,278	1,360	34
Stoke	34	15	1	18	1,304	1,340	31
Boston	34	15	1	18	1,298	1,345	31
Mildenhall	34	15	1	18	1,270	1,378	31
Oxford	**34**	**14**	**1**	**19**	**1,257**	**1,350**	**29**
Weymouth	34	11	2	21	1,186.5	1,454.5	24
Paisley	34	12	0	22	1,152	1,492	24
Scunthorpe	34	11	1	22	1,184	1,379	23
Teesside	34	10	0	24	1,163	1,478	20

1977

The 1977 season was really all about one man, namely Martin Yeates, and the Oxford supporters could thank Roger Jones for the fact that the Salisbury-based racer ended up at Cowley. Jones was mindful of the fact that the Cheetahs had lacked a high-scoring number one rider during 1976, and with Carl Askew returning to Birmingham for 1977, he set his sights on Yeates, and opened negotiations with his parent club, Poole. Having got his man, in the first meeting of the season – a challenge match against Weymouth on 17 March – Yeates opened his account with a fine maximum, as the Cheetahs raced to a 48-30 victory. Most of the lads who had represented the Cheetahs the previous season returned, with Kevin Young, Mick Handley, Phil Bass, Brian Leonard, Colin Meredith and Roy Sizmore all remaining on board. Gerald Smitherman arrived via Ellesmere Port, and waiting in the wings was Pip Lamb, so the Cheetahs appeared to have a competitive edge for their second season of National League racing.

Oxford actually opened their league campaign at Teesside on 7 April, losing a thrilling match by 2 points. The following day, they entertained the Teesside team at Cowley and raced to a decisive 53-25 win, with Martin Yeates recording a paid maximum of 11+1 points. As had happened the previous year, there were several team changes throughout the season. After losing form, the experienced Brian Leonard had gone by the end of June. Another rider to lose form, and subsequently drop out of the side by July, was Gerald Smitherman, while a similar fate befell Roy Sizmore, who was allowed to seek pastures new. Youngster Pip Lamb was subsequently given an opportunity in the side and he grasped it with both hands.

With Martin Yeates continuing to dominate and knocking up high scores everywhere he rode, the management were able to introduce young riders into the side with a degree of confidence. Greg Joynt, a young Australian, made his debut in the away fixture at Crayford on 19 July. However, it was a match where the Cheetahs could only muster 29 points, although the immaculate Yeates scored 15 of his side's tally and rode unbeaten. Unfortunately, Joynt proved to be out of his depth in National League racing, and soon faded from the Oxford scene, but on 28 July, a young former schoolboy scrambler by the name of Richie Caulwell made a wonderful debut against Berwick at Cowley, scoring 7+2 points from three rides. He was given an extended run in the team, but never repeated his debut form, his best score thereafter being a return of 5+1 points against Edinburgh on 22 September.

The home match against Boston on 11 August had seen another rider make his debut for the Cheetahs. This time it was enthusiastic youngster Malcolm Holloway, who arrived on loan from Swindon and weighed in with 6 points. Oxford lost the encounter 40-38, despite the normal 12-point maximum from Martin Yeates. This represented a first home league defeat for the Cheetahs, who had been displaying good form at Cowley, but the following week there was another shock in store when Scunthorpe visited and inflicted a similar 40-38 reverse. Colin Meredith bagged 12 points, while both Yeates and Phil Bass carded 11 apiece. Unfortunately, though, the Cheetahs had a long tail, with Kevin Young, Pip Lamb, Richie Caulwell and Holloway only mustering 4 points between them. The next home meeting against Mildenhall on 1 September saw Oxford drop another point in a 39-39 draw. Winning form at Cowley returned for the match against Peterborough seven days later, though, with Young in fine form, registering an unbeaten 11+1 points in a 51-27 success.

Despite their generally good home form, the Cheetahs just couldn't collect any league points away from Cowley. There were a few near misses at Teesside, Scunthorpe, Stoke, Weymouth and Newcastle, but all too often it was a case of Martin Yeates against the opposition. Meanwhile, in the Knock-Out Cup, Oxford eventually beat Rye House after a replay, before disposing of Newport, but they went down to Ellesmere Port at the quarter-final stage, losing both legs.

The Cheetahs finally finished in thirteenth position, winning fifteen of their home matches, including victories over the Champions Eastbourne and runners-up Rye House. By a long chalk, Martin Yeates was the Cheetahs' number one rider, completely dominating the season, and his win in the Weslake-sponsored Super National at Cowley on 15 September gave the Oxford fans even more to cheer about. Yeates actually finished third in the overall National League averages, scoring 396 points from 35 matches for a massive 10.59 figure. Phil Bass and Mick Handley were good at Cowley, but mediocre away, while Malcolm Holloway and Pip Lamb were excellent prospects for the future. Meanwhile, Kevin Young, who had made good progress, was dismissed after a row with the management in mid-September, following his missing of a tour to Glasgow and Berwick.

Malcolm Holloway arrived at Oxford on loan from Swindon in 1977. The enthusiastic youngster made just 11 appearances in the National League, scoring 49 points to average 5.90.

Banbury-born Phil Bass spent the 1977 season on loan to the Cheetahs from Bristol. He recorded 249 points from 35 league matches to post a 7.53 average.

NATIONAL LEAGUE

Team	Mts	Won	Drn	Lst	For	Agn	Pts
Eastbourne	36	29	0	7	1,752	1,052	58
Rye House	36	24	3	9	1,524	1,273	51
Ellesmere Port	36	22	2	12	1,493	1,303	46
Canterbury	36	23	0	13	1,494	1,307	46
Peterborough	36	22	0	14	1,474	1,332	44
Newcastle	36	21	1	14	1,522	1,274	43
Boston	36	20	0	16	1,462	1,311	40
Mildenhall	36	16	4	16	1,382	1,422	36
Teesside	36	17	1	18	1,264	1,538	35
Crayford	36	17	0	19	1,416	1,375	34
Glasgow	36	16	0	20	1,333	1,442	32
Newport	36	16	0	20	1,311	1,482	32
Oxford	**36**	**15**	**1**	**20**	**1,399**	**1,390**	**31**
Scunthorpe	36	15	1	20	1,293	1,508	31
Edinburgh	36	15	0	21	1,344	1,457	30
Workington	36	14	1	21	1,288	1,512	29
Weymouth	36	11	3	22	1,326	1,476	25
Berwick	36	11	1	24	1,194	1,606	23
Stoke	36	9	0	27	1,295	1,506	18

NOTE: Glasgow took over from Coatbridge upon their withdrawal after completing fifteen matches.

1978

There were significant changes at the top in 1978, with Dan McCormick, Derek Pugh and David Hawkins listed as the directors of Oxford Stadium Speedway Inc. The straight-talking McCormick, who also promoted the sport at Cradley Heath, subsequently installed Chris Van Straaten as his front man, while Bernard Crapper and John Payne, who had previously played vital roles behind the scenes, now had special managerial responsibilities. A further change saw team manager Roger Jones depart, to be replaced by former rider Pete Jarman. On the team front, the immaculate Martin Yeates returned to his British League track, Poole, and Phil Bass departed for Milton Keynes. Meanwhile, Colin Meredith, Mick Handley and Pip Lamb stayed on board from the previous term, to be joined by Australian Carl Askew, who returned after a season away. Another newcomer to Cowley was the promising John Hack, who joined the club via Cradley Heath. Trials were given to Australian Les Sawyer, while Brian Leonard returned to active speedway racing.

The Cheetahs opened the season with a challenge match against Ellesmere Port on 30 March, but went down to a 44-34 reverse. Two National League matches followed, with the Cheetahs suffering crushing defeats at Ellesmere Port, 50-28, and Eastbourne, 51-27. Something drastic had to happen to revitalise fortunes, and two days after the Eastbourne defeat, it did. In a challenge match at Milton Keynes, making his debut as a Cheetah was a pint-sized blond-haired Australian called David Shields. The fact that Oxford were victorious by 43 points to 31, and that Carl Askew recorded a 12-point maximum was great. What was sensational, though, was the performance of Shields, who raced to an unbeaten 11+1 points and also captured the track record at the Groveway Stadium in a dream debut!

John Hack hailed from Manchester and scored 197 points from 31 league matches to average 7.87 for the Cheetahs in 1978.

Co-author Glynn Shailes presents James Moore with his sponsorship cheque prior to the Oxford Stadium Trophy at Cowley on 14 September 1978. Canterbury's Steve Koppe won the meeting ahead of Mildenhall's Mel Taylor, with Moore finishing a creditable third.

A couple of days later, on 6 April, Milton Keynes were at Oxford for another challenge match, which the Cheetahs easily won by 57 points to 20. David Shields had a quieter home debut, scoring 6 points, while Carl Askew, Colin Meredith and Pip Lamb were paid for the lot. Another new signing, the experienced George Hunter from British League Wolverhampton, made a fine home debut, netting 9+1 points. Finally, Oxford looked to have a team able to tackle the league programme and at Newcastle on 10 April, they shook the powerful Diamonds by winning 45-32, and followed that up with a 44-34 victory at Barrow the following evening. The arrival of Hunter and Shields was to signal the retirement of Brian Leonard, who left to concentrate on his business affairs.

On 20 April, Workington were the first visitors to Cowley on league business, with the match resulting in a decisive 57-21 victory to the Cheetahs, and this was followed by a battling 39-39 draw at Boston three days later. Everything seemed to be going well for Oxford, but they came down to earth when Peterborough sneaked a narrow 40-38 victory at Sandy Lane on 4 May, despite 11 points each from David Shields and John Hack. Winning form at home soon returned however, with good victories over Weymouth and Canterbury. Away from home, Scunthorpe were slaughtered 50-28 by the in-form Cheetahs on 22 May, and then Glasgow were hammered unmercifully 58-19 at Cowley on 1 June. But, in a northern tour that followed at Glasgow, Berwick and Workington, the Cheetahs had no luck, losing all three matches. They did enjoy success at Teesside, though, on 15 June with a hard-earned 40-38 win. Three days later at Cowley, the double was completed over Teesside with a 50-27 triumph that featured 12-point maximums for both George Hunter and Carl Askew.

The home league match against Milton Keynes on 6 July saw the debut of a New Zealander of Maori stock, whose full name was James Timy Te-Kerehi Herini-Moore. Thankfully, this was shortened to the much more manageable James Moore! Anyway, the Cheetahs raced to a 58-20 win, with Moore scoring a fine 7+1 points. Remarkably, Oxford now had a surplus of riders, with Mick Handley departing to link up with Scunthorpe.

In 1978, Australian David Shields enjoyed a simply sensational first year of racing in Britain, scoring 300 points from 36 league matches to average 8.83 for the Cheetahs.

July and August proved to be good months on the home front. Both Edinburgh and Barrow were well beaten, although Newcastle secured a 39-39 draw in a fantastic match. Winning form quickly returned when Berwick were thrashed 61-17 on 3 August, with both Boston and Rye House also subsequently falling to the Oxford onslaught. Away from Cowley, however, there wasn't much luck, with the Cheetahs losing at Edinburgh, Stoke and Canterbury. September began badly, as the side slumped to away defeats at Peterborough and Mildenhall, but Oxford still showed their superiority at Cowley by defeating Stoke and Scunthorpe, before beginning the month of October with a tremendous 50-28 home success over Ellesmere Port.

As the season came to its close, Eastbourne were beaten at Cowley, and the home league programme finished with a nail-biting 39-39 draw against Mildenhall on 12 October. On the road, the Cheetahs secured a draw at Milton Keynes, before losing their final away meeting at Rye House on 8 October, when George Hunter notched 16 of his side's total of 31 points. So, a great season of speedway racing ended with the Cheetahs rising to seventh position in the twenty-team National League. At home, they raced to sixteen wins and two draws, and had only a single defeat, whilst away, their form improved considerably with four victories, two draws and thirteen losses. George Hunter registered 333 points from 35 appearances to top Oxford's league averages with a superb 9.93 figure. Meanwhile, the discovery of the season, David Shields, finished on a highly impressive 8.83 average, having tallied 300 points from 36 league matches. John Hack and Carl Askew provided great solidity to the side, achieving averages of 7.87 and 7.26 respectively, whilst Pip Lamb came on in leaps and bounds and finished with a creditable 6.61 figure.

Turning to the Knock-Out Cup, the Cheetahs enjoyed a good run. A bye took them directly into round two, when they edged out Stoke by 82 points to 74 on aggregate. Then, at the quarter-final stage, they narrowly lost 40-38 at Mildenhall on 9 July, before finishing the job with a 43-34 success over the Fen Tigers in the second leg at Sandy Lane on 10 August. Regrettably, Oxford came unstuck in the semi-final, when they suffered a heavy loss at the hands of Eastbourne, going down 56-22 in the first leg at Arlington on 27 August. The second leg took place at Cowley on 7 September, but the Eagles again proved too strong, winning 45-32 to secure a crushing aggregate victory by 101 points to 54.

NATIONAL LEAGUE

Team	Mts	Won	Drn	Lst	For	Agn	Pts
Canterbury	38	30	0	8	1,719	1,240	60
Newcastle	38	29	2	7	1,698	1,261	60
Rye House	38	27	0	11	1,650.5	1,308.5	54
Eastbourne	38	25	1	12	1,704	1,248	51
Ellesmere Port	38	24	0	14	1,576	1,359	48
Peterborough	38	22	1	15	1,578	1,383	45
Oxford	**38**	**20**	**4**	**14**	**1,599.5**	**1,358.5**	**44**
Stoke	38	21	1	16	1,527	1,433	43
Glasgow	38	19	1	18	1,397	1,556	39
Crayford	38	16	2	20	1,437	1,519	34
Berwick	38	17	0	21	1,389	1,565	34
Mildenhall	38	16	1	21	1,538	1,420	33
Weymouth	38	16	0	22	1,460	1,490	32
Workington	38	16	0	22	1,424	1,535	32
Edinburgh	38	15	1	22	1,400	1,557	31
Milton Keynes	38	12	6	20	1,350	1,608	30
Boston	38	13	2	23	1,308	1,644	28
Teesside	38	12	0	26	1,297	1,662	24
Scunthorpe	38	9	2	27	1,291	1,645	20
Barrow	38	8	2	28	1,204	1,755	18

1979

Prior to the season, there was a major shock when the talented Aussie David Shields announced his retirement from the sport. However, with Dan McCormick now occupying the hot seat on behalf of Northern Sports (Oxford) Ltd, the Cheetahs' supporters had little to worry about, and it wasn't long before good replacement riders were signed. The first new acquisition was Les Rumsey via Canterbury, closely followed by John Barker, who came on loan from Eastbourne. With returnees George Hunter, Carl Askew, Pip Lamb, John Hack and Colin Meredith, plus Mick Handley back from his spell with Scunthorpe, Oxford boasted a good line-up with strength in depth. Meanwhile, one other off-track change saw Phil Mountford appointed as team manager and it was always claimed that he was the son of former Bristol rider Jack.

The Cheetahs opened the season with an away challenge match at near neighbours Milton Keynes on 3 April, when they came away with a 42-35 victory. Pip Lamb top-scored with 10.5 points, his performance including a dead heat with teammate George Hunter. The home season began two days later, when Nottingham were the visitors in another challenge fixture, and again Oxford raced to success, winning 47-30. Another win followed at Weymouth on 10 April, with the Cheetahs securing a 45-33 success from a third successive challenge match, so confidence was running high in the camp.

Prior to the start of the league campaign, Oxford enjoyed a couple of international challenge matches, hammering the Swedish Under-23 touring side 49-29 at Cowley on

12 April, before losing narrowly to Red Star of Prague the following evening by 41 points to 37. Ellesmere Port were sent packing, 53-24, in the opening league fixture at Sandy Lane on 19 April, but at Mildenhall three days later, it was the Cheetahs' turn to be on the wrong end of a hammering. The Fen Tigers hit Oxford with everything they had and were decisive victors by 52 points to 26. It didn't take the Cheetahs long to recover, however, and it was visiting Glasgow who were to suffer the power of the side at Sandy Lane on 26 April as Oxford emphatically hammered the Tigers 52-26. Carrying on this wonderful form, they followed that up with a fine 45-33 victory at Nottingham on 7 May.

Rye House came to Cowley on 24 May and shook the Cheetahs by snatching a 41-37 victory, although to be fair John Barker was missing, and Colin Meredith was badly off form. Regrettably, this match was destined to be Meredith's last for the Cheetahs, for he had suffered an early season injury and had never been able to reveal his best form, so announced his retirement from racing. After the setback against Rye House, the Cheetahs enjoyed an excellent period of success, which included a hard-fought 39-39 draw at Weymouth and tremendous home victories over Boston, Canterbury and Crayford. The home triumph over Boston on 21 June will, however, always be remembered with great sadness at Oxford, for Pip Lamb, who had been enjoying a productive season, crashed and received injuries which were to confine him to a wheelchair. The Hereford-born youngster had been ever-present up to that point, averaging 9.33 in the National League, and his injury was a sickening blow.

Following the injury to Pip Lamb, Oxford introduced a few new faces into the side. Robert Dole, a young Australian, was given opportunities, as was South African Denzil Kent, plus Colin Ackroyd, who had had some experience at Eastbourne, and a little later, John Grahame, a member of a famous speedway racing family.

Eastbourne-born John Barker linked with Oxford on loan from his hometown club in 1979, recording 169 points from 32 matches to finish the campaign with a league average of 6.71.

Milton Keynes sprang a surprise, winning 40-38 at Oxford on 15 July, but the Cheetahs responded by defeating Newcastle 41-37 in another home fixture four days afterwards. A northern tour saw losses at Glasgow and Workington, before the Cheetahs gained some consolation at Milton Keynes with a thrilling 39-38 victory on 31 July.

At home, the Cheetahs were a real force in August, hammering Peterborough 50-28, with further big wins following against Weymouth (58-20), Workington (57-21), Berwick (49-29) and Edinburgh (54-23). On their travels, they didn't enjoy such good fortune, however, losing 45-33 at both Rye House and Middlesbrough. September started well, with home victories over Nottingham and Stoke being followed by impressive away wins at both Scunthorpe and Crayford. The run of away successes was halted at Ellesmere Port on 14 September, though, when the Gunners clinched a 45-32 win. Another defeat followed at Boston, but Oxford then enjoyed a great match at Stoke on 22 September, when they won 40-38.

The season drew to its close with home victories over Scunthorpe and Mildenhall, and a defeat at Peterborough. An excellent 42-36 win at Edinburgh was followed by a massacre at Berwick on 6 October, however, when the Cheetahs could only muster 18 points to the Bandits' 60. Oxford soon recovered, though, and two days later, they wound up the season with a fine 41-37 success at Newcastle.

In what had been a marvellous campaign, the Cheetahs finished third in the final National League table, making it their best effort since dropping down from the British League. George Hunter again headed the averages, with a tremendous 10.98 figure, having plundered 309 points from 28 league matches. Meanwhile, new boy Les Rumsey enjoyed a wonderful term, appearing in a full quota of 36 league matches and netting 404 points for a 9.92 average. His huge tally of points actually made him the highest scorer in the entire league. Although it was a much better year for the Cheetahs, it was, nonetheless, marred by the tragic accident that cost them the services of Pip Lamb. The season finished on 21 October with a benefit pairs meeting for the injured rider, with Bruce Penhall and Bobby Schwartz topping a class field to win the trophy donated by Northern Sports.

NATIONAL LEAGUE

Team	Mts	Won	Drn	Lst	For	Agn	Pts
Mildenhall	36	30	0	6	1,658.5	1,139.5	60
Rye House	36	29	1	6	1,684	1,116	59
Oxford	**36**	**24**	**1**	**11**	**1,547**	**1,250**	**49**
Berwick	36	21	3	12	1,540.5	1,261.5	45
Milton Keynes	36	21	0	15	1,441	1,358	42
Newcastle	36	20	0	16	1,480	1,321	40
Glasgow	36	19	0	17	1,432	1,368	38
Peterborough	36	18	2	16	1,422	1,381	38
Ellesmere Port	36	18	1	17	1,435	1,366	37
Canterbury	36	17	2	17	1,401	1,404	36
Middlesbrough	36	17	1	18	1,345	1,457	35
Crayford	36	16	0	20	1,323	1,479	32
Stoke	36	15	2	19	1,321.5	1,477.5	32
Nottingham	36	14	1	21	1,351.5	1,452.5	29
Workington	36	14	1	21	1,319	1,486	29
Boston	36	13	2	21	1,317	1,481	28
Edinburgh	36	13	1	22	1,273.5	1,524.5	27
Weymouth	36	9	1	26	1,243.5	1,560.5	19
Scunthorpe	36	4	1	31	1,068	1,720	9

1980

The 1980 season heralded a number of changes on the team front, with the Cheetahs' two leading riders from the previous year wanting away. George Hunter returned to his first love, Edinburgh, and Les Rumsey, after just one season at Cowley, joined Crayford. Rumsey's move was a real surprise, because the publicity that followed his signing in 1979 indicated that he had come to the Cheetahs' lair on a three-year contract. John Barker was another rider to leave after just one season at Cowley, while Carl Askew remained in his native Australia. There were changes on the promotional front too, with the likeable Bob Wasley put in charge of the Cheetahs' fortunes on behalf of husband and wife directors Derek and Nora Pugh.

With Oxford having to virtually rebuild their side, the signing of Dave Perks from Nottingham ensured that they had an efficient number one rider. Two other newcomers were Chris Sully, on loan from Leicester, and Billy Spiers via Weymouth, who joined John Hack, back for his third season at Cowley, plus old faithful Mick Handley and the two promising youngsters, Colin Ackroyd and John Grahame.

The season opened on 27 March, with a challenge match against Milton Keynes resulting in a 45-33 win for the Cheetahs, with 11 points apiece from Dave Perks and John Hack. Three days later, Oxford began their league campaign at Rye House and found themselves on the wrong end of a 50-27 hammering. An Italian touring team visited Cowley on 4 April, and in an interesting match, the Cheetahs posted a 43-34 success. On 10 April, Rye House were the first visitors to Cowley on league business and the Hoddesdon-based side completed a quick-fire double, winning 43-34. Both Billy Spiers and Chris Sully failed to score for the Cheetahs, with the former disappearing from the Cowley scene after the match, soon to be followed by Sully, who was replaced by former Weymouth rider Mick Fletcher. Mildenhall gave Oxford a terrible mauling at Cowley on 17 April, winning 49-28, with only the immaculate Dave Perks saving his side from an even bigger beating courtesy of a quite brilliant 15-point maximum. Oxford's first league victory arrived on 24 April, when a tense affair against Crayford ended with the Cheetahs snatching a 40-38 win in a thrilling last-heat decider, however, it was obvious that the team needed strengthening.

Derek Harrison began the 1980 campaign with King's Lynn, but was transferred to Cradley Heath, who subsequently loaned him to Oxford. The Suffolk-born rider made 30 league appearances for the Cheetahs, scoring 275 points to average 8.79.

The following week saw Derek 'Super Ted' Harrison link with the Oxford camp, on loan from Cradley Heath. The Suffolk-born rider had been a star with Milton Keynes the previous year, and he was just what the Cheetahs needed. Prior to that, another new face was that of Steve Crockett, loaned to Oxford from Wolverhampton, who, following his debut for the Cheetahs at Stoke on 20 April, held his team place for the rest of the season.

Oxford met the might of British League Leicester in the first round of the Inter-League Knock-Out Cup at Cowley on 15 May and raced to a highly creditable 39-39 draw, with Dave Perks scorching to a 12-point maximum. In the replay at Leicester on 6 June, the Cheetahs put up a battling performance before going down 47-31. Again, it was that man Perks who led the scoring with a superb 11 points from five rides.

Having finally established a useful side, things suddenly began to go wrong for the Cheetahs. Dave Perks, who'd recorded ten league maximums (nine full and one paid) in the Oxford cause, plus a string of other double-figure tallies, sustained serious back injuries in a crash at Birmingham in July and was out of the side, regrettably, for the rest of the season. As if that were not enough, Cradley Heath, the Cheetahs' mentors in the British League, recalled John Hack to their line-up, and by the start of August, Oxford were reduced to just one established heat-leader in Derek Harrison. It was also a busy month on the road with six fixtures on away circuits, so it was small wonder that they lost the lot. The home match against Workington on 21 August did at least give the Cowley fans much in the way of enjoyment, as the Cheetahs won 50-28, but the real pleasure was to see youngsters Colin Ackroyd and Steve Crockett each plunder full 12-point maximums.

New faces to boost the Oxford team came in September via the British League. Experienced Bruce Cribb arrived on loan from Wolverhampton, and the former Oxford Rebel Trevor Geer returned to the club on loan from Eastbourne. Their arrival took some of the pressure off Derek Harrison, and ensured that the Cheetahs were at least competitive in the final weeks of the season.

With all the problems, it was no surprise that Oxford dropped to fifteenth place in the final National League table. They were on a high before the sensational Dave Perks was hurt, but from that moment on, any chance the Cheetahs had of league honours vanished. Despite this, Derek Harrison did a great job in holding the side together, his final league average being 8.79, having gleaned 275 points from 30 appearances. Meanwhile, both Colin Ackroyd and Steve Crockett made excellent progress to average 5.75 and 4.66 respectively. Perks' record really was something special, though, since 226 points from 20 matches yielded an average of 10.94 – the highest in the entire league – while at the Cowley circuit alone, he posted an incredible 11.53 figure. Perks' other claim to fame was the establishing of a new track record at Sandy Lane in heat one of the Silver Helmet Match-Race Championship against Les Rumsey on 19 June, prior to Oxford's league match against Newcastle. His time of 62.2 seconds eclipsed Peter Craven's previous best of 63.0, which had stood since 9 May 1963.

NATIONAL LEAGUE

Team	Mts	Won	Drn	Lst	For	Agn	Pts
Rye House	38	31	0	7	1,735	1,219	62
Newcastle	38	30	1	7	1,714	1,238	61
Middlesbrough	38	27	2	9	1,665.5	1,288.5	56
Berwick	38	24	1	13	1,638.5	1,306.5	49
Boston	38	23	2	13	1,605	1,348	48
Edinburgh	38	23	2	13	1,499	1,457	48
Mildenhall	38	21	2	15	1,543.5	1,415.5	44
Peterborough	38	21	0	17	1,467	1,494	42
Crayford	37	20	1	16	1,542	1,334	41

Ellesmere Port	38	20	1	17	1,561	1,396	41
Glasgow	38	19	2	17	1,538	1,416	40
Exeter	38	17	1	20	1,453	1,505	35
Scunthorpe	38	15	1	22	1,363	1,572	31
Nottingham	38	14	2	22	1,415	1,545	30
Oxford	**38**	**14**	**1**	**23**	**1,339**	**1,608**	**29**
Stoke	38	14	0	24	1,334	1,615	28
Weymouth	37	13	1	23	1,372.5	1,483.5	27
Canterbury	38	10	4	24	1,397	1,555	24
Milton Keynes	38	8	2	28	1,290	1,668	18
Workington	38	2	0	36	969	1,977	4

NOTE: One match, Crayford *v.* Weymouth, was not raced.

1981

The great news that greeted Oxford fans before the start of the season was that skipper Dave Perks had recovered from his injuries and would again lead the Cheetahs' attack. More good news was the fact that Derek Harrison would also be back. Mick Handley returned too, as did the promising Colin Ackroyd, Mick Fletcher and John Grahame, while trials were given to Alan MacLean, the younger brother of Harry, who had ridden for the Cheetahs in 1976. Steve Crockett was missing, though, having moved to Wolverhampton, who were now members of the National League.

Dave Perks recovered from a serious back injury to again lead the Cheetahs' attack in 1981, when he easily topped the club's league averages on a huge 10.26 figure, having scored 361 points from 34 matches.

The management were well aware that the side had a long tail after Dave Perks and Derek Harrison, and a third heat-leader was urgently required. As things turned out, though, the third heat-leader was a long time coming. To try and bring the side up to strength, Oxford turned to former Rebel Bob Kilby, who had retired following a highly successful Testimonial season at Swindon. However, the Swindonian declined the offer and the promotion subsequently looked at Reading's Ashley Pullen. In the event, it was only in the closing weeks of the season that the Oxford-born rider finally became available and joined the Cheetahs' ranks.

The early season matches emphasised the lack of a third heat-leader, with home losses suffered in challenge fixtures against Milton Keynes, Rye House and Weymouth. It wasn't until 23 April, when the league campaign got underway at Cowley, that the Cheetahs tasted success. A 42-36 victory over Boston saw the debut of Arthur Price, who had moved from Nottingham, and he made a quiet start with 4+2 points. Mildenhall beat Oxford 43-35 the following week at Cowley, but on 1 May, the Cheetahs enjoyed a narrow 41-37 success at Workington. Defeats at Stoke and Canterbury followed, with the latter match on 9 May seeing Paul Evitts make a very satisfactory debut for Oxford with 6+1 points.

The home match against Milton Keynes on 14 May saw the Cheetahs really click as a team to record a 49-29 victory. Dave Perks raced to a classy 12-point maximum and Derek Harrison scored 11, while Colin Ackroyd also had a fine meeting, tallying 10+1. Four days later at Newcastle, the Cheetahs thought their third heat-leader problem had been solved with the signing of Arnold Haley from sister track Cradley Heath. Haley had vast experience and Oxford felt he'd be just the man for the job, but, unfortunately, they were to be disappointed, for Haley scored just a single point from two rides, and decided that it was time to retire. Not only that, but the Cheetahs succumbed to a 49-29 loss against the Diamonds.

Defeat at Weymouth was followed by a 41-37 win at Milton Keynes on 9 June, when Oxford used the rider replacement facility for the injured Derek Harrison. A good performance saw Dave Perks ride unbeaten for 15 points, with Colin Ackroyd recording a creditable 10. Throughout June and early July, the Cheetahs enjoyed a period of success, with home wins against Stoke, Glasgow and Edinburgh, plus a 39-36 victory at Wolverhampton. They crashed to defeat, however, at Exeter when, without skipper Perks, they lost 51-27, with Harrison and Ackroyd collectively scoring 24 of the side's dismal total. Newcastle then came to Oxford on 9 July and left with the league points courtesy of a 42-36 scoreline, but when Rye House visited the following week, the Cheetahs returned to winning form by 43 points to 35.

Oxford produced a simply marvellous display at Glasgow on 24 July, when they really shook the home side. Had the Cheetahs not lost the services of the hard-riding Colin Ackroyd to a broken collarbone in heat ten, when the Eastbourne-born rider was involved in a battle royal with the home number one, Steve Lawson, they surely would have won. This piece of cruel luck let the Tigers back into the match and they ran out fortunate victors by 41 points to 37. Right from the opening heat, when Dave Perks had defeated Lawson (and not many visiting riders achieved that), it showed that Oxford meant business. Mick Fletcher had taken heat two, with subsequent race wins posted by Ackroyd and Harrison. Another success followed for Perks, before Harrison crossed the line ahead in heat six. Wins followed for Ackroyd and Paul Evitts in heats seven and eight respectively, and the Cheetahs were on a roll. Oxford led 28-26 and Ackroyd was unbeaten when heat ten began and his accident let Glasgow off the hook, of that there is no doubt. Never was a side more glorious in defeat, with Perks and Harrison heading the scoring on 11 points apiece, both having taken four rides. A home success followed against Berwick on 30 July, although the result was later expunged from the records following the Bandits' premature withdrawal from the National League.

Into August, and despite Oxford operating the rider replacement facility for Colin Ackroyd, they gained a draw at Ellesmere Port, where Derek Harrison blitzed to a magical 18-point maximum. A 43-34 victory at Scunthorpe on 17 August was followed by a home victory over Wolverhampton, 44-34, in a double-header three days later, which also saw the Cheetahs slaughter Workington 62-15 in the second match. Both Dave Perks and Harrison recorded paid maximums (11+1 points) against the luckless Comets, but more pleasing for the Oxford supporters in this uninteresting match was the full 12-point maximum recorded by Paul Evitts, and a paid full-house of 9+3 from John Grahame.

The Cheetahs came down with a bump when visiting Middlesbrough shortly afterwards on 23 August, the home side winning 54-24, and Weymouth sprang a surprise by winning 43-34 at Cowley on 27 August. Success against visiting Ellesmere Port on 3 September was followed by a home defeat at the hands of Middlesbrough, this being one of the few occasions at Cowley when Dave Perks didn't register a double-figure score. Perks was back to his brilliant best for the visit to Crayford on 8 September, however, scoring 15 points from six rides, but despite this, Oxford lost a hard-fought encounter 42-36.

Exeter were beaten 41-37 at Sandy Lane on 17 September, but Canterbury came the following week and recorded a 40-37 victory. The fixture against Exeter saw the return of Colin Ackroyd, while the defeat at the hands of Canterbury was to be the only time Dave Perks really failed at Cowley, as he recorded an uncharacteristic 4 points. Perks was back on form next time out, though, racing to four-ride maximums against Crayford and Scunthorpe in a double-header at Cowley on 1 October. Ackroyd also weighed in with a maximum against Crayford, and just for good measure, he also repeated the feat against Scunthorpe. The very next day at Peterborough, the Cheetahs were heavily beaten 52-26, but the following Thursday, it was their turn to entertain the Panthers. It was to prove a memorable match, not just because Oxford won 42-36, but because it marked the home debut of new signing Ashley Pullen, a man the club had been chasing since day one of the season. The local boy marked his debut with a well-taken 6+1 points.

The league programme ended with defeats at Mildenhall and Edinburgh, although the season at home finished on a high note thanks to a 57-21 victory over Milton Keynes in a challenge match. Oxford's final position was twelfth in the nineteen-team National League and supporters were left wondering what might have been, had they had the services of Ashley Pullen from the start of the campaign. The Cheetahs won thirteen home matches and lost five, while on their travels they won on five occasions, drew just the once and lost a dozen times. Topping the statistical rundown again was Dave Perks, who scorched to 361 points from 34 league matches for an outstanding 10.26 average. Supplying wonderful top-end backing, Derek Harrison recorded 346 points for a 9.51 figure, while Colin Ackroyd's tally of 227 points yielded a solid average of 8.17.

NATIONAL LEAGUE

Team	Mts	Won	Drn	Lst	For	Agn	Pts
Middlesbrough	36	30	1	5	1,692	1,109	61
Weymouth	36	26	1	9	1,570	1,236	53
Newcastle	36	25	1	10	1,566.5	1,232.5	51
Edinburgh	36	25	0	11	1,535.5	1,246.5	50
Glasgow	36	24	0	12	1,500.5	1,294.5	48
Boston	36	22	0	14	1,503.5	1,301.5	44
Exeter	36	22	0	14	1,497	1,305	44
Mildenhall	36	20	0	16	1,417.5	1,383.5	40
Peterborough	36	19	1	16	1,433	1,368	39
Crayford	36	19	0	17	1,361.5	1,432.5	38
Ellesmere Port	36	18	1	17	1,446	1,354	37
Oxford	**36**	**18**	**1**	**17**	**1,392**	**1,407**	**37**
Wolverhampton	36	14	1	21	1,345	1,452	29
Canterbury	36	14	1	21	1,340	1,460	29
Stoke	36	14	0	22	1,343	1,452	28

Rye House	36	11	0	25	1,328	1,472	22
Scunthorpe	36	6	1	29	1,114	1,682	13
Workington	36	6	1	29	1,047	1,752	13
Milton Keynes	36	4	0	32	1,149	1,641	8

NOTE: Berwick withdrew from the league after completing twenty-six matches. Their record was expunged from the table.

1982

As usual, it was all change again at Oxford in 1982, although the Cowley faithful had become accustomed to that over the years. Indeed, the supporters had long since reasoned that being a sister track to a glamour club, Cradley Heath, in the British League meant it was the Heathens who paid the piper and therefore called the tune. The top two from 1981, namely Dave Perks and Derek Harrison, were missing, with the former returning to Long Eaton, while the latter was transferred to Mildenhall. Also Long Eaton-bound was Paul Evitts, who had been so promising for the Cheetahs in 1981, while the equally up-and-coming John Grahame moved into the British League with Reading. Thankfully, Ashley Pullen was back, as was the crowd-pleasing Colin Ackroyd, plus old faithfuls Mick Handley and Mick Fletcher. To bring the side up to strength, Graham Drury was signed from defunct Hull on loan, and Wayne Jackson also arrived at Cowley, following the closure of Workington.

It was hardly surprising that the season opened badly for the Cheetahs, since the side had practically been rebuilt and needed time to settle together. Milton Keynes won at Sandy Lane in the season's opening fixture on 25 March, having already beaten the Cheetahs at the Groveway in the first leg of a home and away challenge fixture two days beforehand, and in addition, Oxford lost another challenge match at Peterborough. At home against Weymouth on 1 April, the Cheetahs secured a 50-46 win in the Dorsox Trophy, only to subsequently lose the second leg at Weymouth by 16 points. Things really looked up at Rye House on 4 April, though, in the first league match of the season, when the Cheetahs were victorious by 53 points to 43. However, it was claimed that Graham Drury's contract had not been registered with the BSPA and this resulted in the match being declared void. The fixture was eventually rerun on 26 September, when the Rye House side made no mistake, winning 64-32.

It soon became clear that Oxford desperately needed bolstering, as Wayne Jackson was hurt in April and sidelined for six weeks with a knee injury. Meanwhile, both Mick Handley and Mick Fletcher were struggling, and Graham Drury wasn't getting the scores the promoters had hoped for. However, the signing of Simon Cross, on loan from Cradley Heath, proved a real boost to the team and it wasn't long before the talented youngster was knocking up double-figure tallies. His arrival gave the Oxford public something to cheer about and the management were quick to give an opportunity to another youngster, namely Kevin Smart, who had seen Central Junior League success with Swindon. He came on loan from the Robins and held his place in the side on merit, and, as such, could be regarded as one of the few pluses enjoyed by Oxford during the season.

Other riders came and went, as Oxford Speedway resembled the revolving doors in a hotel foyer. The experienced Brian Woodward arrived via Weymouth, but hardly had time to settle in before breaking an ankle. No sooner had he recovered than he was sidelined with a back injury, with the result that Oxford hardly knew he'd actually been around. Ian Gledhill arrived via Cradley Heath, but proved to be most disappointing and was gone after barely averaging 4 points per match. Bill Barrett, a young and likeable Australian, was given opportunities to establish himself, but despite his wholehearted efforts, he was never more than a reserve in the line-up. John Frankland, on loan from Long Eaton, was another incoming rider, and although he provided plenty of thrills, he wasn't the heat-leader that the Cheetahs so desperately craved.

Oxford's Ashley Pullen is pictured receiving the Man of the Match award from Bernie Klatt and co-author Glynn Shailes following a home match against Mildenhall on 23 September 1982.

By June, Oxford had collected only a single home league victory against Crayford, and a 48-48 draw against Peterborough. Yet they shook Milton Keynes by winning 49-47 at the Groveway Stadium in the Knock-Out Cup on 11 May, following a home victory in the first leg five days previously. Unfortunately, in the second round against Mildenhall, the Cheetahs suffered a hiding, both at home and away, losing 118-73 on aggregate. The month ended happily, though, with a resounding 60-36 win at Canterbury on 26 June, but there was disappointment as the forceful Colin Ackroyd suffered injury, and Mick Handley retired after struggling to find his best form.

July was a little better for the Cheetahs, and a 53-43 win over Glasgow at Cowley was followed by an excellent 64-31 victory at Stoke. The upsurge in form continued when Berwick came to Oxford on the 22 July and were beaten by 50 points to 46, and the month ended with a home draw against Milton Keynes. Unfortunately, August was a disaster, with both Boston and lowly Scunthorpe being victorious at Cowley, whilst away from home the Cheetahs raced six league matches and lost the lot. As if that were not bad enough, the spectacular Simon Cross and the Oxford skipper Ashley Pullen were involved in a disagreement at Long Eaton on 11 August, with the result that Cross never turned a wheel for Oxford again. To help the Cheetahs' cause, Gary Chessell came on loan from near neighbours Swindon and really played his part in the home win over Stoke on 2 September. However, it was another bad month results-wise. It wasn't until 30 September that the Oxford side had another success of sorts, and that was merely a 48-48 draw at home against Long Eaton.

A season with few memories of note ended at Sandy Lane with a narrow 49-46 victory over Canterbury on 14 October, before the Cheetahs were trounced 72-24 at Berwick three days later in their final match of the campaign. Rather unsurprisingly, the Cheetahs finished at the foot of the nineteen-team league. In all, they won only seven league matches out of the thirty-six raced, and secured three draws, while suffering no fewer than twenty-six losses. Ashley Pullen was the side's best rider, closely followed by Graham Drury and Colin Ackroyd, all three of them ending with averages hovering around the 7-point mark. Incredibly, Oxford used a total of twenty-one riders in an effort to put together a winning combination, but it really was a dismal season, with the efforts of Simon Cross (before he left) and the tigerish Colin Ackroyd being two of the only bright spots.

NATIONAL LEAGUE

Team	Mts	Won	Drn	Lst	For	Agn	Pts
Newcastle	36	30	0	6	2,106	1,345	60
Mildenhall	36	26	1	9	1,967	1,487	53
Ellesmere Port	36	25	0	11	1,848	1,606	50
Middlesbrough	36	24	1	11	1,840	1,605	49
Weymouth	36	22	1	13	1,821	1,631	45
Rye House	36	22	0	14	1,763	1,635	44
Long Eaton	36	20	1	15	1,824.5	1,626.5	41
Boston	36	19	1	16	1,776	1,674	39
Berwick	36	18	1	17	1,784	1,662	37
Exeter	36	17	0	19	1,674.5	1,730.5	34
Glasgow	36	16	0	20	1,592	1,848	32
Milton Keynes	36	14	1	21	1,598	1,843	29
Peterborough	36	13	2	21	1,683	1,768	28
Edinburgh	36	14	0	22	1,631	1,800	28
Crayford	36	13	0	23	1,625	1,814	26
Canterbury	36	12	1	23	1,611	1,833	25
Scunthorpe	36	11	2	23	1,565	1,879	24
Stoke	36	11	1	24	1,510	1,937	23
Oxford	**36**	**7**	**3**	**26**	**1,475**	**1,970**	**17**

1983

The 1983 season heralded yet more changes, both on the team and the promotional front. The change of promotion was to be most significant, because the stadium owners, Northern Sports (Oxford) Ltd, took over the running of speedway, with Bernard Crapper and John Payne becoming the co-promoters. Although it was not fully realised at the time, a new chapter was being written in the history of Oxford Speedway, and little did the supporters know, but it was the beginning of something very special indeed.

The links with British League outfit Cradley Heath were severed, leaving the new promoters to build a team virtually from scratch. Ashley Pullen departed to join Peterborough and, regrettably, the exciting Colin Ackroyd was another absentee. However, Graham Drury was back on loan for a further year and he was elected the Oxford skipper for the new campaign. Wayne Jackson, who had not enjoyed the best of luck during the previous season, was signed on a full transfer from Cradley Heath, and another permanent deal saw Nigel Sparshott move in from nearby Milton Keynes. Further loans were agreed with Swindon for the highly promising duo of Kevin Smart and Gary Chessell, while Dan McCormick agreed to send the spectacular Mike Wilding from Birmingham to Cowley. Mark Summerfield came on loan from Leicester, and to complete the septet, Steve Crockett resumed his speedway career with the Cheetahs.

The opening fixture against Danish touring club Kulsvierne unfortunately fell victim to the weather, so Oxford took to the track for the opening Cowley fixture on Good Friday morning in the second leg of a Knock-Out Cup tie against Milton Keynes. The Cheetahs had previously visited the Knights on 29 March, gaining a 2-point win, and in a very fine match in the Easter sunshine, they raced to a 51-45 success to win overall by 100 points to 92. New boys Mike Wilding and Nigel Sparshott looked good with returns of paid 14 points apiece, while Kevin Smart was a brilliant reserve with a paid 12-point return.

Nigel Sparshott joined the Cheetahs from Milton Keynes in 1983 and was to remain on board following Oxford's elevation back into the British League the following year.

Having lost their opening league fixtures at Canterbury and Exeter, the Cheetahs' first home league match was against Boston on 7 April. The Oxford side was minus Graham Drury, Gary Chessell and Wayne Jackson, who were all injured, and more bad luck hit the makeshift side when Mike Wilding crashed in heat four, breaking a collarbone. Despite this, Oxford still won 49-47, thanks to 14 points from Nigel Sparshott and a well-taken dozen from Steve Crockett.

The match against Mildenhall the following week saw new signing Ian Clark make his debut as a Cheetah, but even his 11-point tally, plus a paid 16 from acting skipper Nigel Sparshott, couldn't stop Oxford losing narrowly by 4 points. Cradley Heath's Simon Wigg won the World Championship qualifying round at Sandy Lane on 21 April, and a week later Graham Drury returned to action in the Cheetahs' 53-43 victory over Long Eaton. League defeats at Stoke and Milton Keynes followed, as did a 5-point loss at Rye House in the Knock-Out Cup. Scunthorpe were beaten 51-45 at Cowley in mid-May, but Weymouth took the league points, winning 53-43 at Oxford as the month drew to a close.

Mike Wilding and Wayne Jackson were now back in action and a full-strength Oxford team took the league points from visiting Peterborough on 2 June. There was a shock, though, when Rye House came to Cowley for the second leg of the Knock-Out Cup and won 51-45 to secure an overall victory. Winning form returned for the Cheetahs with a home league success against Middlesbrough, followed by a 56-40 victory over Milton Keynes. July was a busy month, with the Cheetahs on the road for much of it. They enjoyed a 4-point success at Boston, but visits to Edinburgh, Berwick, Scunthorpe, Middlesbrough and Glasgow proved fruitless. At home, it was a good month, though, with wins over Rye House, Canterbury and Glasgow.

August opened with a gripping match against Newcastle, when the Cheetahs went down by 2 points in a last-heat decider. It was indeed an incredible meeting, as the Diamonds were virtually a two-man side, with Rod Hunter and Joe Owen scoring 40 points between them! On 11 August, a certain John Tremblin brought his British League Swindon side, which included guests Sam Nikolajsen and Andy Grahame, to Cowley for an inter-league challenge. It was small wonder that the powerhouse Robins team won by 73 points to 22. Ian Clark had suffered a broken arm at Rye House and the promising Nigel De'Ath wore the number seven race jacket against the Wiltshire side. Martin Yeates was the winner of the Hartford Motors-sponsored Supporters' Club Trophy on 18 August, and Edinburgh went away from Cowley with a 14-point victory a week later. August had not been a good month away from Oxford, since the Cheetahs had lost at Peterborough and Newcastle in the league, although they did at least manage to secure a point in a 48-48 draw at Long Eaton.

September saw a series of home wins over Crayford, Exeter and Berwick, but this was offset by defeats at Rye House, Crayford and Mildenhall. British League sides Birmingham and Reading came to Cowley at the end of the month for a four-team tournament, with Oxford and a Martin Yeates Select side completing the field. A certain Hans Nielsen was riding for Birmingham and he had little difficulty in recording a 12-point maximum. As the season closed, the whole of Oxford was buzzing with the news that 1984 would see British League racing back at Cowley. Northern Sports director David Hawkins stated: 'Only the best is good enough for Oxford', and proved it by purchasing Hackney's British League licence. 'No effort will be spared to ensure that the 1984 Cheetahs will be an attractive and competitive side,' said Mr Hawkins.

NATIONAL LEAGUE

Team	Mts	Won	Drn	Lst	For	Agn	Pts
Newcastle	34	25	1	8	1,796	1,462	51
Mildenhall	34	23	2	9	1,728	1,516	48
Crayford	34	23	0	11	1,811.5	1,443.5	46
Weymouth	34	19	2	13	1,711	1,546	40
Scunthorpe	34	19	2	13	1,668.5	1,580.5	40
Milton Keynes	34	19	1	14	1,652	1,604	39
Middlesbrough	34	18	3	13	1,652	1,607	39
Berwick	34	17	0	17	1,645	1,615	34
Edinburgh	34	16	1	17	1,614	1,637	33
Exeter	34	16	0	18	1,659.5	1,599.5	32
Rye House	34	15	1	18	1,643	1,605	31
Peterborough	34	14	2	18	1,585	1,676	30
Glasgow	34	14	1	19	1,643	1,609	29
Oxford	**34**	**14**	**1**	**19**	**1,529**	**1,730**	**29**
Canterbury	34	12	2	20	1,554	1,699	26
Boston	34	12	1	21	1,433.5	1,826.5	25
Stoke	34	10	1	23	1,490	1,767	21
Long Eaton	34	9	1	24	1,477	1,769	19

1984

Having finished the 1983 campaign in fourteenth position, the Cheetahs' spell in National League racing was over, with a new and exciting era waiting just around the corner. With everyone looking forward to the new beginning, team building got underway before the 1983 season had actually closed. Already, fans had seen Danish rider Jens Rasmussen of Hackney having a few practice spins around the Oxford circuit, and by October the Cheetahs' management had him signed, sealed and settled. An off-track signing followed, when Len Silver, the former Hackney promoter, joined the Oxford camp to be team manager.

In 1984, Suffolk-born Mel Taylor joined the Cheetahs from King's Lynn for their first season back amongst the big boys in the British League.

David Hawkins of Northern Sports (Oxford) Ltd had made a generous budget available to co-promoters Bernard Crapper and John Payne in order to purchase riders, and they certainly spent the money wisely. Following the signing of Jens Rasmussen, a cheque for £15,000 saw Rye House star Marvyn Cox link with the Cheetahs. This was a marvellous acquisition, since Cox had been one of the top boys in the National League and had a bright future ahead. A few days later, Messrs Crapper and Payne hit the jackpot, though, when a fee, reported as a then record of £30,000, was paid to Birmingham for Danish international Hans Nielsen.

The Oxford promoters' spending spree didn't end there, as they further dipped in the coffers and a reported £25,000 fee brought another international speedster to Cowley. This time, the rider was British and one who would go on to become a legend in the sport, namely Simon Wigg, who arrived via Cradley Heath. Finally, to complete the top five of the line-up, £12,000 was paid to King's Lynn for the services of Mel Taylor. Meanwhile, from the 1983 side, Ian Clark and Nigel Sparshott were retained, and initially both filled the reserve berths in the new team. With an eye to the future, Kevin Smart, who had been purchased from Swindon, and Nigel De'Ath were both loaned to National League Milton Keynes, in order to further their experience.

The 1984 team was now ready to take on all comers, and they certainly made the speedway world sit up and take notice on 24 March. Opening with a League Cup match at King's Lynn, the Cheetahs stormed to victory by 46 points to 32. Then, on Friday 30 March, Oxford made their first home appearance in a challenge match against Poole, and new skipper Hans Nielsen showed his undoubted class, to record the first of many full maximums as the Cheetahs won 43-35. Friday was now to be the regular race night at Sandy Lane, making a change from the traditional Thursday evenings. The new race day was part of the deal when they took over the Hackney licence.

On Wednesday 4 April, Oxford journeyed to Poole and came back with another success, and they went on to record four more victories, including a further two away from Cowley, at Reading and Wimbledon, to make it a wonderful start to the season. Friday 13 April was, however, to prove very unlucky for the Cheetahs. This was when Wimbledon, with former Oxford Rebel Gordon Kennett in their side, came to Cowley and left with the League Cup points following a last-heat decider. The Dons won 40-38, and Kennett showed that he still knew the best way around his former home with a fine tally of paid 13 points, which included a win over Hans Nielsen in a tremendous heat twelve.

With Hans Nielsen absent, Kennett again returned to Oxford as a guest for the brilliant Dane when King's Lynn visited on 27 April, and he proved a worthy replacement in notching 11 points in a super home victory. Nielsen was back for the Knock-Out Cup tie against Belle Vue the following week, but even his paid 15-point maximum couldn't stop the Aces from winning 40-38, and in the return leg, Oxford got a real hammering, scoring only 25 points to Belle Vue's 53.

After their great opening spell, Oxford had now come down to normality. However, they were providing great racing at home, while on their travels they were always very attractive to watch. Hans Nielsen was leading the side by example, and his team riding with Marvyn Cox was a joy to behold. 'Cocker' was riding really well in what was, after all, his first full season in top-flight racing, and no one at Oxford was surprised when he captured the British Under-21 Championship, and followed this by securing the European Junior Championship.

Unfortunately, the injury bug began to bite and at one time there were no fewer than eight Oxford contracted riders who were suffering injuries. To try and rid the track of this problem, the promoters invited an exorcist to Cowley, but despite a seriously conducted service, things didn't improve and this was emphasised when Mel Taylor broke an arm and dislocated a shoulder in a match against Reading. To cover for injuries and help to strengthen the side, Oxford signed German rider Klaus Lausch, who had a fine reputation in his homeland. He certainly showed a great deal of promise, and had he decided on a British League career, he could undoubtedly have become a heat-leader.

The league campaign didn't start at Cowley until 22 June, when the Cheetahs recorded a narrow victory over Newcastle. They had actually begun in the best possible way, with a 6-point victory at Coventry on 9 June, and whilst generally they did well in the quest for league points, injuries caused them to lose some of their sparkle during the second half of the season. Despite their problems, Oxford still managed to finish eighth in the sixteen-team league and had made a fine return to the highest sphere of British racing.

The Cheetahs had two representatives in the Gothenburg-staged World Final on 1 September, when Hans Nielsen notched 13 points to finish as runner-up to Erik Gundersen, while Simon Wigg recorded a 9-point total to occupy sixth place. The same two riders topped the Oxford scoring, with Nielsen notching 296 points from 26 league matches to yield a 10.69 average, which was enough for him to finish the year on the very top of the national averages. Backing the 'Main Dane' all the way was 'Wiggy', who plundered 251 points from 25 appearances to achieve an average of 9.91.

Simon Wigg's route to the World Final had been eventful to say the very least. He had ridden at his home circuit in the British semi-final on Friday 25 May, but really shouldn't have appeared at all due to a broken collarbone. Every lap must have been sheer agony, although he did receive some help from Malcolm Simmons, as revealed in the book, *Simmo – The Whole Truth*, which was published in June 2006. In the publication, Simmons tells how he helped Wigg along the way after he himself had successfully qualified for the British Final, to be held at Coventry. Unfortunately, his help didn't quite ensure Wigg's safe passage through, so

Simmons states that he 'feigned illness', so that the Oxford rider could take his place. Later, in the Overseas Final staged at Belle Vue, Wigg scored 8 points and, by the skin of his teeth, qualified for the Inter-Continental Final at Vojens, Denmark. In this meeting, however, he was just brilliant and notched 12 points to finish as runner-up to Shawn Moran. As a result, he was the only Englishman to qualify for the World Final, although Alan Grahame did make it through as reserve.

However, behind the scenes things were happening, since the *Sunday People* had undercover reporters at work with their brief being to entrap a number of selected riders in order to make sensationalised headlines regarding corruption and race fixing. These reporters were soon after Simon Wigg and Malcolm Simmons, in particular, having got a 'story', or so they thought, of the happenings at the British semi-final and Wiggy's subsequent appearance in the British Final. Both riders were summoned before the Speedway Control Board in 1985 to answer charges relating to the 'exposure' in the *Sunday People*. The Board found both riders, plus Mark Courtney, who it was alleged had received a 'fee' for helping Wigg in the British Final, not guilty of bribery and corruption, but guilty of 'conduct prejudicial to the sport'. Both Wigg and Simmons were banned from the World Championship for a year and fined £1,000 plus £900 costs. Courtney was initially banned from riding until 1 May 1985 and fined £200 plus £200 costs. One can't help thinking back to the Overseas Final at White City, London on 4 July 1982, when Bruce Penhall cruised around at the back of heat nineteen performing wheelies, ostensibly to please the crowd whilst his compatriots qualified for the next stage of the World Championship. This never even made the newspaper headlines, but the fans at White City that day were well aware of what was going on and certainly didn't hold back in giving Penhall the 'bird'.

Completing the story of Oxford Speedway in 1984, as the season finished, plans were announced for the building of a sports complex at the stadium. The super new structure would provide facilities second to none in speedway, while the promoters pledged to spare no effort in strengthening the team. 'We've not had a bad season, all things considered,' said co-promoter Bernard Crapper, 'Next year, we intend to show 'em a thing or two.' Little did he know how true these words would turn out be.

BRITISH LEAGUE

Team	Mts	Won	Drn	Lst	For	Agn	Pts
Ipswich	30	25	2	3	1,343	994	52
Belle Vue	29	23	3	3	1,322	938	49
Cradley Heath	30	21	2	7	1,308	1,031	44
Reading	30	17	1	12	1,202.5	1,126.5	35
Sheffield	30	15	0	15	1,191	1,148	30
King's Lynn	30	15	0	15	1,143	1,196	30
Wimbledon	30	15	0	15	1,139	1,198	30
Oxford	**30**	**14**	**1**	**15**	**1,174**	**1,166**	**29**
Swindon	29	12	2	15	1,142.5	1,119.5	26
Wolverhampton	30	13	0	17	1,141.5	1,193.5	26
Eastbourne	30	12	1	17	1,157	1,178	25
Coventry	30	11	2	17	1,169	1,168	24
Poole	30	10	1	19	1,075	1,258	21
Halifax	30	9	3	18	1,029	1,311	21
Exeter	30	8	2	20	1,045	1,293	18
Newcastle	30	9	0	21	1,036.5	1,299.5	18

NOTE: One match, Belle Vue *v.* Swindon, was not raced.

1985

This was indeed a season to savour if you were an Oxford Cheetahs fan. It was the year that saw the team crowned as British League Champions, while they were also victorious in the Knock-Out Cup and the Midland Cup. The Cheetahs were, without doubt, the team of the season, and it all happened in only their second term back in the British League. The foundations for success had been laid during 1984, and there were a few changes for the 1985 campaign, as money was again made available for the purpose of team strengthening. As in the season before, the cash was spent wisely and Andy Grahame was secured from Wolverhampton, where he had spent the previous season on loan from Birmingham. Nigel Sparshott and Ian Clark, who had filled the reserve berths for the Cheetahs in 1984, were allowed to leave for Exeter and Peterborough respectively. So, to complete the side, Oxford gambled on Troy Butler, a young Australian who had caught the eye of both Hans Nielsen and Simon Wigg whilst they were touring Down Under.

The team to do battle in 1985, therefore, comprised Hans Nielsen, Simon Wigg, Andy Grahame, Jens Rasmussen, Marvyn Cox, Mel Taylor and Troy Butler. In what was a nicely balanced line-up, the Cheetahs had a fine blend of youth and experience. Len Silver had left the club and Bernard Crapper took over as the team manager of the senior side, with John Tremblin taking charge of the junior team. For one reason or another, the British League was now reduced to eleven sides, with Newcastle closing, while Poole, Eastbourne, Exeter and Wimbledon opted for National League racing.

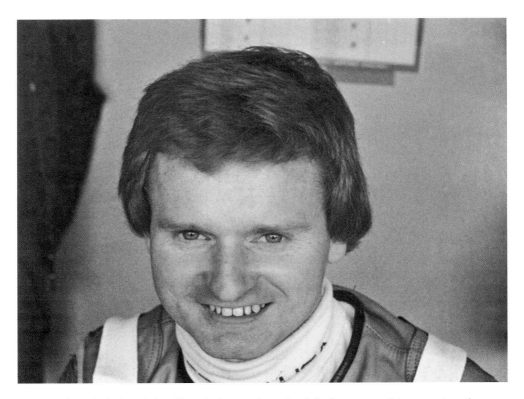

Andy Grahame linked with the Cheetahs in 1985, but missed the latter part of the campaign after breaking a wrist. The rider who hailed from Birmingham scored 69 points from ten league matches to average 7.70.

The season opened with the League Cup competition, and a narrow 2-point win over Coventry was followed by a 39-39 draw against Cradley Heath. Away success came at King's Lynn by a 47-30 scoreline, but having won at home against Wolverhampton, the Cheetahs went down by 2 points at Halifax, prior to securing an excellent draw at Coventry. Home wins against Sheffield and Belle Vue, and an away victory at Wolverhampton saw Oxford riding high, but mid-May saw defeat at Belle Vue. The Cheetahs suffered home and away losses at the hands of Ipswich, before Swindon caused a surprise by winning 40-38 at Cowley on 24 May. However, the next day, Oxford gained revenge by claiming a 41-37 victory at Blunsdon. At Sheffield, the Cheetahs went down by 6 points, but followed this with a home victory against King's Lynn and an away win at Cradley Heath. Thames Valley rivals Reading defeated Oxford at Smallmead on 24 June, but the Cheetahs then enjoyed home victories over Halifax and Reading to finish second in the League Cup table and qualify for a semi-final clash against Ipswich.

In the Knock-Out Cup, Oxford went to town with a vengeance, securing home and away victories over Coventry. A 2-point defeat at Belle Vue, followed by a 10-point home win over the Aces, saw the Cheetahs drawn against Reading in the semi-final. Things were looking very good indeed, and an aggregate 81-74 success against the Racers meant they would meet Ipswich in the final.

The British League campaign had begun at Belle Vue on 22 June, and this time the Cheetahs secured a 40-37 win. This was to be the first of many away triumphs, as Oxford strolled their way to the Championship. The Cheetahs lost only three matches, all very narrow defeats – 40-38 at Halifax, 41-37 at Sheffield and 41-37 at Cradley Heath – while only Ipswich took a league point from Cowley, after snatching an excellent draw on 18 October.

Happily, the team saw few changes, although Mel Taylor moved out to Mildenhall in August, with German racer Klaus Lausch recalled, and when he broke a collarbone there was the promising Alastair Stevens waiting in the wings. As the season moved to its close, the question on everyone's lips was 'Could Oxford secure the Grand Slam?' and having beaten Ipswich both at home and away in the League Cup semi-final and secured a home win against Coventry in the first leg of the final, things looked very promising. Regrettably, Andy Grahame had broken his wrist on 4 September, and without him the Cheetahs crashed to defeat at Brandon in the second leg on 26 October, losing by 50 points to 28, so it was Coventry who took the League Cup honours.

The Cheetahs made no mistake in the Knock-Out Cup, however, as they beat mighty Ipswich 42-35 at home, having lost the first leg 41-37 at Foxhall Heath, thereby securing a marvellous 79-76 aggregate victory. In the Midland Cup, Oxford didn't taste defeat. They beat Wolverhampton in both legs, and followed it up with victory over Swindon at home and a draw at Blunsdon. For the final against Cradley Heath, Andy Grahame returned to the side with his damaged wrist heavily bandaged and played his part in a 45-33 success at Cowley. This was followed by a magnificent 40-38 win at Dudley Wood on 31 October.

Hans Nielsen was a magnificent leader of the Cheetahs and the whole team responded to his sheer brilliance. In British League matches alone, the Dane again topped the national averages with an astounding 11.43 figure, having recorded 231 points from nineteen matches. He was well backed by Simon Wigg, who remained ever-present over the twenty-match campaign to notch 212 points for an average of 9.70. Again, Nielsen was runner-up to Erik Gundersen in the World Final held at Bradford, but Wiggy won the World Long-Track title at Korskro, Denmark, and celebrated by arriving at Cowley in a helicopter.

The city of Oxford rewarded the Cheetahs' success with a civic reception to mark their outstanding speedway achievements, when the team paraded through the streets in an open-top bus. Who can forget the crowds that waited outside City Hall to receive the team that had achieved so very much? Oxford Cheetahs – 1985 British League Champions, Knock-Out Cup winners and Midland Cup winners.

BRITISH LEAGUE

Team	Mts	Won	Drn	Lst	For	Agn	Pts	Bon	Tot
Oxford	**20**	**16**	**1**	**3**	**849**	**708**	**33**	**10**	**43**
Sheffield	20	13	1	6	816	741	27	6	33
Coventry	20	11	2	7	817	740	24	7	31
Halifax	20	9	1	10	783	774	19	5	24
Ipswich	20	9	2	9	781	778	20	4	24
Belle Vue	20	10	0	10	778	777	20	4	24
Cradley Heath	19	10	0	9	740	740	20	4	24
Swindon	20	8	1	11	796	762	17	6	23
Reading	19	6	4	9	734	743	16	6	22
Wolverhampton	20	5	2	13	715	843	12	2	14
King's Lynn	20	5	0	15	677	880	10	0	10

NOTE: One match, Reading *v* Cradley Heath, was not raced.

1986

Prior to the campaign, the Cheetahs paid the price for their success of the previous year. In order to comply with the maximum points ceiling, popular Dane Jens Rasmussen had to move and linked up with Ipswich. Meanwhile, Troy Butler, who had won the Australian Championship, returned suffering from the after effects of a badly broken leg, which effectively sidelined him for the whole of the season. A new face at Cowley was another Aussie, Mark Carlson, and the introduction of a compulsory junior saw the promising Jon Surman given a berth in the Oxford line-up. A further change saw Nigel De'Ath return to the team after two seasons with Milton Keynes in the National League. Off track, the year saw the opening of a super new home straight grandstand, complete with a sports complex.

The Cheetahs didn't make a particularly good start to the term, losing the Premiership to Coventry, with defeats at both Sandy Lane and Brandon. Mark Carlson scored 4 points at Coventry, before finding himself the victim of an assessed average, which forced him to leave and eventually join Milton Keynes in the lower sphere of racing. In the League Cup, Oxford also got off to a bad start, losing by 6 points at home to Belle Vue on 4 April. Coventry also won again at Cowley on 23 April, although the Cheetahs were victorious in their other eight home meetings, and with five away successes, along with a 39-39 draw at Swindon, they managed to qualify for the final.

The rather shaky start convinced the promoters that the team needed a bit more bite. It was at Swindon on Sunday 11 May, on the occasion of the World Championship semi-final meeting, that Bernard Crapper and John Payne took the decision that was to transform the Cheetahs from a good team into a great team. Young Danish rider Per Sorensen had been forced out of the Swindon side, following the return from injury of compatriot Finn Thomsen. Fortunately, Sorensen's average was such that he would fit into the Cheetahs line-up, so the Oxford promotion made an offer, which was accepted. The management reasoned that Sorensen, under the guidance of Hans Nielsen and backed by the tremendous team spirit in the Cheetahs camp, would blossom at Oxford. It was something of a gamble, but it was to pay off handsomely. The young Dane was made partner to Nielsen and, following his signing, the Cheetahs never really looked back. Although a couple of academic League Cup fixtures were lost during June – at Wolverhampton by 2 points and at Ipswich by just a single point – and a 12-point defeat was suffered at Sheffield in the so-called Challenge Cup, from 4 July onwards, Oxford were not to taste defeat again in 1986!

It was an amazing winning sequence, and following a victory against Ipswich on 4 July, the Cheetahs went to Cradley Heath twenty-four hours later and won 45-33. Sheffield came on 11 July in the second leg of the Challenge Cup, and although the Cheetahs won 44-34, they just failed to triumph on aggregate. Belle Vue were beaten at Cowley in a British League match, and this was followed by a League Cup victory at Hyde Road a day later, before July finished with a home victory over Cradley Heath. August saw King's Lynn severely mauled 60-18 at Cowley in the British League, and away wins at Belle Vue, Bradford and Reading followed. September brought more success, starting with a narrow 40-38 victory over Ipswich in the League Cup semi-final at Sandy Lane. Swindon were defeated at Blunsdon in the Knock-Out Cup, and Wolverhampton fell to the Cheetahs at Monmore Green in a league encounter.

Coventry were beaten when they visited Cowley on 12 September and still the Cheetahs steamrollered on. Swindon lost 48-30 at Sandy Lane in the second leg of the Knock-Out Cup, and Bradford were hammered 58-20. On their travels, the Cheetahs won at King's Lynn in a British League fixture, Ipswich in the League Cup semi-final, and finally, they took Sheffield to the cleaners by 49 points to 29. The month ended with a home double-header, which saw continued league success over local rivals Swindon and Reading. In October, Sheffield were beaten 45-33 in the Knock-Out Cup semi-final, and the Cheetahs recorded the same score in the return leg at Owlerton to book a place in the final against Cradley Heath. Local rivals Swindon were hammered 56-21 at Blunsdon in a league match, then Cradley Heath were beaten by 2 points in the League Cup final at Dudley Wood, and finally, Ipswich fell to the powerful Cheetahs in the British League.

Oxford again climbed the ladder to success as they brilliantly took the British League Championship for a second successive season in 1986. From top to bottom: Hans Nielsen, Simon Wigg, Marvyn Cox, Per Sorensen, Andy Grahame, Nigel De'Ath, Jon Surman, Bernard Crapper (team manager).

Whilst it was win, win, win on the track, the high-flying Cheetahs couldn't defeat the weather and, unfortunately, the home league matches against Wolverhampton and Sheffield were never ridden, but such was Oxford's dominance, they still emerged as Champions. Not only were the two league matches wiped out, the weather also prevented the home matches against Cradley Heath in both the League Cup and the Knock-Out Cup from being ridden. The Cheetahs had actually journeyed to Cradley Heath for the first leg of the Knock-Out Cup final on 1 November and had come away with a fine draw. Previously, on 18 October, Oxford had secured a 40-38 victory at Cradley Heath in the first leg of the League Cup final, but with it proving impossible to complete both competitions, the decision was made that the two clubs would share the prestigious trophies!

The Oxford success story also received a tremendous boost when Hans Nielsen claimed the World Championship in Katowice, Poland on 30 August, and it was pleasing to have Marvyn Cox as a competitor in the World Final as well. Nielsen had a tremendous season, and in addition to his World title success, he took the British League Riders' Championship and never tasted defeat in all ten British League matches away from Cowley. Having recorded 198 points from seventeen appearances, the brilliant Dane's league average of 11.83 speaks for itself, although Oxford's overall success was a great team effort. Also performing wonderfully well for the Cheetahs was Simon Wigg, who tallied 191 points to average 11.01, while Marvyn Cox achieved a brilliant 8.79 figure. Per Sorensen also covered himself in glory and recorded a paid maximum (10+2 points) in the thumping win at Swindon on 11 October, a performance which must have given him tremendous satisfaction. Once again, Oxford City Council honoured the Cheetahs with a civic reception. As in 1985, crowds lined the route as the riders toured the city in an open-top bus.

BRITISH LEAGUE

Team	Mts	Won	Drn	Lst	For	Agn	Pts	Bon	Tot
Oxford	18	18	0	0	863	540	36	8	44
Cradley Heath	20	13	3	4	854	706	29	9	38
Wolverhampton	19	13	0	6	771	710	26	6	32
Sheffield	19	10	2	7	783	697	22	6	28
Coventry	20	10	1	9	829	731	21	6	27
Bradford	20	8	1	11	758	799	17	4	21
Reading	20	7	3	10	757	801	17	4	21
Swindon	19	8	1	10	693	784	17	4	21
Ipswich	20	7	1	12	729	831	15	3	18
Belle Vue	19	5	0	14	675	805	10	2	12
King's Lynn	20	2	0	18	626	934	4	0	4

NOTE: Three matches were not raced: Belle Vue *v.* Swindon, Oxford *v.* Sheffield and Oxford *v.* Wolverhampton.

1987

It was asking a great deal of the Cheetahs to follow their success of the previous two years, and regrettably they couldn't do it. As in the past, they paid a price for their achievements on track, and speedway's rules ensured the break-up of the 1986 title-winning side. Although the points limit, set at 45, remained in place, the Cheetahs, whose total average topped 50-plus, still had to lose riders and this gave the promotion the heart-searching job of deciding who was to be retained and who had to go. Eventually it was Simon Wigg who left, joining Hackney, the London club having decided to give British League racing another go. It was interesting to note that the BSPA were pleased to welcome another track into speedway's top competition, and pledged that help would be given to re-establish the Kestrels. Unfortunately, in the event, it was only Oxford who released an established heat-leader to assist them, and no one else seemed too concerned. Wigg's release created other problems, because whilst the debate over his joining Hackney went on, the Cheetahs missed out on the popular Per Sorensen. The young Dane had the offer of a very good job in his native Denmark, and in the end accepted it, so he too was lost to Oxford.

Good news for the campaign came when an attractive sponsorship deal for the team was announced, with Halls Brewery providing excellent backing, initially in a two-year deal. Oxford, therefore, became known as the SKOL Cheetahs, proudly displaying the Halls emblem on their race jackets. The release of Simon Wigg and the unavailability of Per Sorensen saw the return of Jens Rasmussen, and to complete the line-up, the promising Alastair Stevens came into the side after a season on loan at Rye House in the National League. Another change in the Cowley organisation saw the race night changed back to Thursdays.

The season started well for the Cheetahs, as they went to Cradley Heath on 21 March in the first leg of the Premiership and won 41-37, and on 3 April at Cowley they made sure that overall success was theirs, winning the return leg 41-36. The injury bug struck in a three-team tournament, which saw Oxford, Reading and Swindon in competition over the Easter period. Ali Stevens suffered a broken arm in a heat nine spill at Cowley, which ruled him out of the saddle for a few weeks. Kevin Smart, on loan to Milton Keynes, and Troy Butler, happily recovered from his broken leg and also on loan to the Knights, covered during Stevens' absence. The Cheetahs' bright start continued through the League Cup competition, as they gained away victories at Hackney (40-38), Reading (45-33), Cradley Heath (41-37) and Wolverhampton (40-38). At home, only Coventry took points away from Oxford, winning 41-37 on 17 July. Oxford went through to the semi-final again, and they'd done it by not only having to cover Stevens' enforced lay-off, but also injuries to Nigel De'Ath, Marvyn Cox and Jens Rasmussen as well.

The only blot on the landscape came on 15 May, in a League Cup match against Belle Vue, when Bernard Crapper resigned from his job as team manager following a row in a very stormy meeting. The Cheetahs won the match 45-33, but Crapper, whose motivation of the side had really played its part in 1985 and 1986, said 'enough is enough,' with junior manager John Tremblin taking over for the next match against Hackney.

For the fourth straight year 'Main Dane' Hans Nielsen topped Oxford's league averages in 1987, scoring 252 points from 20 matches for a mammoth 11.73 figure.

The league campaign began on 23 July at Sheffield, which saw Oxford defeated 43-35. Two days later, Coventry took the points from the Cheetahs at Brandon with a 44-34 victory. Things looked up a tad when Oxford defeated King's Lynn at Cowley on 29 July, and followed it up with a fighting draw at Wolverhampton. Both results were achieved without the services of Jens Rasmussen, who had been hurt in a Knock-Out Cup match against Belle Vue on 5 June. Little did Oxford supporters know, however, that the victory over King's Lynn would be one of just six home wins in the league, while the draw at Wolverhampton would turn out to be the only point achieved away from Cowley!

After beating Ipswich in the Knock-Out Cup and losing to Belle Vue in the League Cup final, the rot really set in at Cowley, with wins only being achieved against Bradford, Sheffield, Wolverhampton, Belle Vue and Cradley Heath. The returning Simon Wigg inspired a shock Hackney victory by 45 points to 33 at Sandy Lane on 14 October, with the HL1 Kestrels proving very worthy winners indeed, and the season ended with the Cheetahs only just avoiding the bottom spot. Cradley Heath defeated Oxford on aggregate in the Knock-Out Cup semi-final, so there was nothing much to show for what had been an extremely frustrating year.

However, it wasn't all doom and gloom, as Marvyn Cox reached the Inter-Continental final, and generally enjoyed a good season with an average in excess of 8 points per match. There was also, of course, the magnificent Hans Nielsen, whose achievements at international level made up for the Cowley fans' disappointment at club level. The brilliant Dane retained the World Championship in Amsterdam in speedway's first ever two-day World Final and, just for good measure, he also retained the British League Riders' Championship. He also topped the entire British League averages for a fourth successive season, with 252 points from 20 meetings, yielding a mighty 11.73 figure. At international level, there was further success for Nielsen in the World Team Cup and World Pairs events when representing his country.

BRITISH LEAGUE

Team	Mts	Won	Drn	Lst	For	Agn	Pts	Bon	Tot
Coventry	22	19	3	0	970	746	41	11	52
Cradley Heath	22	13	1	8	917	796	27	9	36
Swindon	22	12	2	8	884.5	828.5	26	7	33
Sheffield	22	13	0	9	871	840	26	6	32
Bradford	22	10	3	9	882	832	23	7	30
Ipswich	22	10	3	9	874	840	23	6	29
Reading	22	11	2	9	874.5	840.5	24	4	28
Belle Vue	22	10	1	11	843	872	21	5	26
Hackney	22	7	3	12	795	917	17	3	20
Wolverhampton	22	6	2	14	790	923	14	3	17
Oxford	**22**	**6**	**1**	**15**	**825**	**891**	**13**	**3**	**16**
King's Lynn	22	4	1	17	758	958	9	2	11

1988

After the frustrations of the previous year, the 1988 season was better for the Cheetahs, although still not good enough for the ambitious Oxford management. They had promised changes in the side and, as good as their word, alterations were made in an attempt to build a title-winning team. The points ceiling was raised to a maximum of 48, which helped, while the compulsory junior ruling was scrapped, so it gave Oxford room to manoeuvre. Simon

Wigg returned to the team after his stint at Hackney, with the London side opting for a return to National League racing, while Peter Lloyd was another returnee, following a spell with Milton Keynes. The Cheetahs' major signing was Martin Dugard, who arrived via Eastbourne. Dugard, a young rider of outstanding potential, was totally dedicated to making it to the top in speedway and had been the target of practically every team in the British League, so it was a real coup when he pledged his future to Oxford.

So, the Oxford team read Hans Nielsen, Simon Wigg, Marvyn Cox, Martin Dugard, Nigel De'Ath, Alastair Stevens and Peter Lloyd, with John Tremblin as the team manager. The combined average of the squad was 47.37, and the rebuilding of the side meant that there had to be departures from the previous season's line-up. Thanks to the points system, the Cheetahs released Andy Grahame, Jens Rasmussen and Jon Surman. The former, Grahame, returned to Wolverhampton on loan and Surman went to National League Eastbourne, but surprisingly, no British League track came forward for Rasmussen. There was no doubt that the Dane could have done a useful job for any team, and Oxford were prepared to offer him on a free loan to get him fixed up, but still no one was interested. So, being an EEC rider and married to a British girl, 'Razzer' exercised his right to race in the National League and linked with Rye House, where his presence undoubtedly saved the Rockets from going under.

The season at Cowley began with a challenge match against Swedish touring side Getingarna, which the Cheetahs won 53-37, but in their first British League match at Coventry on 30 March, Oxford crashed to defeat by 51 points to 39. The return fixture on Good Friday morning was a cracker, with Oxford winning 46-44 after a last-heat decider. Despite a series of home wins during the early weeks of the season, one thing became obvious: that at the lower end of the side the Cheetahs were vulnerable. Ali Stevens was struggling to produce his best form, while Peter Lloyd was finding British League racing understandably tough. Something had to be done, so the go-ahead Oxford promotion took a chance on Norwegian Einar Kyllingstad, who had been released by King's Lynn. His signing allowed Nigel De'Ath to drop to a reserve berth, and the management hoped that Kyllingstad would do what Per

Following a season at Hackney, Simon Wigg returned to the Cheetahs' lair in 1988 and posted an 8.66 average, having registered 363 points from 37 league appearances.

Sorensen had done in 1986. The changes resulted in Stevens being released to join National League Wimbledon, where he quickly found his form. Regrettably, the Kyllingstad move didn't come off. The Norwegian flopped and was quickly released, but despite this failure, the promoters were not put off and they took another gamble with Dane Lars Munkedal, who had been released by Wolverhampton. But he faired little better and with De'Ath continuing to find points hard to come by, the Cheetahs were still vulnerable in both the number two position and the reserve department.

Despite their problems, the progress of Martin Dugard gave Cowley fans plenty to cheer about. It didn't take the mustard-keen youngster long to settle into British League racing and his enthusiasm kept everyone happy. Frequently during the year, Dugard came good when his teammates – Hans Nielsen apart – were struggling, and he was undoubtedly the signing of the season in British racing. Overall, it was a term that promised much, but achieved little, and it ended with Oxford occupying fourth spot in the British League standings, although this was certainly an improvement on the 1987 campaign. Nielsen again led the scoring, with 563 points from 40 league matches producing an average of exactly 11.00. Amazingly, that was enough to see the Main Dane top the national averages for the fifth successive year since linking with the Cheetahs.

Hans Nielsen lost the World Championship title in his native Denmark to his old nemesis Erik Gundersen, but at least joined forces with his great rival to win the World Pairs crown. The triumphant Danes also won the World Team Cup at Long Beach in the USA, with Nielsen scorching to a 14-point tally. Nielsen and Marvyn Cox teamed up to take the British Open Pairs Championship at Reading, which was one of the few honours in the season to find its way to Sandy Lane. Unfortunately, Cox seemed to lose some of his sparkle along the way and at the end of the season, there were rumours that he fancied a move to a larger track. Meanwhile, Simon Wigg, who made a welcome return to the Cheetahs' lair and totalled 363 points to average 8.66 in the British League, also qualified for the World Final, where he notched 9 points.

BRITISH LEAGUE

Team	Mts	Won	Drn	Lst	For	Agn	Pts	Bon	Tot
Coventry	40	31	2	7	1,978.5	1,618.5	64	18	82
Belle Vue	40	26	1	13	1,912	1,686	53	13	66
Cradley Heath	39	22	1	16	1,831	1,675	45	15	60
Oxford	**40**	**20**	**6**	**14**	**1,850**	**1,743**	**46**	**13**	**59**
Reading	40	20	3	17	1,857	1,736	43	12	55
Sheffield	39	19	2	18	1,731.5	1,776.5	40	8	48
Swindon	40	17	1	22	1,706.5	1,888.5	35	8	43
Wolverhampton	40	15	3	22	1,781	1,817	33	8	41
King's Lynn	40	14	3	23	1,718.5	1,878.5	31	7	38
Ipswich	39	13	0	26	1,651	1,854	26	4	30
Bradford	39	10	0	29	1,580	1,924	20	2	22

NOTE: Two matches, Bradford *v.* Ipswich (BLB) and Sheffield *v.* Cradley Heath (BLB), were not raced.

1989

During the winter break at the end of the 1988 season, the Oxford management began the task of constructing the Cheetahs team in readiness for another tilt at the league title. The points limit had been lowered to a maximum of 46, with an agreement from the BSPA that it would initially last for three years, which made the task of putting a competitive side together just a little bit harder. Hans Nielsen was quickly signed up to lead the team for a sixth successive season, with Martin Dugard and Simon Wigg quickly following to ensure the Cheetahs had as solid a trio of heat-leaders as any of the nine tracks now left in the British League. An important signing for the first team was that of Paul Dugard, the brother of Martin, who had come into the Oxford junior side in October 1988, just after his sixteenth birthday. This talented young rider decided it was the British League for him, and, like his elder brother, pledged himself to the Cheetahs.

Good news for Oxford was that Marvyn Cox, after a somewhat unsettled winter where a move to another track was on the cards, agreed to stay at Cowley to the joy of his many fans on the terraces. Andy Grahame, who'd not enjoyed a very good season at Wolverhampton, leapt at the chance to return, which left Oxford with just 3.32 points to play with. It was now that the Oxford promoters' keen knowledge of the rulebook paid off, because an intense study revealed that they could include Troy Butler in the side. The Aussie had spent two seasons on loan at Milton Keynes and had captured the National League Riders' Championship title in 1988. There was no doubt that he was now ready for the higher level of racing, and the fact that he could legitimately return to the Oxford team on his previous British League assessed average of 3.00 was a real boost. Naturally, Butler's inclusion in the final line-up provoked quite a bit of reaction from other promoters, but the fact was that the rider's inclusion was well within the rules.

The season got off to a poor start weather-wise, when both of Oxford's opening away fixtures, a Gold Cup match at King's Lynn and a challenge match at Wolverhampton, fell foul to inclement weather. But the Cheetahs showed great form in their opening home fixture on Good Friday morning, recording a fine 55-35 victory over Wolverhampton in a challenge match. The Gold Cup began at Swindon the following day, with Oxford again in great form, winning 49-41. To make it a very happy festival period for the Cheetahs, they enjoyed two further successes on Easter Monday, beating Swindon 56-34 in the morning, before winning 49-41 at Reading in the evening. Oxford once more topped 50 points, when they completed the double over Reading on 31 March, but a surprise was in store when they went to Coventry on 8 April and suffered a 49-40 reverse. However, revenge over Coventry came quickly on 14 April, when the Cheetahs won 58-32 at Sandy Lane, and the Gold Cup competition finished with a draw at King's Lynn on 15 April, plus a storming win over the Stars at Cowley on 28 April. So, Oxford qualified to meet Cradley Heath in the Gold Cup final, and the chance of their first pot of the season.

The British League campaign began well courtesy of a good win over Cradley Heath, and a draw in the return at Dudley Wood in late April was followed by an outstanding 51-39 victory at Swindon on 6 May. Oxford fans had seen Simon Wigg win the World Championship semi-final at Sandy Lane on 5 May, and for good measure, Wiggy went on to capture both the British and Commonwealth titles on the way to booking his passage to Munich for the World Final on 2 September. Talking of Munich – what a night that was! Hans Nielsen had already qualified, and an injury to Jan O. Pedersen meant that Troy Butler moved up from reserve to take his place. So, Oxford had three competitors and the joy of the supporters and management simply overflowed when Nielsen put in a tremendous performance to score maximum points and collect his third World Championship. To complete a marvellous night for Oxford, Wigg, who had already captured the World Long Track Championship, put in a great display to finish as runner-up after defeating fellow Englishman Jeremy Doncaster in a run-off, both having tallied 12-points. Meanwhile, Butler finished well down the field on 4 points.

Prior to the World Final, Oxford had journeyed to Cradley Heath on 26 August for the first leg of the Gold Cup final. The Cheetahs came away with a 6-point victory, and in the second leg on 15 September they took the Heathens to the cleaners, winning 54-36, to clinch the trophy by 102 points to 78 on aggregate. Who can forget Martin Dugard's superb

Paul Dugard, the younger brother of Martin, was
handed a first-team spot in 1989, having claimed
a place in Oxford's junior side the previous
October, just after his sixteenth birthday.

third-to-first ride in heat eleven, which set Oxford up for a storming finish? While all that was
going on, the Cheetahs were still very much on course for the British League Championship,
but their hopes received a setback on 20 September when old rivals Swindon came to Cowley.
Marvyn Cox was absent, having broken his collarbone in a home fixture against Bradford on
6 September, so Oxford used Belle Vue's Chris Morton as a guest. Unfortunately, the Cheetahs
crashed to defeat, with the Robins doggedly carving out a 49-41 success.

Winning form returned in the home matches against Wolverhampton and Reading, while
in between, the Cheetahs gained revenge for their home defeat at the hands of Swindon by
taking a narrow 2-point victory at the Abbey Stadium to keep their title hopes alive. However,
defeats at Coventry and Bradford, along with a home match against Coventry that fell victim
to the weather, kept the Oxford camp on tenterhooks. Then came the GM Classic on Sunday
22 October and more frustration when the track was declared unfit, with no racing possible.
Further problems with the Cowley circuit saw the important league matches against Cradley
Heath and Coventry postponed, and it was then that stadium owner David Hawkins took a
hand in events. In a meeting called to discuss track problems, the riders claimed that granite
could provide a solution. Within hours, granite and the necessary equipment had arrived,
with Mr Hawkins himself heading a squad of workers to ensure that the track was in perfect
shape for Oxford's final meeting, a British League double-header against Cradley Heath and
Coventry, on Wednesday 1 November.

Prior to that, Oxford had visited King's Lynn on 26 October and won in tremendous style
by 56 points to 34. That victory meant they had only to win one of their two remaining
home matches to clinch the Championship. With the racing strip in superb condition for
the showdown on 1 November, the Cheetahs made no mistake. Marvyn Cox returned to
the side, and Belle Vue's American sensation Gary Hicks replaced Troy Butler who had made
the trip home. The first match against Cradley Heath was a tight affair, but with Martin
Dugard in great form, Oxford made sure of the league title by winning 48-42. In the second
match, the Cheetahs kept up the pressure, with Andy Grahame, who had not had the best
of luck against Cradley Heath, really coming into his own. In a great performance, the

Birmingham-born rider notched paid 14 points to head the scorechart and ensure an Oxford victory over Coventry by 49 points to 41. The Cheetahs thus became League Champions for the third time since returning to top-flight racing in 1984. As usual, Hans Nielsen not only headed the side's scoring with 436 points from 32 league appearances, but also topped the national averages on a huge 10.97 figure. Solid support came from Simon Wigg, who notched 233 points to average 7.82, while Martin Dugard tallied of 253 points to yield a 7.69 figure.

BRITISH LEAGUE

Team	Mts	Won	Drn	Lst	For	Agn	Pts	Bon	Tot
Oxford	32	22	1	9	1,580	1,293	45	13	58
Wolverhampton	32	19	2	11	1,511	1,366	40	12	52
Cradley Heath	32	19	3	10	1,550.5	1,327.5	41	10	51
Belle Vue	32	19	2	11	1,496	1,378	40	10	50
Coventry	32	15	3	14	1,389	1,486	33	8	41
Swindon	32	12	1	19	1,395.5	1,483.5	25	8	33
Reading	32	13	1	18	1,356	1,521	27	5	32
Bradford	32	9	2	21	1,347	1,529	20	3	23
King's Lynn	32	8	1	23	1,319	1,560	17	3	20

1990

The 1990 season began with a real shock for all Oxford supporters. With just weeks to go, there came the news that Hans Nielsen and the club's management had been unable to agree a new contract, and for a time it looked as though the Cheetahs would enter the campaign without their World Champion and number one rider. Such a thing was unthinkable, but with Nielsen not really wanting to leave, and the promotion not wanting him to go, there was a sound basis for negotiation. After further talks, everyone connected with the club was happy when the Main Dane eventually signed up to lead the Cheetahs once again. It was, therefore, a very relieved bunch of supporters who journeyed to Belle Vue on 16 March and saw Nielsen and his new partner, Dean Barker, line up for Oxford in heat one of a challenge match. Barker had been signed from National League Eastbourne and was a rider with a very bright future, but whilst the Oxford bosses realised signing him would present problems in finalising their side, they also knew that they could not let the opportunity of gaining such a promising rider slip away.

Putting the team together gave the promoters several headaches. However, one problem was solved when Marvyn Cox asked for a move and was loaned to Bradford for the season. Due to the 46-point limit, it still meant that another member of the title-winning side had to go and, after much soul-searching, it was decided that Andy Grahame was to be released. Somewhat surprisingly, no British League track came in for Grahame, with the result that he sought pastures new at National League Wimbledon. So, for 1990, Oxford lined up with Hans Nielsen, Dean Barker, Martin Dugard, Troy Butler, Paul Dugard, Simon Wigg and Alastair Stevens, who had been recalled from Poole. Meanwhile, an off-track change saw Peter York join Bernard Crapper and John Payne as co-promoter, albeit for only the one season.

The season got underway at Cowley, with an impressive win over Wolverhampton, and although it was just a challenge match, the Cheetahs looked mightily impressive. New boy Dean Barker rode well for a paid 7 points and returnee Ali Stevens really shone with a tally of 11. The following day, 24 March, Oxford began their Gold Cup campaign at Swindon and emerged convincing winners by 51 points to 38. The Premiership matches against Cradley

Dean Barker was born in Isleworth, Middlesex and joined the Cheetahs from Eastbourne in 1990, initially filling the number two berth in the team alongside Hans Nielsen.

Heath provided two excellent meetings, with a 45-45 draw at Oxford, followed by defeat at Dudley Wood, when Simon Wigg surprisingly failed to score at a track where he was usually good for double figures. On 6 April, local rivals Swindon came to Cowley for the return Gold Cup fixture and surprised the Cheetahs by avenging their defeat at Blunsdon with a storming 51-39 success. Hans Nielsen experienced all sorts of problems and could only muster 4 points, but Oxford thankfully returned to winning form on Easter Monday morning, easily beating Reading by 53 points to 37. Martin Dugard had been hurt in an accident at King's Lynn, suffering a damaged ankle and a wrist injury, and although he returned for the evening match at Smallmead, Barker was ruled unfit, with his place being taken by a junior, Sean McCullagh. Oxford were trailing 40-26 when the track lights went out, causing the match to be abandoned.

Oxford were proud to stage the first Test match between England and Denmark on 18 April, which the home nation won 63-45. The meeting commemorated the Diamond Jubilee of Test matches in this country, and many former capped riders were welcomed along to be part of the event. Most importantly, Oxford's first Great Dane, Arne Pander, returned to Sandy Lane as a special guest, and was given a tremendous reception.

The Cheetahs completed their home Gold Cup fixtures with a narrow victory over King's Lynn on 27 April, and began their league matches with a fine win over Bradford at Cowley. The league campaign had actually begun for Oxford at Swindon on 21 April, when the Cheetahs had crashed to a 57-31 defeat. It was a loss that wasn't totally unexpected, for the side was minus Dean Barker, Ali Stevens and Paul Dugard, who were ordered to compete in a rearranged World Championship qualifying round at Stoke. Therefore, Oxford were forced to track three juniors, plus Kelly Moran as a guest for the injured Martin Dugard.

May saw a special meeting staged for the dependants of the late Oxford junior Paul Muchene, who had tragically died on 4 July the previous year, after a track accident at

Hackney four nights earlier. There was a shock for Oxford on 18 May, when Coventry came for a rearranged Knock-Out Cup match. The Cheetahs had raced to a 45-45 draw at Coventry on 4 April and were cruising to overall victory when the Bees staged a brilliant comeback, riding out of their skins in the last three heats to take victory by 2 points. The month ended on a happy note for Oxford, however, as both Martin Dugard and Simon Wigg made it through to the Commonwealth Final, while the league double was completed over Cradley Heath.

June began badly when Belle Vue, tracking three guest riders, defeated the Cheetahs in a league match by a single point. The Commonwealth Final at Belle Vue on 10 June saw three Oxford riders, namely Martin Dugard, Simon Wigg and Troy Butler, battle their way through to the Overseas Final. Hans Nielsen, meanwhile, was already on the World Final trail via the Nordic Final.

Having secured the bonus point in the rearranged Gold Cup match at Reading, the Cheetahs qualified for the final where they would face Bradford, and on 22 June, the Dukes came to Cowley for the first leg. Oxford clinched a narrow 4-point win, but in the return match Bradford went on the rampage, hammering the Cheetahs 63-27 to win the trophy amidst an atmosphere never before witnessed at the Odsal Stadium.

The Overseas Final at Coventry saw Martin Dugard and Troy Butler progress to the Inter-Continental Final in Denmark. However, it was the end of the line for Simon Wigg, who just failed to qualify, having ridden with a collarbone injury sustained in the home hammering of King's Lynn on 15 June.

In the league campaign, July and August heralded a difficult time for the Cheetahs. Reading and Coventry secured victories at Sandy Lane, and Oxford were surprised when Paul Dugard retired, claiming he had lost interest in the sport. Former Cradley Heath rider John Bostin replaced the youngster, but he was never able to pick up as many points as Dugard and it left Oxford extremely vulnerable at reserve. Swindon and Wolverhampton tasted success at Cowley, and although the Cheetahs raced to a win at King's Lynn on 7 July, the Zetor Stars caused a surprise by forcing a draw in the return match at Sandy Lane on 17 August. Rubbing salt into the wounds, Reading, who were riding high in the league, won by 3 points at Cowley on August Bank Holiday Monday to end a lean month for Oxford.

September saw the Cheetahs return to form with a vengeance. At home, there was success against Bradford, Belle Vue, Cradley Heath and Coventry, while on the road the Cheetahs tasted victory at Swindon, Wolverhampton and Cradley Heath. Unfortunately, there were also disappointments during the month. Hans Nielsen and Martin Dugard had qualified for the World Final at Bradford but, in a tremendous meeting, the Dane was unable to retain his title, which went instead to Per Jonsson of Reading. Nielsen ended up finishing in fourth position, while Dugard made a most satisfactory World Final debut, scoring 6 points. The month ended with Simon Wigg, who had retained his World Long Track Championship, suffering a serious injury to his neck whilst racing in Italy, which regrettably put him out of racing for the remainder of the season.

The season finished on a high note at Cowley, with convincing wins over Cradley Heath and Wolverhampton, and there was an away victory at Belle Vue to ensure that Oxford finished fourth in the final British League standings. Reading emerged as Champions, and the Cheetahs were left thinking how different things could have been had they not suffered that string of home defeats in July and August, since their away record was the best in the league. Hans Nielsen, with his World Final disappointment behind him, won the British League Riders' Championship for the third time, with a superb 15-point maximum. The immaculate Dane once again led the scoring for his club and in the league as a whole, totalling 413 points from 32 appearances for a league average of 10.32. Meanwhile, Martin Dugard continued his rapid progress to record an 8.39 figure, having scored 290 points from 30 matches. Simon Wigg was third in the club's scoring stakes, with 187 points from 24 league appearances yielding an average of 7.55. Prior to the season's end, the Oxford promoters had opened negotiations with National League Poole for the transfer of their number one rider, Australian Craig Boyce.

On 2 November, on the occasion of the Supporters' Club Dinner and Dance, it was officially announced that Boyce had signed on the dotted line and would line up with Oxford for the 1991 season.

BRITISH LEAGUE

Team	Mts	Won	Drn	Lst	For	Agn	Pts	Bon	Tot
Reading	32	19	3	10	1,513.5	1,360.5	41	13	54
Wolverhampton	32	17	5	10	1,446	1,431	39	10	49
Belle Vue	32	19	2	11	1,454	1,418	40	7	47
Oxford	**32**	**17**	**2**	**13**	**1,467**	**1,405**	**36**	**10**	**46**
Bradford	32	16	1	15	1,470	1,407	33	8	41
Swindon	32	15	2	15	1,462	1,416	32	8	40
Cradley Heath	32	12	1	19	1,425.5	1,454.5	25	7	32
Coventry	32	10	3	19	1,386	1,487	23	7	30
King's Lynn	32	7	5	20	1,315	1,560	19	2	21

1991

There were more team changes at Oxford in 1991, as Bernard Crapper and John Payne strove to put together a competitive side. Simon Wigg went on loan to Bradford, who in turn, and somewhat surprisingly, released Marvyn Cox – another Cheetahs asset – who was subsequently purchased by Poole. Changes to the set-up of British speedway saw the formation of Divisions One and Two, with Poole, Ipswich, Wimbledon and Berwick opting to move up from the lower level to the higher sphere of racing. The Oxford team for the year was made up of Hans Nielsen, Martin Dugard, Craig Boyce, Dean Barker, Mark Carlson, plus Aussie Tony Primmer and Darren Grayling, who joined via Eastbourne to stiffen the reserve berth. New signing Boyce had become Australian Champion at Alice Springs, Northern Territory on 27 January, when recording a brilliant 15-point maximum.

The opening meeting of the season, a Gold Cup fixture against King's Lynn on 22 March, fell victim to the weather. So, Oxford opened the following day at King's Lynn, with the scheduled return Gold Cup fixture, and to the pleasure of their travelling fans, they won a thrilling encounter by 47 points to 43, with new boy Craig Boyce making a sensational debut, scoring 17 points. The Cheetahs then belatedly opened at Cowley on Good Friday morning, with a Thames Valley Trophy match against Swindon, which they won by 48 points to 42. On Easter Monday, they had home and away fixtures against Reading, winning at Cowley by 48 points to 42 again, but suffering defeat at Smallmead. Oxford then lost at Swindon, the scores being 52-38 in both matches against their Thames Valley rivals. The weather prevented the Gold Cup fixture with Wimbledon from going ahead on 5 April, and it was eventually run on 17 May. It was at this meeting that it was announced that the team nickname SKOL Cheetahs had to be dropped, since Allied Breweries had decided that motorsport and alcohol did not go together, so Oxford lost the brand name, but happily retained the sponsorship.

In the meantime, Oxford had beaten Swindon and Poole at Sandy Lane in Gold Cup matches, but, unfortunately, they lost their first home league match against Belle Vue by 47 points to 42. Away from Cowley, Gold Cup results were quite encouraging, with victories at Wimbledon, Reading and Swindon, while defeats were suffered at Poole and Ipswich. Moving along, Peterborough visited Oxford for a BSPA Cup tie on 29 May, and whilst the Second Division side were soundly beaten 63-27, it was Swedish rider Mikael Blixt who caught the eye with a 9-point tally. On 2 June, the Ancit-sponsored Commonwealth Final was held at

Three of the Cheetahs from 1991: Mark Carlson, Darren Grayling and Craig Boyce.

King's Lynn, with Oxford having two representatives in Craig Boyce and Martin Dugard. Unfortunately, Boyce was involved in a nasty spill, which saw him receive back injuries and he was subsequently ruled out of the Oxford side for some weeks. Meanwhile, Dugard, who had qualified from the British Final on 19 May with 8 points, rode his heart out at Saddlebow Road, but could only muster 4 points.

With Boyce out of action, Oxford covered his absence in the main by using rider replacement, but when Wolverhampton came visiting for a Division One match, former favourite Marvyn Cox replaced the Australian. The Cheetahs instead used rider replacement for Hans Nielsen, who had to be at the compulsory practice for the Scandinavian Final. With a weakened team, the Cheetahs lost 55-35, despite an outstanding 18-point maximum from 'Cocker'. Nielsen, however, was successful in winning the Scandinavian Final in his homeland at Brovst, with 13 points. Regrettably, Tony Primmer had found the pace of top league racing beyond him, and Dean Barker was proving terribly inconsistent. So, with no Boyce, it was often down to just Nielsen and Dugard to score for the Cheetahs, but two men cannot cover for five, and there was also a weakness at reserve. There was a glimmer of hope on the horizon though, as medical opinion suggested that Boyce should be back in action by early August.

In the Reserve League match against King's Lynn on 14 June, Bristol-born novice Glenn Cunningham made a most satisfactory debut, scoring a paid 7 points. He was signed up on the spot by the Oxford management, and was certainly considered a rider for the future. On 2 August, Craig Boyce returned to track action, scoring a paid 6 points against Cradley Heath. However, it wasn't enough to stop the Cheetahs losing 47-43, and this was despite a 14-point return from Hans Nielsen and 10 from Martin Dugard. Following that defeat, the Cheetahs had a reasonable time in home league matches, with wins over Swindon, Poole and Reading, but saw the Gold Cup go to Berwick, after losing on aggregate to the Northumberland outfit in the final.

The end of the season saw Oxford finish the league campaign in ninth position, although losing no fewer than five matches at home certainly didn't help their cause. With 340 points from twenty-two league matches, the ultra-professional Hans Nielsen sauntered to a fantastic 10.66 average, while the sensational Martin Dugard achieved a 9.12 figure. In league matches, Nielsen failed to top the national averages for the first time since 1984, with 'Sudden' Sam Ermolenko finishing slightly above the Main Dane on a 10.74 figure. Nielsen finished third in the World Final at Gothenburg, Sweden, but together with newly crowned World Champion and fellow Dane Jan O. Pedersen, he won the World Pairs title in Poznan, Poland. The dynamic duo were also part of a Danish success in the World Team Cup, held in their own backyard at Vojens.

BRITISH LEAGUE DIVISION ONE

Team	Mts	Won	Drn	Lst	For	Agn	Pts	Bon	Tot
Wolverhampton	24	19	1	4	1,205.5	952.5	39	10	49
Bradford	24	15	4	5	1,184.5	973.5	34	9	43
Cradley Heath	24	15	1	8	1,118	1,032	31	10	41
Belle Vue	24	12	3	9	1,042	1,082	27	6	33
Berwick	24	13	0	11	1,073	1,053	26	6	32
Ipswich	24	12	1	11	1,065.5	1,089.5	25	7	32
Coventry	24	12	0	12	1,076	1,079	24	6	30
King's Lynn	24	12	1	11	1,013.5	1,139.5	25	5	30
Oxford	**24**	**8**	**3**	**13**	**1,069**	**1,085**	**19**	**6**	**25**
Poole	24	8	2	14	1,053	1,103	18	5	23
Reading	24	9	0	15	1,030	1,123	18	3	21
Eastbourne	24	6	3	15	1,027	1,125	15	3	18
Swindon	24	5	1	18	1,018	1,138	11	2	13

NOTE: Eastbourne took over the results and fixtures of Wimbledon, who withdrew after completing two matches.

1992

The 1992 season featured a change to the management, with Kevan Hedderly, one of the directors of Northern Sports (Oxford) Ltd, replacing John Payne as co-promoter of the Cheetahs' affairs. On track, however, it wasn't a good term for Oxford, yet when the side was put together, the supporters had every reason to believe that a serious challenge would be made for league honours. After just one year at Cowley, Australian rider Craig Boyce was on his way back to Poole on a full transfer and this left the Cheetahs without an established third heat-leader and, as the season progressed, this weakness became more and more obvious. Meanwhile, prior to the season, Dean Barker was made available for transfer, although the Isleworth-born rider's name was removed from the list before the action got underway.

In Hans Nielsen and Martin Dugard the team had two of the best riders in the league, and both did everything that was expected of them. From 23 league matches, Nielsen scored 315 points to achieve a 10.25 average, while Dugard notched 215 points for an impressive 8.94 figure. Unfortunately for Nielsen, he fractured a collarbone at a mid-May meeting in Denmark, and although he was quickly back in track action, he failed to make the World Final in Poland. Remarkably, this was the first time the Danish superstar hadn't reached the big night since 1980. Dugard was another to suffer a collarbone injury, but like his skipper, he

Martin Dugard spent a fifth successive season with Oxford in 1992, scoring 215 points from twenty-one league appearances to average 8.94.

soon returned to action. The battling Englishman did make it to the World Final, but only as a reserve and he failed to get a ride.

The back-up department of the Oxford team, on paper anyway, looked good, with Dean Barker, Troy Butler, Mark Carlson and Glenn Cunningham, plus young Dane Morten Andersen. With Craig Boyce gone, the Cheetahs looked to Dean Barker to fill the vacant berth of third heat-leader, but things didn't work out. As the season progressed, 'Deano' developed something of a complex about the Cowley racing strip, and his scoring became somewhat erratic. It was no surprise to anyone really, when he returned to his old club, Eastbourne, at the end of the season. It has to be said, however, that there was substance in Barker's feelings about the Oxford track, as it did provide some problems and this point was emphasised in early May when Cradley Heath were the visitors. In each of the first three heats, the Heathens had a rider fall, and after a failed attempt to run heat four, the match was called off. A practice session was then held in order to prove that conditions were not that bad, and Oxford believed that they had permission for the practice, but they were called before the Control Board and fined.

The Oxford promoters were never happy to just sit back if they thought that team changes were necessary. Attempts to sign former star Gordon Kennett failed, though, thanks to the rulebook. Kennett wanted to come, but as a backup to the heat leaders. However, if he had returned to Cowley, one of the existing heat leaders would have had to be released, and that was something that just wasn't an option. Glenn Cunningham was struggling to come to terms with top-flight racing and in an attempt to strengthen the reserve berth, Spencer Timmo was signed to take the Bristolian's place. Timmo, the son of former Oxford rider, Rick, tried very hard, but like Cunningham, he was way off the pace, and finally Daz Sumner was drafted in from Middlesbrough.

Tenth position in the First Division was something of a disappointment for everyone at Sandy Lane. Yet, despite the problems with the track, which were solved to a degree with the help of Cradley Heath promoter Colin Pratt, the racing was very exciting indeed. At home, the Cheetahs won seven matches and recorded four draws – against Belle Vue, Cradley Heath, Poole and Swindon – while losing just once, to Wolverhampton on 2 September. Away from home, it was a different story, with a lone success, a 48-38 win at Coventry. The Oxford bosses tried hard to strengthen the side when they thought it necessary, but they failed, thanks to the constraints of the points limit. Had the rules permitted them to add Gordon Kennett to the side, things could have been very different. Little did the faithful supporters realise when the season ended that they were due for a most dramatic winter, with the Cheetahs' very existence in jeopardy. The end of an era of unrivalled success came about in October 1992, and no one had an inkling, but things were destined to never be quite the same again.

BRITISH LEAGUE DIVISION ONE

Team	Mts	Won	Drn	Lst	For	Agn	Pts	Bon	Tot
Reading	24	19	1	4	1,199	944	39	11	50
Bradford	24	15	0	9	1,132	1,027	30	8	38
Poole	24	15	2	7	1,129	1,028	32	6	38
Cradley Heath	24	14	2	8	1,118.5	1,038.5	30	8	38
Wolverhampton	24	14	1	9	1,106	1,051	29	9	38
Belle Vue	24	14	1	9	1,144	1,011	29	8	37
Ipswich	24	11	2	11	1,090	1,065	24	6	30
Coventry	24	10	1	13	1,057.5	1,097.5	21	5	26
King's Lynn	24	9	0	15	1,005	1,136	18	7	25
Oxford	**24**	**8**	**4**	**12**	**1,053**	**1,103**	**20**	**4**	**24**
Arena-Essex	24	7	0	17	1,008	1,149	14	3	17
Eastbourne	24	6	2	16	965	1,191	14	1	15
Swindon	24	5	2	17	996	1,162	12	2	14

1993

The fact that Oxford operated at all in 1993 was due entirely to Kidderminster businessman and speedway enthusiast Tony Mole, who stepped in at the eleventh hour to save the track. The club had been through a troubled winter, due to the introduction of the BSPA pay policy. Despite sterling efforts by the management, led by promoter Kevan Hedderly, Oxford were unable to come to terms with star man Hans Nielsen. Mr Hedderly made it clear that there was no way Oxford Speedway would risk the heavy fines – a figure of £10,000 had been mentioned – by breaching the pay code, other than through sponsorship for their multi-World Champion and the number one rider in British racing. It is ironic that after the decision to impose a pay policy, it was Mr Hedderly who expressed the view that he 'just did not see how the pay policy could work,' and had actually voted against it at the BSPA Conference.

With the season beckoning, Oxford had just three riders, one of whom was Martin Dugard, who were prepared to take a pay cut and had been able to agree a deal, thanks to the tremendous efforts by the Cheetahs Supporters' Club, who had secured sponsorship. The other two riders were novice Darren Andrews, and outstanding Danish youngster Morten Andersen. It was, therefore, a sad day on 23 February, when Kevan Hedderly announced that, having been unable to put together a competitive team, the Oxford Speedway club would cease to function. It was then that Tony Mole took over the promotion under the umbrella of Oxford

Oxford Cheetahs 1993. From left to right, back row: John Tremblin (team manager), Darren Andrews, David Clarke, Rene Madsen, David Smart, Mark Blackbird, Bernard Crapper (co-promoter). Front row: Tony Langdon, Andy Hackett (on bike), Garry Sweet.

Speedway (1993) Ltd, having made an acceptable offer to the stadium owners, Northern Sports Ltd. In the beginning, Mr Mole tried to get things moving for the continuation of First Division racing, but through no fault of the new promoter, things had moved too fast. Hans Nielsen was on the brink of signing for Coventry, and being unable to put together a competitive Division One side, Mr Mole settled for Second Division racing. It was a new era and Oxford were, effectively, in the same position that they were in at the beginning of 1976, when they joined the National League. Bernard Crapper and the returning John Payne were installed as the day-to-day promoters and their first task was to put together a new side.

Mark Blackbird, one of twin brothers, was the first to sign for the new Cheetahs, with his brother Paul following a few weeks later. Further signings quickly followed in the shape of Andy Hackett from Coventry and David Smart via Swindon. 'Smartie', in fact, could not be fitted in at his home track, Swindon, in what was actually his Testimonial year! Young Dane Rene Madsen, who was spotted by Bernard Crapper at Belle Vue in a World Under-21 meeting, came over, impressed in practice, and was duly signed. David Clarke, formerly of Coventry, was another new acquisition for the Cheetahs' camp. With the team beginning to take shape, a good number one was urgently needed and Oxford found that man in Poole rider Tony Langdon, who came on loan for the season. Langdon was to enjoy an outstanding term and always led the team from the front.

Oxford stunned the speedway world on 22 April, when their new side won the league match at Sheffield by 55 points to 53, this after beating the Yorkshire side by 10 points at Cowley a week earlier. However, as the season went on, injuries began to play havoc. Andy Hackett, who had struggled to find his best form, was badly hurt in a match against Swindon on 9 July. Meanwhile, Mark Blackbird decided to retire and made way for a new signing, as the Oxford bosses shuffled and reshuffled their pack. In came the experienced Alan Grahame, along with Spencer Timmo and Andy Meredith, plus, as the averages determined, Chris

Cobby. Unfortunately, the various team changes that the management were forced to make meant that the side was never settled. Throughout the traumas, Tony Langdon kept on going, scoring 451 points and eight maximums from 37 league matches to yield an average of 9.10. Even he couldn't escape the injury bug, though, for he suffered a knee problem, while David Smart, who was a real success, broke a collarbone towards the end of the season. David Clarke held his team place and provided excitement with his style of racing, but he ought to have done much better at Second Division level. Clarke, in fact, was actually dropped for a spell, as the Oxford bosses tried strenuously to assemble a winning combination.

Having struggled all year, it was little wonder that Oxford finished at the very bottom of the Division Two table, but at the end of a difficult season, at least John Payne was able to announce that a three-year agreement had been reached with Northern Sports. With the racing during 1993 being exciting and well worth watching, Payne was confident that after the initial year, the promoters would seek to improve in 1994, with a return to First Division racing being the long-term objective.

BRITISH LEAGUE DIVISION TWO

Team	Mts	Won	Drn	Lst	For	Agn	Pts	Bon	Tot
Glasgow	40	27	I	12	2,416	1,900	55	19	74
Long Eaton	40	25	0	15	2,302	1,970	50	13	63
Peterborough	40	24	0	16	2,260	2,012	48	13	61
Swindon	40	23	I	16	2,217.5	2,088.5	47	13	60
Edinburgh	40	20	I	19	2,272	2,041	41	15	56
Newcastle	40	21	2	17	2,138.5	2,133.5	44	8	52
Middlesbrough	40	21	0	19	2,125	2,189	42	8	50
Rye House	40	20	0	20	2,133	2,177	40	9	49
Sheffield	40	15	0	25	1,959	2,320	30	5	35
Exeter	40	12	0	28	1,881	2,429	24	3	27
Oxford	**40**	**9**	**I**	**30**	**1,934**	**2,378**	**19**	**4**	**23**

1994

Oxford could only go in one direction in 1994, and that was up! The first task facing promoters Bernard Crapper and John Payne was team building, since many of the 1993 outfit were, for one reason or another, unavailable. A particular body blow was the fact that Tony Langdon wasn't available. Langdon was a Poole asset, of course, and with the management of the Pirates also now promoting Second Division racing at Swindon, it was obvious that they would need the Aussie at Blunsdon. It was tough for Oxford to lose their number one rider, but the closure of Rye House meant that Martin Goodwin was available, and he was quickly snapped up. Mick Poole sought a move from Peterborough and he too was swiftly added to the Oxford team. An important backroom appointment was that of 1991 World Champion Jan O. Pedersen as team manager, with the Dane enjoying his first experience of life on the other side of the safety fence.

The season began with a few problems, as Martin Goodwin suffered concussion and a leg injury, which caused him to miss a number of matches in early May. Another matter for concern was the fact that Mick Poole was taking time to settle on the Oxford raceway. It turned out to be a bad month, with the Cheetahs losing all their matches, but perhaps the blackest happening was when Andy Meredith suffered a bad injury at Glasgow on 29 May. The Coventry-based rider unfortunately received back and neck injuries and was out for the season, but as soon as he was able, the youngster was back, cheering on his teammates from the terraces.

Team manager Jan O. Pedersen welcomes Daz
Sumner back to Cowley midway through the
1994 season.

It was obvious that new faces were needed, and two arrived from Sweden in the shape
of Stefan Ekberg and Niklas Karlsson, although efforts to bring back former favourite Jens
Rasmussen failed. Happily for the Cheetahs, Mick Poole gradually discovered his best form,
and as the season progressed, he became very much the number one around the Cowley
circuit. Indeed, a special tribute should be paid to the Australian for the hard work he put in
to rediscover his best form, after initially finding life on the Sandy Lane racing strip tough. The
blonde-haired rider just gritted his teeth and, having set to work with great determination, it
took a very good rider to beat him in the last few months of the season. Poole certainly proved
that riding the Oxford track should be a pleasure, not a nightmare.

David Smart had been riding well, even though he was troubled by a series of niggling little
knocks, but he was allowed to move on when the returning Daz Sumner was snapped up via
Middlesbrough. Smartie wasn't altogether happy with the management and left for Exeter in
late July, a rather disillusioned young man. Throughout the year, there were several changes
to the team, as the management tried to juggle their riders and find the feel-good factor. At
one point, they actually tried to replace Stefan Ekberg with Niklas Karlsson, but the BSPA
vetoed the idea and ruled that the Cheetahs had to ride both Swedes at the same time or not
at all. One further change occurred as the season drew to its close when veteran racer Alan
Grahame, who had been a steady points compiler, lost form and was dropped.

Oxford were to finish eighth in the ten-team league, which showed a slight improvement
on the previous year, but although they had good riders, the problem was getting them all
to strike form together and successfully gel as a team. The Cheetahs would certainly have
fared better in their quest for league honours had they been able to track a settled side, but
regrettably this wasn't the case. Mick Poole took over the mantle of top man at Oxford,
scoring 398 points from 36 league matches for an average of 8.59. Giving good support was
the solid scoring 'Burt' Goodwin, whose tally of points reached 285 from 32 appearances and
produced a 7.72 average. Although league form was patchy, a real highlight for the Oxford

faithful was the Cheetahs' success in the Four-Team Championship at Peterborough, when Goodwin headed the scoring as they beat Long Eaton, Peterborough and Edinburgh in the final. Later on, both Poole and Alan Grahame rode in the Jawa/Barum-sponsored Division Two Riders' Championship, scoring 10 and 9 points respectively.

During the year, perhaps the most bizarre of accidents happened to promoter Bernard Crapper, when he was accidentally knocked over in the Sandy Lane pits by junior team manager Colin Clarke, who was moving his car at the time. The end result was that the Cheetahs' boss suffered fractures to both legs.

BRITISH LEAGUE DIVISION TWO

Team	Mts	Won	Drn	Lst	For	Agn	Pts	Bon	Tot
Glasgow	36	26	1	9	1,955	1,494	53	14	67
Long Eaton	36	24	2	10	1,835	1,614	50	15	65
Edinburgh	36	20	1	15	1,760	1,690	41	10	51
Swindon	36	18	1	17	1,752	1,698	37	12	49
Peterborough	36	18	2	16	1,752	1,681	38	10	48
Middlesbrough	36	19	1	16	1,744.5	1,706.5	39	9	48
Newcastle	36	15	1	20	1,729.5	1,714.5	31	9	40
Oxford	**36**	**15**	**1**	**20**	**1,691**	**1,743**	**31**	**7**	**38**
Sheffield	36	10	1	25	1,537	1,914	21	3	24
Exeter	36	9	1	26	1,474	1,975	19	1	20

1995

There was a shake-up, both on and off the track in 1995, with Tony Mole, who had saved the club from going under in 1993, putting the promoting rights up for sale. In the event, Mr Mole didn't sell the club immediately; instead an agreement was reached with former Ipswich boss Chris Shears to handle the affairs of the Cheetahs, alongside Bernard Crapper and John Payne. However, as this change came within weeks of the new season beginning, it gave the management little time to put a side together, although somehow they succeeded. All the tracks from both the First and Second Divisions had joined forces to form one big Premier League, with Oxford taking their place amongst no fewer than twenty-one teams, so it was imperative that the promotion put together a competitive team.

Martin Goodwin and Rene Madsen remained from the 1994 line-up, and were joined by Swede Jimmy Nilsen, who came via Bradford, and the exciting Italian Armando Castagna, who arrived from Reading. Linking with these signings was former Belle Vue rider Michael Coles, together with David Steen, who had turned up for a practice session and was duly handed a reserve berth. Once the season was underway, Chris Shears pulled off a super signing when young Swede Daniel Andersson (known as Dalle) came to Cowley and went on to become an outstanding success.

Mick Bell, the former Reading, Oxford and Coventry rider, became the team manager and there is no doubt that he instilled a grand fighting spirit amongst his charges. The Cheetahs opened with a well-deserved win in a Bank Holiday challenge match against Wolverhampton, but lost their opening Premier League match at Reading in the rain, going down 52-42. However, in the first leg of the Knock-Out Cup at Poole on 19 April, Oxford rode brilliantly to keep the Pirates' victory down to a 3-point margin, 54-51, with David Steen notching a brilliant 13+2 points from seven outings. This was quite a triumph for Steen, who hadn't even been named in the programme, the number seven berth in the Cheetahs' side instead being

Swedish ace Jimmy Nilsen linked with the Cheetahs in 1995 and notched 404 points from 39 league matches to finish the year with an average of 8.31.

a blank space. In the return leg at Cowley two days later, Jimmy Nilsen, Michael Coles and Rene Madsen each recorded double figures as Oxford really went to town, with a massive 72-36 victory on the night giving them an aggregate success by 123 points to 90.

Oxford continued to put up great performances as the team gelled together well, even when Martin Goodwin suffered a shoulder injury at Hull in May and was sidelined for some weeks. The Cheetahs became a pretty formidable outfit at their Cowley base, and on 10 May produced their biggest league success of the season, when they hammered visiting Sheffield 62-34. The match was memorable for the marvellous 13-point tally from Swedish sensation Dalle Andersson. The youngster enjoyed a tremendous year and looked a real world-beater, however, he moved to Cradley Heath the following year, and subsequently tried to make it at a number of other venues, although, regrettably, he never repeated the outstanding promise and ability he had shown at Oxford.

After beating Poole in the opening round of the Knock-Out Cup, the Cheetahs defeated Arena-Essex in round two, before losing to Cradley Heath at the quarter-final stage by 12 points on aggregate. In the league, Oxford won fifteen matches at home, while also losing five, and their form away from Cowley wasn't good, highlighted by just a single victory at Coventry and a draw at Long Eaton. Unsurprisingly, this form saw the Cheetahs end the campaign in seventeenth position, after a particularly poor spell in mid-season when Mick Bell had to ask for more commitment from his men. Jimmy Nilsen finished up as the team's top rider, having recorded 404 points from 39 league appearances to post an 8.31 average. Armando Castagna was runner-up to Nilsen in the scoring stakes with 388 points from 38 matches, giving the Italian an average of 7.90. Dalle Andersson was a deserving third in the statistical rundown, his impressive tally of 333 points from 36 appearances yielding a 7.62 average.

With the season ending and everything looking good for 1996, it came as a shock when Jimmy Nilsen indicated that he wanted to go back to Swindon, the track where he made his name in British racing. There was further drama when Tony Mole, within the rules of speedway, reclaimed the promotion, and within weeks had sold it on to former Ipswich and Hackney boss Dave Pavitt. As could be expected, rumours were rife at the time, but apart from Mr Mole's announcement, nothing was said, and no statement was ever forthcoming from Chris Shears. One cannot help but pay tribute to the hard core of Oxford fans who, despite the many promotional changes, still stuck by their team and gave them, in whatever level of racing they rode, the very maximum of support and encouragement.

PREMIER LEAGUE

Team	Mts	Won	Drn	Lst	For	Agn	Pts	Bon	Tot
Eastbourne	40	28	3	9	2,041	1,785	59	18	77
Bradford	40	25	2	13	2,072.5	1,761.5	52	17	69
Cradley Heath	40	25	1	14	2,058	1,771	51	17	68
Peterborough	40	25	0	15	1,982.5	1,848.5	50	12	62
Wolverhampton	40	23	0	17	1,981	1,831	46	14	60
Ipswich	40	23	0	17	2,000	1,835	46	13	59
Glasgow	40	21	1	18	1,957.5	1,876.5	43	14	57
Belle Vue	40	20	1	19	1,968	1,841	41	14	55
Edinburgh	40	20	4	16	1,904.5	1,923.5	44	10	54
Arena-Essex	40	21	0	19	1,935	1,903	42	10	52
Swindon	40	20	3	17	1,908	1,925	43	9	52
Poole	40	18	2	20	1,920	1,911	38	9	47
Reading	40	17	4	19	1,876	1,959	38	9	47
Sheffield	40	19	0	21	1,858	1,977	38	9	47
Coventry	40	17	1	22	1,929	1,905	35	8	43
Hull	40	17	2	21	1,822	2,014	36	4	40
Oxford	**40**	**16**	**1**	**23**	**1,858**	**1,976**	**33**	**6**	**39**
Long Eaton	40	14	4	22	1,848	1,984	32	7	39
King's Lynn	40	14	4	22	1,867	1,966	32	6	38
Middlesbrough	40	10	2	28	1,728	2,094	22	2	24
Exeter	40	8	3	29	1,705	2,132	19	2	21

1996

The 1996 season heralded a new promoter in Dave Pavitt, and Keith 'Buster' Chapman joined him in the running of the club, since his own track (King's Lynn) had temporarily closed down. Chapman brought with him Czech riders Tomas Topinka and Bohumil Brhel, while former Oxford favourite Marvyn Cox, together with Mark Lemon, both arrived on loan from Poole. Meanwhile, Lawrence Hare joined via Ipswich and Martin Goodwin was retained from the outgoing promotion, with young Poole loanee Martin Willis being brought in to complete the side. John Tremblin became clerk of the course and assistant team manager, whilst Chapman took on the important role of team boss. Oxford started the season well and were generally impressive at home, but their away form remained suspect. In a stuttering start, Swindon forced a 45-45 draw in the opening Premier League match of the season, before the Cheetahs went on a winning streak at Cowley, which ended on 3 May when composite side Cradley Heath and Stoke were victorious.

Shortly after the season began, promising youngster Mark Frost was signed, after being recommended to Oxford by London rider Paul Hurry, who had spotted Frost during a tour of South Africa. Frost forced his way into the side and replaced Martin Willis. In the end, however, he only appeared in thirteen league matches for the Cheetahs, scoring 35 points, and was injured before the season ended. Although Frost was initially retained in 1997, he was subsequently released without donning a Cheetahs race jacket again. He then disappeared from the speedway scene, but in 1999 he was seen in the World Team Cup semi-final at Poole, when he rode for Hungary under what turned out to be his real name of Attila Stefani! It was a pity that he didn't return to compete in British racing since, in his short stay at Cowley Stadium, he showed himself to be a very able young rider.

Frenchman Philippe Berge was signed, but found himself in and out of the team, when an extended run could have worked wonders. The Cheetahs, sponsored by John Tarr of JT Commercials from Poole, won by 10 points at near neighbours Reading, and then forced impressive draws at Poole and Exeter. The divisional Four-Team Championship commenced on 14 June, and the Oxford boys did brilliantly to qualify for the final at Peterborough on 4 August. As they had done in 1994, they went on to win the tournament, with the result being: Oxford 23, Peterborough 17, Hull 16, Ipswich 16.

The side finished in thirteenth position in the league, having won just twelve of their thirty-six-match programme. When the statistics were calculated at the end of the campaign, Tomas Topinka was the Cheetahs' top man, his 27 league appearances having yielded 287 points and an average of 8.63. Oxford could point to being somewhat unlucky with injuries, for besides the aforementioned Mark Frost, four regulars suffered injury during the course of the season, namely Bo Brhel, Mark Lemon, Marvyn Cox and Martin Goodwin. An example of Oxford's bad luck with injuries ironically occurred on Friday 13 September! The Cheetahs were racing against London and looked to be in with a good chance of winning. However, the match was only a quarter-of-an-hour old when Oxford were reduced to a five-man team. Both Brhel

Mark Frost joined Oxford in 1996, having been spotted in action in South Africa. He only appeared in 13 league matches for the side and it subsequently turned out that his real name was Attila Stefani. He was later seen representing Hungary in the World Team Cup.

and Cox suffered falls in their first outings and were taken off to hospital, with the Cheetahs subsequently losing 53-43.

Talking of Marvyn Cox, it is worth remembering that he became the first Oxford rider to make it through to the Grand Prix series in 1996. Regrettably, though, Cocker found the going too tough, and could only muster 15 points from the five rounds in which he participated. At the end of the season, promoter Dave Pavitt claimed to have lost money during the course of the campaign, but said that Oxford would run in 1997, albeit in the revamped Premier League. In other words, the Cheetahs would not be joining the ten teams that opted to form an Elite League (or First Division), but would compete in the lower level of racing offered by the Premier League. So, for the third time in little over twenty years, Oxford supporters would have to settle for Division Two-style racing, as had happened previously in 1976 and 1993.

The Czech duo of Tomas Topinka (*above*) and Bohumil Brhel (*right*) could be seen in Oxford's colours in 1996. Topinka was to end the campaign as the side's top man, averaging 8.63 from the league programme.

PREMIER LEAGUE

Team	Mts	Won	Drn	Lst	For	Agn	Pts	Bon	Tot
Wolverhampton	36	29	0	7	1,941	1,504	58	18	76
Peterborough	36	23	0	13	1,834	1,615	46	15	61
Eastbourne	36	23	1	12	1,808	1,634	47	12	59
Swindon	36	22	2	12	1,777	1,657	46	12	58
Cradley Heath & Stoke	36	21	1	14	1,819	1,633	43	13	56
Belle Vue	36	21	1	14	1,775	1,651	43	12	55
Hull	36	20	3	13	1,774	1,675	43	11	54
Ipswich	36	20	0	16	1,799	1,654	40	12	52
London	36	20	0	16	1,732.5	1,693.5	40	11	51
Coventry	36	16	2	18	1,770	1,679	34	10	44
Bradford	36	16	0	20	1,692	1,717	32	9	41
Scottish Monarchs	36	16	0	20	1,673	1,780	32	5	37
Oxford	**36**	**12**	**4**	**20**	**1,676**	**1,748**	**28**	**8**	**36**
Poole	36	13	2	21	1,633	1,801	28	5	33
Exeter	36	13	2	21	1,614	1,841	28	4	32
Middlesbrough	36	11	1	24	1,607	1,843	23	6	29
Long Eaton	36	12	0	24	1,615	1,807	24	4	28
Sheffield	36	13	0	23	1,533	1,871	26	2	28
Reading	36	11	1	24	1,590.5	1,859.5	23	2	25

1997

Dave Pavitt acted quickly to assemble an attractive and competitive team for the 1997 season of Premier League racing, retaining Lawrence Hare, Philippe Berge and the promising Mark Frost from the 1996 team. The promoter made his top priority a number one rider, and whilst his search went on, he signed Krister Marsh on loan from Swindon. Rumour was rife around Oxford as to the name of the number one signing, so much so that Pavitt was forced to admit his target was Kelvin Tatum's younger brother, Neville. The former Canterbury, Wimbledon, Coventry, Eastbourne, Ipswich, Peterborough and London rider duly arrived on board, and was closely followed by Swede Mikael Teurnberg, which certainly made the Cheetahs look a very good side on paper. In the event, Frost wasn't retained, his place being taken by Jason Bunyan (on loan from Poole), who had spent the greater part of 1996 on the injured list.

The JT Commercials Cheetahs began the season well in the Premier League Cup (a rebranded version of the Knock-Out Cup), with the months of April and May being particularly fruitful. A draw at Long Eaton on 2 April was followed by four victories, including a 2-point success at Exeter. A slight wobble occurred on 2 May, when Oxford lost 46-44 in a very tight encounter with near neighbours Reading, although the Control Board later amended the result to a draw. Favourable results followed, including draws at both Reading and Arena-Essex in the Premier League Cup on 19 May and 23 May respectively. However, the Cheetahs' opening league match was staged on 25 May, and it was a surprise when they lost 46-44 at home to Edinburgh. Winning form quickly returned, though, courtesy of an away 55-34 success against Skegness in a Premier League Cup encounter that was actually ridden at Peterborough. On 8 June, Oxford lost a controversial league match at Newport by 50 points to 40. The Cheetahs were upset by the constant track watering on a hot afternoon, which was done without their consent or any reference to them. Promoter Dave Pavitt claimed that the conditions certainly upset Neville Tatum, who returned a tally of just 6+1 points and that, in many respects, was when the Oxford season began to change for the worse.

Certainly, the months of July and August were not good for the Cheetahs. A 46-43 home win against Long Eaton was followed by a Premier League Cup defeat at Hull. Newcastle came to Cowley on 11 July, and left on the wrong end of a 50-39 defeat. Then came the crunch, a home league match against Reading seven days later, when the Cheetahs suffered another close defeat, 47-43, despite a real captain's part being played by Neville Tatum with a paid maximum, 14+1 points. Krister Marsh, who was taking a long time to settle, received a shoulder injury at Newport and although he returned to track action, his form let him down and he soon disappeared from the Oxford scene. Another rider to depart was Jason Bunyan, who moved to the Isle of Wight and was replaced by local boy Darren Andrews.

Two sides operated from Cowley during the season, for apart from the main Cheetahs team, Oxford Cubs participated in the Amateur League. The junior side completed twenty-four league matches and ended up in ninth position out of thirteen teams. First-team riders Krister Marsh and Darren Andrews also appeared in the Cubs' side, while other regulars in the Amateur League side included Phillip Ambrose, Lee Driver, Simon Wolstenholme, Lance Sealey, Jason Newitt, Jason McKenna, Andrew Appleton and Gary Fawdrey. With 167 points, Ambrose topped the Cubs' scoring, receiving good support from Driver (120 points) and Wolstenholme (111).

Back to the Cheetahs, and Exeter were beaten 54-36 at Cowley on 8 August, but regrettably this was to be the only Oxford win for some time. Indeed, it wasn't until 5 September that the side again tasted the sweet smell of success, courtesy of a 52-38 home win over Sheffield. Thankfully, the Cheetahs managed to follow that up with two more league victories against Newport (52-38) and Berwick (55-34), before the Isle of Wight left Sandy Lane with a 49-41 victory under their belts. Defeats followed at Stoke and Glasgow, before the Cheetahs completed their home fixtures by thumping Arena-Essex 56-34 on 28 September.

It had been a season of two halves for Oxford, and if only they had ended the campaign as they had begun, they might well have taken league honours. As it was, they finished eleventh in a fourteen-team league. As had happened in previous seasons, the Cheetahs couldn't escape the injury bug, with Mikael Teurnberg being particularly affected. Oxford finished third in the Four-Team Championship at Peterborough, and Neville Tatum won the British semi-final of the World Championship at Exeter with 14 points, and subsequently qualified for a British Final place by scoring 5 points at Sheffield in the second semi-final. In the big event at Coventry on 1 June, he could only manage a couple of second places on his way to a 5-point tally and twelfth position overall.

Despite everything, Oxford did reach the final of the Premier League Cup, only to lose both legs by an identical scoreline of 47-43 against Edinburgh, giving the Scottish outfit an aggregate success by 94 points to 86. Philippe Berge was the most productive rider for the Cheetahs in the final, netting 11 points at Cowley in the first leg on 29 August and a sensational 15+2 tally at Armadale in the second leg twenty-four hours later. Tatum also scored well over the two meetings, hitting 13+1 and 12 points respectively, while Lawrence Hare contributed returns of 11 and 8+1 points. Unfortunately, they lacked the necessary backing and the Monarchs took victory by having that tad extra strength in depth.

Lawrence Hare was Oxford's best performer overall and was selected as the club's Rider of the Year by the loyal Cheetahs supporters. In league matches, the Suffolk-born racer notched 253 points from 24 appearances for an average of 8.60. Fractionally behind, Neville Tatum posted an 8.59 figure, having racked-up a higher total of 274 points from 26 matches. Philippe Berge was third in the club's league records for the year, his 21 appearances yielding 194 points and an average of 7.96. Meanwhile, injuries restricted Mikael Teurnberg to seventeen matches, from which he netted 149 points for a final figure of 7.27.

Dave Pavitt, at the end of the season, claimed he would be returning for his third year at the helm, but in the event, it was yet another traumatic winter for Oxford, with the promotion

Martin Goodwin completed a three-year stint with Oxford in 1996, scoring 120 points from 26 league matches.

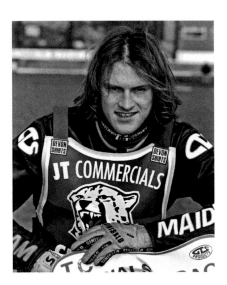

In 1997, Lawrence Hare was retained from the previous season's line-up and he went on to scoop the Rider of the Year award after scoring 253 points from 24 appearances to head the Cheetahs' league averages on an 8.60 figure.

changing hands again. This time, Southampton-based businessman Steve Purchase and his wife, Vanessa, bought the promotional rights. The Cheetahs would, it was explained, be joining the Elite League, so yet again, it was a case of all change at Cowley, although the loyal Oxford public had seen it all before and were accustomed to it.

PREMIER LEAGUE

Team	Mts	Won	Drn	Lst	For	Agn	Pts	Bon	Tot
Reading	26	22	0	4	1,323	1,011	44	13	57
Long Eaton	26	18	1	7	1,227	1,107	37	11	48
Edinburgh	26	17	1	8	1,235	1,102	35	8	43
Newcastle	26	15	0	11	1,201	1,134	30	8	38

Exeter	26	14	0	12	1,213	1,125	28	6	34
Glasgow	26	12	2	12	1,158	1,179	26	6	32
Arena-Essex	26	12	0	14	1,157	1,179	24	7	31
Isle of Wight	26	12	0	14	1,149	1,184	24	7	31
Hull	26	13	0	13	1,134	1,195	26	5	31
Sheffield	26	12	0	14	1,116	1,219	24	5	29
Oxford	**26**	**9**	**0**	**17**	**1,116**	**1,219**	**18**	**6**	**24**
Stoke	26	8	2	16	1,111	1,222	18	3	21
Berwick	26	7	1	18	1,105	1,223	15	4	19
Newport	26	7	1	18	1,095	1,241	15	2	17

NOTE: Isle of Wight took over the results and fixtures of Skegness, who withdrew after completing two matches.

AMATEUR LEAGUE

Team	Mts	Won	Drn	Lst	For	Agn	Pts
Peterborough	24	22	1	1	1,064	729	45
Berwick	24	17	2	5	999	767	36
Ryde (IOW)	24	15	1	8	987	857	31
Buxton	24	15	0	9	948	901	30
Mildenhall	24	13	2	9	961	874	28
St Austell	24	13	0	11	963	871	26
M4 Raven Sprockets	24	10	3	11	820	848	23
Welsh Western Warriors	24	10	0	14	909	946	20
Oxford	**24**	**9**	**0**	**15**	**901**	**909**	**18**
Shuttle Cubs	24	9	0	15	799	969	18
Belle Vue	24	7	0	17	798	967	14
Lathallan	24	7	0	17	819	1,024	14
Anglian Angels	24	4	1	19	725	1,031	9

NOTE: M4 Raven Sprockets was a composite side formed by Reading and Swindon; similarly, Welsh Western Warriors was formed by Exeter and Newport; Shuttle Cubs were formed by Long Eaton and Wolverhampton; Anglian Angels were formed by Ipswich and King's Lynn.

1998

With Steve and Vanessa Purchase in position at the helm as the club's new owners, the 1998 season also saw Terry Russell come on board as a co-promoter, mainly in an advisory capacity during their first term in charge. Mr Purchase was determined that the club should be participating in Elite League racing when he took over and, as such, he knew the importance of putting together a good, competitive side; a task he set about achieving with great gusto. Lawrence Hare, a star of the 1997 side, was taken over by Purchase, who also came up with a new team skipper in Steve Schofield from Poole. Other incoming riders were Paul Hurry (via King's Lynn) and Jan Staechmann, who had been sacked by Peterborough after a few matches in 1997. Steve Johnston also came on board after a spell at Ipswich, while former Oxford favourite Martin Goodwin was brought in as team manager. There was a need for an established number one rider, and Jason Crump was signed when the Peterborough management opted for Premier League racing. Sponsorship arrived when Gresham Computing agreed to back the Cheetahs, so it was all systems go down Cowley way.

As the season got underway for the new Gresham Cheetahs, there was a home draw against Coventry on 3 April in the Knock-Out Cup, and their first home win in the competition occurred a full month later against Belle Vue on 3 May. Local rivals Swindon came the following week, and Oxford recorded their most convincing result to that point, winning 58-32. Success away from home was non-existent in the early weeks of the season, while a couple of home league defeats in June, against Coventry and Eastbourne, convinced Steve Purchase that his side definitely needed improving upon. For the away fixture against King's Lynn on 24 June, Australian Todd Wiltshire, who had been out of British speedway since 1991, following a bad injury in his native land, made his debut for Oxford. He scored just a single point from four outings, but this was to be his poorest score in a Cheetahs race jacket. Wiltshire netted a tally of 7+2 points in a narrow 46-44 home league win over Swindon on 3 June and, as the season progressed, he just got better and better, until on 21 August, he recorded a marvellous six-ride paid maximum of 16+2 points in a home victory over Eastbourne.

July was greeted with mixed feelings by all those associated with Oxford. Jason Crump suffered ankle ligament damage in the home match against Swindon on only the third day of the month, and had an unfortunate confrontation with teammate Todd Wiltshire. The World

Jason Crump was outstanding for Oxford in 1998, ending the league campaign with a 9.10 average, having recorded 292 points from 24 appearances.

Long-Track Championship at nearby Abingdon saw excellent performances from Paul Hurry (who finished as runner-up), Steve Schofield and Crump. On 16 July, the Cheetahs made the short journey down the road to old rivals Swindon, and there was great joy when they came away with a 52-38 victory, thanks to a mesmeric 18-point maximum from guest Billy Hamill, who was standing in for Crump. The following day, however, there was a surprise in store when Wolverhampton came to Cowley and left with a 46-44 victory, and although Hamill again stood in for Crump, his 14 points couldn't help Oxford avoid defeat. Having apologised for his attack on Wiltshire, 'Crumpie' returned for the home match against Poole on 24 July and quickly showed his best form with 14+1 points in a 47-43 success.

Coventry beat Oxford at Cowley on 31 July, but the following week saw a cracker of a match when Ipswich visited. The Cheetahs grabbed victory in the final heat, with the Jason Crump/Steve Johnston pairing scorching to a magnificent 5-1 over the Ipswich duo of Tony Rickardsson and Tomasz Gollob. This so inspired the Cheetahs that they went to King's Lynn on 12 August and came away with a 10-point victory, thanks to a full 15-pointer from Crump and 13+1 from Paul Hurry. Crowd favourite 'Lol' Hare had left for Premier League Newport in early July, but in his very first home meeting for the Wasps he suffered a serious injury and was out of action for the rest of the season, due to chipped bones in both ankles. With Elite League teams now being made up of six riders only, Hare didn't have to be replaced and the arrival of Wiltshire enabled him to move on.

Oxford completed the season in seventh position and Jason Crump was, as to be expected, the club's number one rider, as emphasised by 292 league points from 24 appearances and an average of 9.10. Crumpie was also a big success in the Grand Prix series, actually winning the British round at Coventry on 7 August and scoring a series total of 62 points to occupy eighth position overall. To round off a brilliant campaign, he finished as runner-up to the victorious Tony Rickardsson at Swindon in the Elite League Riders' Championship. At the end of the term, it was a very disappointed Steve Purchase who, having done all he could to re-establish top league speedway at Oxford, announced that he had lost a great deal of money, and in order to complete the season, had had to cancel a fiftieth anniversary meeting. Nevertheless, he was prepared to give speedway a go again in 1999, when once again he would endeavour to put together a winning side.

ELITE LEAGUE

Team	Mts	Won	Drn	Lst	For	Agn	Pts	Bon	Tot
Ipswich	32	26	1	5	1,653.5	1,211.5	53	16	69
Belle Vue	32	20	0	12	1,524.5	1,353.5	40	12	52
Coventry	32	18	1	13	1,474	1,401	37	11	48
Swindon	32	15	1	16	1,429	1,450	31	7	38
Eastbourne	32	15	0	17	1,430	1,449	30	7	37
Wolverhampton	32	14	1	17	1,421	1,444	29	8	37
Oxford	**32**	**13**	**2**	**17**	**1,388**	**1,490**	**28**	**5**	**33**
Poole	32	11	1	20	1,348	1,529	23	5	28
King's Lynn	32	8	1	23	1,270	1,610	17	1	18

1999

Promoters Steve and Vanessa Purchase had every reason to be optimistic in their second season in charge of the club. True, the return of Peterborough to the Elite League saw the top man from 1998, Jason Crump, rejoin his parent track, but the backbone of the side was still there, led by the immaculate Todd Wiltshire. With Crump gone, Mr Purchase looked for a top-class replacement and took a chance with former Cheetah Craig Boyce, on loan from Poole. To strengthen the reserve department, the promoter added another Poole rider (again, on loan) in the shape of perky Alun Rossiter. Team manager Martin Goodwin was forced to step down due to pressure of business and, to replace him, Purchase appointed track supremo Colin Meredith, together with centre-green presenter Richard Palmer in a dual role.

Oxford began the campaign with a Craven Shield match at Ipswich, but with Craig Boyce an absentee, still suffering from the after-effects of an injury, the Gresham Cheetahs crashed to a 52-38 defeat. A week later, Oxford visited Coventry, again in the Craven Shield competition and, with reserve Lawrence Hare giving the best performance of his speedway career to record an unbeaten 15-point tally, the Cheetahs were victorious by 54 points to 34. Following that, the team were to get better and better as the Craven Shield progressed. In fact, their run in the competition was outstanding, and it really was no surprise when they finished first in the qualifying table and met old rivals Coventry in the semi-final. Unfortunately, the last-four encounter wasn't held until October and, by that time, the Cheetahs had run out of steam and went down on aggregate by 100 points to 80. One thing worth mentioning regarding the Craven Shield was the match against Hull at Cowley on 9 April. This was when Alun Rossiter, who certainly had his critics on the terraces, recorded an unbeaten 12 points – the first time he'd scored a maximum in top-flight racing. 'Rosco' was, in fact, offered another ride in the meeting, but declined, and was reported as saying, 'I didn't want to push my luck!'

The season's opening meeting at Oxford had been a big farewell for former Cheetahs' legend Simon Wigg. The meeting on 28 March, quite rightly billed as the World Champions' Jawa Challenge, saw a fabulous field turn out to pay tribute to Wiggy, including meeting winner Greg Hancock, along with Jason Crump, Armando Castagna, Billy Hamill, Jimmy Nilsen, Sam Ermolenko, Tony Rickardsson, Hans Nielsen, Leigh Adams, Todd Wiltshire, Gary Havelock and Chris Louis.

Oxford's league campaign began at Ipswich on 27 May, when the side went down fighting by 48 points to 41, with Steve Johnston and Paul Hurry giving excellent performances to notch tallies of 14+2 and 10 respectively. At home, Oxford started well, with victories over Belle Vue and King's Lynn, and their good form at Cowley lasted into the month of August, with a fine 56-34 win against Hull. Away from home, the Cheetahs' form wasn't as dominating as it had been in the Craven Shield, a particularly low point being a 61-29 hammering at Poole on 1 September.

Just prior to that, on 27 August, Eastbourne came to Cowley for a league match and the Cheetahs lost by a single point, 47-46. Little did the supporters realise, but that was the beginning of the end as far as any title aspirations were concerned. After that evening, Oxford didn't enjoy any kind of success until 8 October, when they clinched a thrilling draw against Coventry in the home leg of the Craven Shield semi-final. The Cheetahs did finish their league fixtures with a narrow 47-43 win over Ipswich at Sandy Lane on 15 October, but by that time most folk on the terraces had lost interest in the Elite League competition.

In summary, it was a season of two halves; for in the Craven Shield the Oxford boys were magnificent, but when the Elite League came along the side was found wanting. Sometimes, it was hard to think that the team of riders struggling was in fact the same side that had been so dominant in the early months of the campaign. However, the racing was very exciting, and Todd Wiltshire gave Oxford fans much to cheer about. It was the Aussie's first full season in Britain for a number of years, and he did very well to total 170 points from his eighteen league appearances for a highly satisfactory 7.70 average. Wiltshire, to add to his honours in 1999, won the Inter-Continental final at Poole and gave a polished performance when feeling far from well in the Elite League Riders' Championship, finishing second to Jason Crump at Coventry on 23 October.

Craig Boyce, an ever-present over the eighteen-match Elite League programme, showed patchy form and wasn't quite the force that had been expected. Despite this, the Australian still occupied second spot in the team's final averages, his 143 points yielding a 7.01 figure. Steve Johnston, the third of Oxford's Australian contingent, looked like a world-beater on occasions, but the post-July period often saw him struggling. Both the reserve riders, Lawrence Hare and Alun Rossiter, were capable of doing anything, the problem being that no one was sure just when they were going to do something really special, although to be fair, they gave of their best at all times. Regrettably, the final position for the Cheetahs was eighth in the ten-team Elite League, but the good news at the end of the season was that the Purchases indicated they would be prepared to carry on, with the priority for the team being an established number one rider.

ELITE LEAGUE

Team	Mts	Won	Drn	Lst	For	Agn	Pts	Bon	Tot
Peterborough	18	12	2	4	889	734	26	8	34
Poole	18	12	0	6	899	724	24	9	33
King's Lynn	18	11	1	6	823	804	23	6	29

The chirpy Alun Rossiter rode for the Cheetahs in 1999 and recorded the first top-flight maximum of his long career, when he scored 12 points in a Craven Shield match against Hull at Cowley on 9 April.

Coventry	18	11	1	6	821	804	23	5	28
Ipswich	18	11	0	7	815	810	22	4	26
Belle Vue	18	9	1	8	848	773	19	5	24
Hull	18	6	1	11	785	834	13	3	16
Oxford	**18**	**5**	**0**	**13**	**754**	**869**	**10**	**3**	**13**
Eastbourne	18	6	0	12	745	879	12	1	13
Wolverhampton	18	4	0	14	736	884	8	1	9

2000

The 2000 season was promoter Steve Purchase's third year in charge, and he again worked hard to assemble a winning side, but whilst he hadn't met with the success his efforts deserved, he was due considerable praise for his endeavours. On the team front, Craig Boyce had gone, snapped up by King's Lynn, and to replace him came former Cheetah Jimmy Nilsen, on loan from parent club and local rivals Swindon. Purchase then took a risk by signing the young Czech brothers Ales and Lukas Dryml, who arrived with falsely inflated assessed averages of 7.50 and 5.00 respectively. Russian Roman Povazhny came to Cowley from Eastbourne, with Paul Hurry heading in the opposite direction. The brilliant Todd Wiltshire returned, along with Steve Johnston, who was to skipper the side. Meanwhile, to keep within the points limit, young Jon Underwood, a grass-track rider and a member of the Oxford junior side, was drafted in to fill the second reserve berth. Sponsorship of the team came from Poole-based company JT Commercials, who had previously backed the side in 1996 and 1997.

Straight away, Oxford opened their league programme with a match at Coventry on 25 March and promptly lost by 55 points to 34. Todd Wiltshire and Jimmy Nilsen looked good, but both the Dryml boys and Jon Underwood appeared way off the pace. Cowley subsequently opened for business on 31 March when a challenge fixture was staged against Wolverhampton. The Cheetahs took a narrow 46-44 victory and lost the second leg at Monmore Green by just 4 points. Before the Oxford public saw another meeting at Cowley, the Cheetahs were to race a league fixture at Ipswich, which they lost 52-38. Already a pattern was emerging, but it was telling promoter Steve Purchase something that he already knew, or at least suspected; that the Dryml brothers, whilst displaying plenty of promise, were not yet of Elite League standard. Meanwhile, young Jon Underwood was in desperate need of a stint at Premier League level, and Roman Povazhny hadn't built on his experience at Eastbourne the previous year.

Team strengthening was a top priority, and as soon as the Oxford boss could, he made changes to the line-up. Some juggling saw Mark Lemon return, on loan from Poole, and Jan Staechmann came back from exile. Moving in the opposite direction, Jon Underwood was posted to Premier League Arena-Essex, where he began to settle down, but then tragedy struck. Regrettably, the youngster was killed in a motor accident whilst returning to this country from a grass-track meeting on the continent. Everyone was shocked at the loss of such a popular lad, and condolences poured in to his family and friends from the speedway and grass-track fraternity. To accommodate the team changes and stay within the points ceiling, Steve Purchase was forced to let Roman Povazhny go out on loan to Wolverhampton, but at least, on paper, the Oxford boss had improved his side. However, there was an early exit from the Knock-Out Cup, when a 4-point defeat at Poole on 10 May was followed by an exciting draw in the second leg at Sandy Lane two days later.

As the season progressed, the Cheetahs proved to be very inconsistent at home and didn't have much luck on their travels. They enjoyed a rare 50-40 away success at Belle Vue on 25 June, but during July, Oxford lost six away matches in a row. July proved a bad month at home too, because although just two matches were raced, against Wolverhampton and Poole, the Cheetahs lost them both. To break up the fixtures, a Young England *v.* Young Australia Test match was held at Cowley on 28 July, when the English lads enjoyed a good win in a rain-affected match that, disappointingly, just didn't pull the punters. Business interests were taking up more and more of Steve Purchase's time and it became obvious that he was getting increasingly disillusioned with speedway. The upshot was that his wife, Vanessa, took a more prominent role in the running of the club.

August began in promising style for the Cheetahs when they won a gripping league match by 2 points against eventual League Champions Eastbourne early on and followed it up with a tremendous 47-43 success at Wolverhampton. Unfortunately, the rest of the month was a disaster, with home losses against Coventry, Peterborough and Ipswich. The month also saw the arrival of Brian Andersen, on loan from Coventry, as Vanessa Purchase worked hard to put some more pep into her side. The Dane took his bow for the club in the win at Wolverhampton on 7 August, when he tallied 9+1 points, before following it up with a brilliant 13+3 points in his home debut against his old club four evenings later, although his efforts couldn't prevent an Oxford defeat.

As the season approached its close, the Cheetahs rode with great determination to take a league point from Poole on 6 September, before defeating the Dorset side in a very wet return match at Cowley. The season ended with Oxford finishing eighth in the nine-team league, with an unstaged match at Belle Vue being declared null and void by the Control Board. The Cheetahs were, however, awarded the aggregate bonus point as a result of their home victory. Looking back, it has to be said that the Oxford management tried so hard to do their best for the supporters. Amazing comeback man Todd Wiltshire topped the Oxford scoring with 322 points from 31 league appearances for an 8.29 average. Jimmy Nilsen occupied second spot in the club's statistical rundown, having recorded 192 points from 23 matches for an average of 8.12 average; this despite a shoulder injury sustained in a home match against Peterborough on 16 June, which completely disrupted his season.

In the Grand Prix series, Oxford boasted three representatives, with Todd Wiltshire proving to be the best. It was a great credit to the Aussie that he could live with the world's best and 63 points from the six rounds was sufficient to see him finish in eighth position. Jimmy Nilsen scored 42 points for eleventh place overall, while Brian Andersen had to be satisfied with just 15 points from his six rounds.

There was great sadness when former Oxford legend Simon Wigg died on 15 November after a battle with illness. He was an all-round professional motorcyclist and his record was tremendous, having been crowned World Long-Track Champion on no fewer than five occasions. Wiggy also won the British Championship twice and was runner-up to Hans Nielsen in the 1989 World Final. His record with Oxford was marvellous, as he was an inspirational team member and helped the side to their British League Championship successes in 1985, 1986 and 1989, as well as their victories in the Knock-Out Cup and Gold Cup of 1985 and 1989 respectively. With the Aylesbury-born rider on board, the Cheetahs also shared both the Knock-Out Cup and League Cup with Cradley Heath in 1986, when inclement weather prevented the completion of the finals of each competition. A Service of Thanksgiving was held for Wigg at the Church of Christ the Cornerstone in Milton Keynes on Monday 27 November. As a measure of his popularity, the church was packed for the occasion, with many friends recalling fond memories of the rider. Sometime later, when preparations were being made for the special reunion of the 1985 and 1986 title-winning teams in 2005, former promoter John Payne recalled how parents of sick or injured children would sometimes ring up to enquire if it could be arranged for a rider to make a hospital visit. Wiggy, being locally based, was often asked if he could help. Naturally, he was a very busy man, but he always managed to make time and fit a visit into his hectic schedule. He regarded this as a very personal matter and insisted on no publicity, yet the Oxford management knew just how much the families appreciated what he did and how very grateful they were.

A Service of Thanksgiving
for the life of

SIMON ANTONY WIGG

15/10/1960 - 15/11/2000

Church of Christ the Cornerstone
Central Milton Keynes

Monday 27th November 2000 at 2.00 PM

The brochure from the Service of Thanksgiving for Simon Wigg, held at the Church of Christ the Cornerstone in Milton Keynes on 27 November 2000.

ELITE LEAGUE

Team	Mts	Won	Drn	Lst	For	Agn	Pts	Bon	Tot
Eastbourne	32	24	1	7	1,544	1,322	49	13	62
King's Lynn	32	22	2	8	1,564	1,321	46	14	60
Ipswich	32	16	3	13	1,456.5	1,409.5	35	11	46
Coventry	32	16	3	13	1,442	1,427	35	8	43
Poole	32	14	4	14	1,437	1,426	32	8	40
Wolverhampton	32	15	3	14	1,396	1,467	33	6	39
Peterborough	32	11	2	19	1,431.5	1,425.5	24	7	31
Oxford	**31**	**9**	**1**	**21**	**1,296**	**1,477**	**19**	**4**	**23**
Belle Vue	31	5	3	23	1,249	1,541	13	1	14

NOTE: One match, Belle Vue *v.* Oxford (ELB), was not raced.

2001

During the winter, Vanessa Purchase made clear her intentions for the 2001 season. The first priority would be a world-class number one rider to lead the scoring, and the second was to win the Elite League Championship. Happily for the Cowley faithful, the Cheetahs succeeded on both fronts, securing Leigh Adams on loan from his parent club Swindon and, after a nail-biting finish to the domestic campaign, capturing the Elite League title by just a single point.

The signing of Leigh Adams was a masterstroke. The talented Australian international and Grand Prix rider had been at King's Lynn for two seasons, during which time he had established himself as the master of the Saddlebow Road circuit. However, Adams lived just outside Swindon and it was obvious that if Vanessa Purchase could agree terms with him, then a track just down the road as a home base would surely appeal to him. That, of course, was just what happened and the Aussie put pen to paper and became an Oxford rider for the 2001 campaign. There were the so-called speedway experts who believed that the Cowley circuit wasn't Adams' type of track and that he would never be able to dominate in the manner he had at King's Lynn. However, they should have known better, as he quickly became the new Cowley King, giving the Oxford team a stability that the club hadn't enjoyed since the days of Hans Nielsen.

Mrs Purchase also kept faith with the two Czech signings from the 2000 season – the Dryml brothers, Ales and Lukas, who had both gone through a tough first year in the Elite League. The Oxford boss reasoned that if she had stood by them as they came to terms with the high standard of top-flight racing, then she should stand by them after they had enjoyed a season's experience. This was another shrewd move; Lukas, although suffering from a leg injury that actually required surgery (which he kept putting off), rose to the rank of heat-leader, and his elder brother, Ales, also had his moments in 2001, being a more than useful reserve-cum-second-string for the Cheetahs. Backing the efforts of Leigh Adams and the Dryml brothers were Grand Prix riders Brian Andersen, who was on loan from Coventry, and Todd Wiltshire. The fast-gating Wiltshire was a steady scorer for the Cheetahs, who as a club were backed by JT Commercials and a local radio station, Fox FM. However, as the season drew to its close, the Aussie suffered a painful shoulder injury, but kept going for the sake of the club with the injury strapped up, when he really ought to have been resting.

Another Australian, Steve Johnston, captained the 2001 Cheetahs, and proved to be a very popular skipper. You never knew just what 'Johno' would do, as he was somewhat inconsistent in his scoring, but he created a fine team spirit and gave of his best in every race. The side was completed with young Andrew Appleton, who had done much of his early training at Cowley, but came back on loan via Premier League side Newport. It was a baptism of fire for the youngster, but he stuck to his task and made such an impression that Oxford were keen to make his move a permanent one.

The Cheetahs began the season with a 53-37 defeat at Coventry, although it was just a challenge match, with the Aussie duo of Leigh Adams and Steve Johnston showing good form. Oxford then went to Belle Vue for an Elite League encounter on 26 March, and lost by just 5 points, despite a superb 18-point maximum from Adams. The team's first Elite League success came on 30 March, when they defeated Wolverhampton 47-43 at Cowley. After that, the Cheetahs put together a great run and didn't taste defeat again until 30 April, when they lost the return match against Wolverhampton by 53 points to 37. In between, Oxford had shown that they were a force to be reckoned with, having raced five matches in the league, winning three and drawing two. However, the real purple patch began on 18 May, when they beat visitors Poole 54-36, after which they did not lose again until 15 August. Ironically, that was when they travelled to Poole and found the Pirates in a mean mood, and succumbed to a heavy 52-38 reverse.

During their fantastic unbeaten run, Oxford raced fifteen matches, winning fourteen and drawing a superb encounter at Poole on 27 June. Success was tasted away from home at Coventry, Peterborough, King's Lynn (twice) and Wolverhampton. After such a period of triumph, speedway pundits were talking seriously of Oxford as possible Elite League Champions, but the hopes of the supporters received a jolt on 24 August, when Eastbourne stole the points from Sandy Lane courtesy of a thrilling 46-44 success. Coventry then beat Oxford 47-43 the following night at Brandon, but the Cheetahs came back strongly, taking revenge at Eastbourne with a 51-41 victory on 1 September, and that was closely followed up with a 48-42 win at Belle Vue a couple of evenings later.

In 2001, Czech racer Lukas Dryml showed improvement during what was his second season with the Cheetahs to post a league average of 6.82, having scored 102 points from 18 appearances.

Having dispatched Eastbourne in the first round of the Knock-Out Cup, Oxford faced Ipswich at the semi-final stage, with the Witches visiting Cowley on 14 September and riding to an exciting 45-45 draw. Meanwhile, Poole, who were quietly picking up points and were to prove that they too had an interest in the final destination of the Championship, scuppered any hopes Oxford may have had in the Craven Shield competition, beating the Cheetahs both home and away. It was a trying time for Oxford, who appeared to lose a little of their early season sparkle. However, they dug deep, and even though Poole won their final two Elite League matches – both, incidentally, at Peterborough – Oxford had matches in hand, although, of course, they still had to be won.

Finally, the great day came. Tuesday 9 October saw a double-header at Ipswich, and in a super-charged initial clash that went right to the wire and a last-heat decider, Oxford clinched a 45-45 draw and the Elite League point that gave them the Championship by the narrowest of margins. The final heat of the match saw the pairing of Leigh Adams and Todd Wiltshire keep the ever-pressing Chris Louis behind them, while Scott Nicholls sailed off into the night air to win the race. The Cheetahs had secured a total of 58 league points with a match to go, whereas Poole had finished with a total of 57. The second part of the double-header then saw the teams turn around and do the whole thing again, in the second leg of the Knock-Out Cup. This time, however, it was success for the Witches, who won another close contest by 46 points to 44, thereby gaining a place in the final. Having already made sure of the league title, few of the Oxford fans in the large crowd were too bothered about going out of the Knock-Out Cup.

On 19 October, the Cheetahs raced their final Elite League match of the season at Cowley, against Coventry. Unfortunately, it was the visitors who took victory, and they did it brilliantly by 53 points to 37, with only Leigh Adams showing anything like normal Cowley form on his way to a 14-point tally. The result didn't dampen the celebrations after the match, though, when television presenter Kirsty Gallacher handed over the Sky Sports Elite League trophy to jubilant skipper Steve Johnston. The Cheetahs were deserved winners, since they had set the pace right from the opening weeks of the season. It was a just reward too for Vanessa Purchase, who had spared no effort or expense to bring the title back to Cowley.

Looking through the riders, the brilliant Leigh Adams led the way, scoring an amazing 411 points from 32 league matches for a 10.07 average. As a measure of the Cheetahs' solidity, they then boasted no fewer than five riders who finished the season with averages between 6.05 and 7.45. The highest of these was Todd Wiltshire, while the others were Brian Andersen (7.19), Lukas Dryml (6.82), Steve Johnston (6.49) and Ales Dryml (6.05). Oxford had three representatives in the Grand Prix series, with Adams enjoying his highest ever finish in the event, recording 69 points to finish a very creditable fifth overall. After starting well in the first three rounds, Wiltshire tailed off a little, although he could still be reasonably satisfied with 56 points and eighth position. Like his teammates, Brian Andersen took part in all six rounds, scoring a total of 23 points for eighteenth place in the final reckoning.

ELITE LEAGUE

Team	Mts	Won	Drn	Lst	For	Agn	Pts	Bon	Tot
Oxford	**32**	**20**	**5**	**7**	**1,495**	**1,367**	**45**	**13**	**58**
Poole	32	21	2	9	1,538	1,325	44	13	57
Coventry	32	21	2	9	1,518	1,356	44	11	55
Ipswich	32	17	2	13	1,444	1,429	36	7	43
Peterborough	30	12	2	16	1,356	1,329	26	7	33
King's Lynn	32	12	1	19	1,381	1,467	25	7	32
Eastbourne	32	11	3	18	1,373	1,463	25	7	32
Wolverhampton	32	12	0	20	1,397	1,478	24	4	28
Belle Vue	30	7	1	22	1,196	1,484	15	1	16

NOTE: Two matches, Peterborough *v.* Belle Vue (ELA) and Peterborough *v.* Belle Vue (ELB), were not raced.

2002

This was, to say the least, a strange season for the Cowley faithful. Early on, there were signs that the club owners, Steve and Vanessa Purchase, were becoming disillusioned. It was easy to see why. This was the fifth season with the duo in charge and during that time they had bought wisely, culminating in their Championship success of the year before. There were also signs of increased numbers on the terraces. Of course, they were well aware that it is one thing to construct a side that wins a league title, but it is another matter entirely to hold on to it, especially since the system that operates in speedway often ensures that doesn't occur. Added to that, in 2002, there was the introduction of a rule that meant each Elite League outfit could track just one Grand Prix rider.

It therefore became obvious that the Cheetahs would have to release one of their Championship-winning line-up, who was also involved in the GP series, and it was clear that the man to go would be popular Australian Todd Wiltshire. There was no way that his compatriot Leigh Adams would be released. Indeed, Adams' superb scoring again throughout 2002 fully justified his being retained. He was truly magnificent, and only on a solitary occasion during the campaign did he fail to hit double figures. This happened in a league engagement at Coventry on 8 May, when Adams recorded 8+1 points in a narrow 48-42 defeat. Now, a tally of paid 9 points really isn't that bad but, by the impeccable scoring standards the brilliant Australian had set for himself over many years of racing, it was a low return.

Anyway, Leigh Adams was in, whilst Todd Wiltshire was out. This was all too reminiscent of what had occurred after the Oxford successes in 1985 and 1986. There wasn't the Grand Prix to worry about in those days, but David Hawkins, one of the then Northern Sports (Oxford) Ltd directors, could never understand how the rules could take away one of the team's riders almost without reference, and one that the promotion could well have shelled out a hefty fee for too.

Apart from the 'system' leaving the Oxford bosses somewhat fed up, the sport's biggest enemy, namely injuries, also hit the team. Brian Andersen began the league fixtures with 10+2 points at Peterborough on Good Friday, 29 March, when the Cheetahs went down to a single-point defeat, 45-44. Leigh Adams registered 13 points in the match and, to all intents and purposes, Oxford were desperately unlucky not to have tasted victory at the East of England Showground. Regrettably, in the return match at Sandy Lane later that same day, the Cheetahs capitulated and were hammered 52-38. Adams fought a lone battle, scoring 15+1 points, but couldn't prevent the hefty home defeat. After his bright opening at Peterborough, the year quickly became a nightmare for Andersen. The Dane crashed heavily at King's Lynn on 10 April, sustaining a displaced disc in his neck. He was absent from the side until 29 April, when he bravely returned for an away match at Wolverhampton. Clearly, he wasn't fit and following an appearance at Coventry on 8 May, his season was over. Unfortunately, he was still receiving treatment for the injury in 2003 and was forced to quit active racing.

Ales Dryml was another Cheetah to miss meetings, his absences caused after an operation to a shoulder. The Czech often rode in great discomfort and doubtless this was a major factor in a string of disappointing on-track returns. Meanwhile, his brother Lukas was a real puzzle. It would be fair to say that, although the younger of the two Czechs generally impressed in the Grand Prix series, he certainly didn't perform as well as he ought to have done when representing Oxford. Despite his inconsistent form, he did occupy third spot in the Cheetahs' end-of-term averages, with 201 points from 29 league matches achieving a 6.23 figure. However, it surprised none of the regulars on the Sandy Lane terraces when he subsequently moved to Poole for the 2003 season.

Andrew Appleton plugged away until July, but the pace of Elite League racing was understandably hard and he dropped down to the Premier League, linking with Reading, where he became an instant success. His move saw the return to Cowley of the chirpy Alun Rossiter, who began with a score of 3+1 points in a home league match against Belle Vue on 17 July. Rosco struggled in the main, though, and his season finished abruptly on 26 August, when he made a guest appearance for his old side, Poole, against King's Lynn in what was actually the second of two meetings that day against the Norfolk outfit at Wimborne Road. A frightening spill in heat two saw him sustain a serious knee injury after he had been dumped into the safety fence on the pits bend, when King's Lynn's Jernej Kolenko had lost control. Regrettably, this effectively brought the curtain down on Rossiter's racing career.

German racer Joachim Kugelmann was drafted into the Oxford team, followed by Pole Krzysztof Jablonski. The former looked likely to come good, but Jablonski was the better of the two. Had he been available from the start, he could well have developed into a good back-up rider.

Leigh Adams was the out-and-out number one for Oxford in 2002, as emphasised by a total of 444 points from 31 league matches for a hefty 10.23 average.

The away Elite League 'B' fixture at Peterborough never took place and with only fourteen victories to show from the thirty-one matches that did go ahead, the Cheetahs ended up in sixth position amongst the nine participating teams. At the business end of the table, play-offs were introduced to decide the destiny of the Championship and although Eastbourne had topped the table, it was Wolverhampton who landed the major silverware after defeating the Arlington-based club over two legs in the final. In the Knock-Out Cup, Oxford went out at the first hurdle to Wolverhampton, being held to a 45-45 draw at home on 26 April, before losing heavily, 61-29, in the return match at Monmore Green three days afterwards. In the end-of-season Craven Shield competition, the Cheetahs fared little better, finishing last in their group of three. This, despite hard-fought 46-44 wins over both Poole and Eastbourne at Cowley, which were offset by big losses in the away fixtures at Wimborne Road and Arlington respectively.

The backbone of the 2002 side was an Australian triumvirate, headed by the brilliance of Leigh Adams, with solid support from skipper Steve Johnston and the dependable Mark Lemon, who returned to Oxford, having previously represented the side in 1996 and again in 2000. The remarkable Adams remained ever-present over the Cheetahs' 31 league matches and totted up 444 points to achieve a 10.23 average. Meanwhile, Johno, a real Cowley favourite, was always capable of pulling something special out of the bag. A perfect example of this was when he went through the card unbeaten in a home league fixture against King's Lynn on 26 July, netting 17+1 points from six outings. The flamboyant rider finished second in Oxford's statistical rundown, with 246 points from 29 appearances yielding an average of 7.19. Lemon, like Adams, was also ever-present and he had his moments too, especially when he recorded 12+2 points at home to Belle Vue on 17 July, his performance helping the Cheetahs to a 47-42 success. Overall, Lemon totalled 187 points to post a solid 5.57 average.

Individually, in the Grand Prix, Leigh Adams gleaned 127 points from the ten-round series to finish fourth overall, while Lukas Dryml totalled 95 points for tenth spot. Finally, Steve Johnston certainly gave the fans their moneys worth to earn 7 points when he was drafted into the Australian round at Sydney on 26 October.

With the Purchases bowing out at the end of the season, yet another winter of uncertainty lay in store for the diehard Oxford supporters.

ELITE LEAGUE

Team	Mts	Won	Drn	Lst	For	Agn	Pts	Bon	Tot
Eastbourne	32	20	3	9	1,562	1,316	43	15	58
Wolverhampton	32	20	2	10	1,548	1,311	42	12	54
Coventry	32	19	3	10	1,492	1,383	41	9	50
Poole	32	17	1	14	1,455	1,406	35	11	46
Peterborough	31	15	0	16	1,394	1,395	30	7	37
Oxford	**31**	**14**	**2**	**15**	**1,369**	**1,407**	**30**	**5**	**35**
Ipswich	32	11	3	18	1,375	1,494	25	5	30
Belle Vue	32	11	3	18	1,379	1,484	25	4	29
King's Lynn	32	7	1	24	1,247	1,625	15	3	18

NOTE: One match, Peterborough *v.* Oxford (ELB), was not staged.

PLAY-OFFS
Quarter-finals: Wolverhampton 50 Peterborough 39; Coventry 59 Poole 31.
Semi-final: Wolverhampton 51 Coventry 39.
Final (aggregate result): Wolverhampton 93 Eastbourne 87.

2003

After a traumatic close season, following the decision of club owners Steve and Vanessa Purchase to step down, the supporters of Oxford welcomed a new line-up, a new promoter and, indeed, a new team name in 2003. The new boss was Nigel Wagstaff, who had previously been in charge at King's Lynn, where his side had been known as the Silver Machine. Having negotiated a three-year lease with the Purchases, the incoming promoter brought the moniker with him to Sandy Lane, meaning the team would ride as Oxford Silver Machine during his tenure. Although the name change wasn't popular in every quarter, the main thing for the fans was that with 'Waggy' at the helm, it meant speedway in the university city had been saved yet again.

The side had an interesting blend and was led by Nicki Pedersen, the spectacular and tough riding young Dane, who could ride any track well. In support of Pedersen there was stylish Pole Sebastian Ulamek, who, on his day, could beat the best. They were joined by gritty Australian Travis McGowan, Swede Niklas Klingberg, Slovenian Jernej Kolenko, with the big signing, as far as many supporters were concerned, being the return of Todd Wiltshire. Completing a cosmopolitan line-up, the Danish duo of Charlie Gjedde and Jan Staechmann were brought on board to share a reserve berth in a 'doubling up' capacity from their respective Premier League clubs, Swindon and Stoke. Meanwhile, a new competition saw all the sides in the Elite and Premier Leagues racing for the British League Cup, and for this the Oxford asset base was extended to include Andy Smith, a man of many tracks, who the speedway system seemed to move on each year. Effectively, the top-flight teams had to de-strengthen for this particular competition in order to close the gulf between the two leagues and it was felt that Smith's vast experience would be of great benefit. Happily for Oxford, the enthusiasm of Nigel Wagstaff was infectious and, as the season unfolded, the club began to buzz again.

Following a challenge match at Coventry, the season got underway officially with a British League Cup encounter at the Isle of Wight on 18 March, when Oxford suffered a 47-43 defeat to their lower league opponents. The Elite League campaign began at Belle Vue on 31 March and, in a wonderful start, the boys from Cowley returned home with a 46-44 victory. Nicki Pedersen topped the scoring on 11+1 points, while Charlie Gjedde and Todd Wiltshire made telling contributions with tallies of 10 and 9+1 respectively. Oxford opened their home league programme on 4 April, when Wolverhampton were sent packing by 58 points to 32. In notching 13+2 points, Pedersen was paid for the lot, while Wiltshire scored 13+1 and Seba Ulamek romped to a brilliant four-ride maximum to send the fans home in a buoyant mood. However, defeats were to follow at Poole in a league fixture and at Swindon in the British League Cup. The match against their oldest rivals at Blunsdon on 10 April ended in a 48-41 loss on the night, but the result was later amended to 48-37 in favour of the Robins since Oxford's use of Polish rider Lukasz Jankowski was deemed ineligible and the 4 points he scored were deducted.

The team returned to winning ways at home to Belle Vue and followed it up with another Sandy Lane success against Coventry a week later. In between, though, they lost on the road at both Eastbourne and Peterborough. Unfortunately, Jernej Kolenko was finding points hard to come by, while Niklas Klingberg wasn't showing the form that everyone knew he was capable of. The match at Peterborough proved to be the Swede's last appearance for the side and in the return fixture at Coventry on 19 April former Oxford Cheetah Craig Boyce replaced him. The meeting resulted in another defeat by 49 points to 41, with the Aussie having a quiet time in recording just 5 points from five starts.

After beating Ipswich in a league match at Cowley, the Silver Machine travelled to the home of the Witches for a Knock-Out Cup tie on 5 May and claimed a 49-41 victory as they finally broke their away duck. Oxford completed the job against Ipswich four days later, with a comprehensive 55-35 scoreline taking them safely through to the semi-finals. The match was particularly memorable for a fantastic 15-point maximum from Todd Wiltshire, dubbed by many as 'Mr Oxford Speedway'.

Having lost at Wolverhampton on 12 May, it was Poole who provided the opposition in the next home fixture eleven days afterwards. In a meeting to forget, Oxford were beaten 49-41, leaving many folk shaking their heads. The general feeling amongst the patrons was that the team needed a tweak or two. Despite this, home and away victories followed against Reading in the British League Cup, with Travis McGowan impressing in both matches, courtesy of 11+1 points at Smallmead and an unbeaten 14+1 at Cowley. The Silver Machine were to overcome Peterborough in a home league match on 11 June, but then went on a losing streak, suffering four straight defeats on the road. During this spell, Steve Masters and highly rated Dane Niels-Kristian Iversen had linked with the side to share a reserve berth, and the latter had given a very good account when netting 10 points at Eastbourne. The dismal run concluded with a 54-36 reverse at Peterborough on 25 June, when Nicki Pedersen's stint with the club came to an unceremonious end after a heated argument with Nigel Wagstaff. The Oxford promoter acted quickly to replace the axed Dane, bringing in charismatic American ace Greg Hancock. In what amounted to quite a reshuffle of his pack, Waggy also ousted Masters, Iversen and Craig Boyce, with Slovenian Matej Ferjan joining the side, while Andy Smith assumed a full-time role.

Andy Smith celebrated his full team position with a sensational 15-point maximum against Swindon in the British League Cup at Sandy Lane on 27 June, when another newcomer to the squad was young Czech rider Lubos Tomicek. Shortly after this, a league encounter at Poole on 2 July marked the club debut of both Greg Hancock and Matej Ferjan. It wasn't a winning start for the pair, though, as the Pirates edged the match 46-44, with Ferjan scoring 10 points and Hancock 9+1. Undoubtedly, the man of the match for the Silver Machine was Charlie Gjedde, who tallied 15 points and had become the darling of the Oxford supporters. The arrival of Hancock sparked an upturn in team spirit and the side went on a five-match winning run in the Elite League, before crashing to a 54-36 loss at Wolverhampton on 18 August. They recovered well from that setback, however, and didn't taste defeat again in their remaining league fixtures. The strong finish hoisted Oxford to fourth place in the table, as the signing of Hancock was hailed a stroke of genius. A place in the play-offs was theirs and to Poole the side travelled for a one-off semi-final on 22 September. In front of a reported 3,500 gate, the Silver Machine lads rode their socks off and after heat eleven, the match score was deadlocked at 33-33. Regrettably, for the travelling Oxford fans, the Pirates came up with the goods when it mattered and eventually clinched victory by 48 points to 42.

The club's final league averages, unsurprisingly, saw Greg Hancock in pole position, with 123 points from eleven matches giving the American a 9.50 figure. Whilst with the club, Nicki Pedersen's efforts gleaned 181 points from 15 appearances to yield a 9.20 average, putting the Dane second in Oxford's statistical table. Todd Wiltshire occupied third position on a solid 8.37 figure, having recorded 276 points from 27 matches. The mega-popular Charlie Gjedde also posted an excellent league average, with 164 points from 19 appearances giving the cheerful Dane a final figure of 8.09. Behind Gjedde in the statistical rundown was Seba Ulamek, who wasn't able to repeat his early-season maximum against Wolverhampton, yet all the same often caught the eye with his superb riding style at Cowley. The polished Pole registered 134 points from 19 matches to average 6.94.

In the British League Cup, Oxford finished third in their group of five, having won four and drawn one of their eight matches. Meanwhile, in the Knock-Out Cup, the Silver Machine suffered another semi-final defeat at the hands of Poole, going down by 100 points to 80 on aggregate.

The year also saw Nigel Wagstaff enter a second team in the Conference League, with the side branded as the Silver Machine Academy. Former Peterborough rider Pete Chapman was put in charge of the youngsters and guided them to third position in the thirteen-team division. The side won fourteen of their 24 matches and lost on ten occasions, using a variety of riders including Darren Andrews, Ben Barker, Joe Cook, Carl Downs, Chris Johnson, Chris Mills, Jason Newitt, Ricky Scarboro and Chris Schramm. Bizarrely, Andy Smith also appeared in one match at home to Carmarthen on 6 June, when he comfortably racked-up an 18-point maximum. This

Todd Wiltshire gave great service to the Oxford Silver
Machine throughout 2003, scoring 276 points from 27
league appearances for a solid 8.37 average.

came about because the veteran racer was only getting rides for the senior Oxford team in the
British League Cup and was therefore eligible to appear in the Conference League. Although
the inclusion of 'Smudger' in the side raised many eyebrows, in truth it was meant more as a
statement that Smith was still ready and able to ride. Not long after, of course, he did attain a full-
time position in Oxford's main side. The youngsters in the Silver Machine Academy certainly
impressed, with Cook tallying 218 points from 18 appearances to top the side's scoring and
average 9.76. Meanwhile, Schramm posted a 9.65 figure, while the diminutive Barker performed
brilliantly to achieve an 8.34 average. Mills and Johnson also did very well too, finishing with
league averages of 7.78 and 7.62 respectively. Finally, in the Knock-Out Cup, Oxford lost to
Mildenhall in the first round, going down 97-82 on aggregate.

ELITE LEAGUE

Team	Mts	Won	Drn	Lst	For	Agn	Pts	Bon	Tot
Poole	28	20	1	7	1,335	1,182	41	11	52
Coventry	28	17	0	11	1,295	1,224	34	10	44
Peterborough	28	16	0	12	1,325	1,195	32	8	40
Oxford	**28**	**16**	**0**	**12**	**1,295**	**1,224**	**32**	**8**	**40**
Wolverhampton	28	14	1	13	1,248	1,265	29	6	35
Eastbourne	28	12	1	15	1,261	1,250	25	8	33
Belle Vue	28	9	1	18	1,219	1,298	19	5	24
Ipswich	28	6	0	22	1,088	1,428	12	0	12

PLAY-OFFS
Semi-finals: Coventry 60 Peterborough 30; Poole 48 Oxford 42.
Final (aggregate result): Poole 100 Coventry 79.

CONFERENCE LEAGUE

Team	Mts	Won	Drn	Lst	For	Agn	Pts	Bon	Tot
Mildenhall	24	18	1	5	1,236	917	37	10	47
Rye House	24	18	0	6	1,178	936	36	9	45

Oxford	24	14	0	10	1,179	959	28	11	39
Boston	24	15	0	9	1,103	1,017	30	8	38
Swindon	24	14	0	10	1,042	1,036	28	5	33
Buxton	24	12	1	11	1,095	1,054	25	7	32
Newcastle	24	13	0	11	1,072	1,070	26	5	31
Sheffield	24	10	2	12	1,115	1,016	22	8	30
Wimbledon	24	9	1	14	1,028	1,126	19	5	24
Wolverhampton	24	10	1	13	1,005	1,116	21	2	23
Carmarthen	24	8	0	16	956	1,177	16	4	20
Peterborough	24	6	1	17	950	1,187	13	3	16
Newport	24	5	1	18	895	1,243	11	1	12

2004

Nigel Wagstaff looked forward to his second term as the Oxford promoter with optimism and, after a good season of racing, earned a place in the play-offs by sheer hard work and belief. At the beginning of the campaign, Waggy put together a very fair side. Naturally, Greg Hancock was back and there were few better captains in the sport than the vastly experienced Californian. Also back were Travis McGowan and Seba Ulamek, while from Newport, where he had been on loan, came another of Wagstaff's assets, namely the all-action youngster Niels-Kristian Iversen. The Dane had briefly appeared for the Silver Machine in 2003, but linked with the club on a full-time basis in 2004, having served his British speedway apprenticeship in the Premier League. Swede Emil Kramer was used at the start of the season, but he didn't last long and returned on loan to Hull in the second tier of racing. However, before departing, he did give notice of his ability when beating Mark Loram in a Knock-Out Cup tie against Arena-Essex at Cowley on 26 March. To complete the initial starting line-up, Swedish youngster Jonas Davidsson was secured via Reading, while American Ryan Fisher came on loan from Coventry. Dane Tom P. Madsen also joined as a squad member to be used as and when necessary, when his Premier League commitments with King's Lynn would allow.

Rafal Dobrucki was to replace Emil Kramer after Nigel Wagstaff had gone 'shopping' in Poland. By all accounts, the rider wasn't too keen on coming to Britain to start with, but he was to do well and his hard-riding style proved very popular with the fans. The signing of the Pole was typical of Wagstaff, who wasn't one to let the grass grow under his feet. Indeed, if there was a need for strengthening his side at any time, then he was always on the lookout for talent.

Oxford's season got underway at Poole on 17 March, when they went down 51-44 in the first leg of the so-called Air-Tek Challenge. This saw the riders giving their services on a voluntary basis in order to offset the costs of having air safety barriers installed at all Elite League circuits. The action began at Sandy Lane with the Knock-Out Cup fixture against Arena-Essex, when a cracker of a match finally resulted in a narrow 47-46 success for the Silver Machine. Defeat followed three days later at Wolverhampton in the side's first league meeting of the season, despite a sublime 18-point maximum from Greg Hancock. Oxford quickly gained revenge, when beating the West Midlands outfit 52-43 in the return match on 2 April. A home victory followed against Ipswich, before the Silver Machine headed out of the Knock-Out Cup at Arena-Essex on 7 April, albeit by the smallest of margins. A tight affair ended in a 48-46 win for the Hammers, meaning Oxford went out of the competition by 94 points to 93 on aggregate.

The club's oldest rivals, Swindon, had returned to top-flight racing at the start of the season, having last competed at Elite League level in 1998, and it was the Wiltshire side who recorded a 54-42 win at Blunsdon on 8 April. However, in a tense return match the following day, it was Oxford who emerged on top courtesy of a 49-44 scoreline. Rafal Dobrucki gave a wonder show to net 14+1 points, while Lukas Dryml, riding as a guest replacement for Greg Hancock, tallied 10 as the Silver Machine dug deep to dispatch the local enemy. Dobrucki was again in excellent form a week later, notching 15+1 points in a 48-45 success over Poole in the second leg of the Air-Tek Challenge.

Concerns over the initially low returns from Ryan Fisher were allayed by Oxford's good home form, which saw successive victories posted against Belle Vue, Arena-Essex, Eastbourne and Peterborough. Fisher was a battler, though, and by the last of those four matches the Californian had turned the corner, scoring 9+1 points in the 54-38 win over Peterborough on 24 May. Away success was proving elusive, however, and following losses at Poole and Arena-Essex, the Silver Machine endured a complete and utter nightmare at Coventry on 27 May. The match saw the Oxford team reduced to only four riders by the fourth race of the contest. Jonas Davidsson was hurt in heat two when his machine landed on top of him after he had laid it down to avoid a stricken opponent. Two races later, Seba Ulamek was inadvertently struck by teammate Tom P. Madsen after partially locking up in front of the Dane. All three injured riders ended up going to hospital and, with no reserve riders left on track, the Silver Machine went down to a hefty 58-36 defeat. Regrettably, Ulamek sustained the worst of the injuries from the carnage, receiving a broken collarbone.

Thankfully, Jonas Davidsson was fit enough to ride when Oxford entertained Coventry in the corresponding Elite League 'A' fixture on 5 June, although the line-up did include two guests in David Norris and Andrew Moore. The rider replacement facility was also in operation for Rafal Dobrucki, but despite not being at full strength, the side went on the rampage to crush their opponents 71-21 and eradicate the memory of that dreadful evening at Brandon. Travis McGowan, Norris and Greg Hancock headed the scoring with paid maximums, scoring 17+1 points, 16+2 and 11+4 respectively, while the remaining three team members were also paid for double figures: Ryan Fisher 11+1, Davidsson 9+2 and Moore 7+3. The confidence gained from that performance was evident at Belle Vue two evenings later, when Oxford claimed their first away win of the season by 46 points to 44, the side being superbly led by 13 points from the imperious Hancock.

Oxford's inspired form continued unabated at Ipswich on 10 June, when they again clinched a 46-44 victory. Greg Hancock once more led from the front with a 15-point maximum, while Niels-Kristian Iversen gave an excellent performance to register 11+1. Another determined showing followed at Eastbourne four days later, although the Silver Machine fell just short of completing a hat-trick of away wins, going down 47-46. After gaining a home success over Wolverhampton, Seba Ulamek returned to the side for the return match at Monmore Green on 28 June. The Pole looked understandably tentative on his way to just 1 point from four starts, as Oxford were eclipsed 58-35.

A powerful Poole side arrived at Sandy Lane on 2 July, when the patrons were treated to a speedway classic that saw the lead fluctuate before the Pirates sealed a 47-46 victory. This was in spite of Ryan Fisher's heroics from a reserve berth, which culminated in a tally of 15+2 points from seven outings. Oxford got back to winning ways at home to Eastbourne, with defeats following at Peterborough and Ipswich. Unfortunately, the latter match at Foxhall Heath on 15 July was to be Seba Ulamek's final appearance for the side, as he subsequently crashed at Torun in his homeland and re-broke his collarbone. The Silver Machine were to operate the rider replacement facility in his absence for the rest of the season.

There was a particularly special night at Cowley on 23 July, for not only did the Silver Machine defeat old foes Swindon 53-41, but a reunion of former riders also took place, organised by Pete Seaton and co-author Glynn Shailes. Adding significance to the occasion was the fact that Swindon Speedway had opened on the same date back in 1949, when Oxford had first locked horns with the Robins, so it wasn't just a reunion, but an anniversary as well. Amongst a whole host of former riders who gathered together for the occasion were Dennis Gray, Jim Wright and Alf Viccary, who had all ridden for Oxford in the Blunsdon opener, as well as Ivor Atkinson, who had represented the Robins on that special day fifty-five years previously. The media attention this generated was wonderful, with both South Today on the

BBC and Central News (Sport) from ITV covering the event, as well as BBC Radio Oxford and local newspaper the *Oxford Mail*.

Home wins were recorded against Peterborough, Arena-Essex and Coventry, before the Elite League 'B' fixture came around against Poole on 27 August. The Pirates had taken the league points on their previous visit on 2 July, but this second encounter was to dispel the often misplaced theory that speedway is predictable, as Oxford thrashed the league's table-topper's 65-29. The amazing Greg Hancock raced through the card to post an undefeated 13+2 points, whilst the rest of the side all contributed strongly, thus: Travis McGowan 15+2, Ryan Fisher 10+3, Niels-Kristian Iversen 9+3, Rafal Dobrucki 9+1 and Jonas Davidsson 9. Although they were to defeat Belle Vue at Cowley the following week, on their travels it was a different story and Oxford were to make it nine straight defeats in a row on the road since the win at Ipswich on 10 June. Making matters worse, they slipped to a 45-44 defeat at home to Ipswich on 10 September, leaving their play-off hopes hanging in the balance.

Somehow, Nigel Wagstaff got his troops to perform when it mattered most, as Oxford travelled to Coventry on 13 September and secured a vital 48-42 win. Greg Hancock returned to his former home track to notch 12+1 points, being ably backed by an identical tally from Niels-Kristian Iversen and a determined 10+1 from another ex-Coventry rider, Ryan Fisher. Finally, in order to cram in all the Elite League fixtures, Peterborough's 'home' match against the Silver Machine was held at Arena-Essex on 15 September and this saw Oxford clinch a place in the play-offs with a gritty 46-44 success. Home track rider Mark Loram replaced

Inspirational American Greg Hancock headed Oxford's league averages in 2004 with a 9.94 figure, having raced to 374 points from thirty-one matches.

Hancock and proved a shrewd choice of guest in registering a 15-point maximum, while Iversen again came good in tallying 14+1.

Wolverhampton beckoned for the play-off semi-final on 20 September, when Greg Hancock was again an absentee. Fellow American Josh Larsen deputised for Hancock, but on the night there was little the Silver Machine representatives could do to stem the tide as the Wolves swept to an emphatic 61-33 triumph. Only Niels-Kristian Iversen, riding like a tiger, was able to take the fight to the home men, all of whom were in great form. Iversen never stopped trying and his 13+1 points were earned in spectacular style.

The season at Cowley ended with an emotional night on 15 October, with the staging of a meeting billed as the Todd Wiltshire Farewell – The Final Ride. As a measure of the Australian's standing within the speedway, some of the sport's greats participated, including Sam Ermolenko, Billy Hamill and Nicki Pedersen, as well as many of his compatriots such as Adam Shields, Craig Watson, Craig Boyce, Steve Johnston, Mark Lemon and Davey Watt. Meanwhile, former Oxford legend Hans Nielsen and recently crowned World Champion Jason Crump were also in attendance to pay tribute to Wiltshire. Despite inclement weather, there was a good turn-out on the terraces, although the wet stuff eventually came out on top and the meeting was abandoned after heat twelve, with Mikael Max, who had been victorious in all three of his races at that stage, declared a deserving winner.

Looking through the league averages for the season, Greg Hancock again finished on top of the pack, with 374 points from 31 appearances yielding a 9.94 figure. Seba Ulamek occupied second place in the rundown, having accrued 107 points from 16 matches for a 6.88 average. Third spot was filled by Travis McGowan, who recorded a 6.74 figure, having plundered 254 points from his 36 appearances. In the Grand Prix series, Hancock enjoyed a superb year and also maintained his ever-present record in the competition, with 137 points from the nine rounds giving him third place overall. Meanwhile, Niels-Kristian Iversen made a wildcard appearance in the Danish GP at Parken, Copenhagen on 26 June and acquitted himself well, scoring 13 points. Prior to that, Rafal Dobrucki had appeared in the Czech Republic round at the Marketa Stadium in Prague on 15 May, when registering 5 points.

Oxford's other team, the Silver Machine Academy, replicated their performance of the previous season by again taking third place in the Conference League. In mid-season, Pete Chapman, who had done so much to establish Conference level racing at Cowley, stood down to be replaced as team manager by Bryn Williams, a respected and important member of Nigel Wagstaff's back-up department at Sandy Lane. The side included a young Australian named Sam Martin, whose father, Mark, had ridden for Canterbury at National League level in 1981 and 1982. Also new to the set-up were Danny Norton and Craig Branney, while Jamie Courtney came on board after a brief spell with Swindon Sprockets. From the team of 2003, Ben Barker, Chris Mills and Chris Schramm were retained, making the Academy a very potent force.

Craig Branney topped the side's averages on a 9.97 figure, having netted 280 points from 23 matches. Chris Schramm wasn't far behind, with 231 points from 19 appearances achieving a 9.78 figure. Chris Mills also had a high 9.10 average, having recorded 84 points from ten matches, his appearances in the team being unfortunately restricted by a number of injuries. Aside from those already mentioned, others who appeared for the side included Paul Cooper, Carl Downs, Jason Newitt, Ricky Scarboro and Mark Woods. In the Knock-Out Cup, the youngsters reached the semi-final, but came up against all-conquering Mildenhall, losing 96-91 on aggregate.

ELITE LEAGUE

Team	Mts	Won	Drn	Lst	For	Agn	Pts	Bon	Tot
Poole	36	23	2	11	1,721	1,603	48	13	61
Wolverhampton	36	21	0	15	1,729	1,586	42	16	58

Ipswich	36	21	0	15	1,701	1,626	42	11	53
Eastbourne	36	18	3	15	1,699	1,632	39	11	50
Oxford	**36**	**19**	**0**	**17**	**1,679**	**1,672**	**38**	**10**	**48**
Swindon	36	18	3	15	1,657	1,667	39	6	45
Belle Vue	35	17	0	18	1,630	1,597	34	9	43
Arena-Essex	36	16	0	20	1,651	1,679	32	8	40
Peterborough	35	12	2	21	1,514	1,722	26	2	28
Coventry	36	9	0	27	1,565	1,762	18	3	21

NOTE: One match, Belle Vue *v.* Peterborough (ELB), was not ridden.

PLAY-OFFS
Quarter-finals: Wolverhampton 61 Oxford 33; Ipswich 55 Eastbourne 39.
Semi-final: Wolverhampton 45 Ipswich 45 (Wolverhampton's Mikael Max subsequently defeated Scott Nicholls in a run-off to take his side through to the final).
Final (aggregate result): Poole 112 Wolverhampton 71.

CONFERENCE LEAGUE

Team	Mts	Won	Drn	Lst	For	Agn	Pts	Bon	Tot
Mildenhall	24	21	0	3	1,254	952	42	10	52
Rye House	24	19	0	5	1,206	991	38	9	47
Oxford	**24**	**17**	**0**	**7**	**1,199**	**979**	**34**	**10**	**44**
Armadale	24	15	0	9	1,185	990	30	8	38
Boston	24	14	1	9	1,171	1,034	29	8	37
Buxton	24	13	1	10	1,093	1,100	27	7	34
Wimbledon	24	11	0	13	1,138	1,080	22	6	28
Weymouth	24	10	1	13	1,047	1,143	21	5	26
Stoke	24	9	1	14	1,054	1,139	19	4	23
Swindon	24	8	0	16	1,063	1,158	16	5	21
Newcastle	24	7	0	17	998	1,203	14	2	16
Carmarthen	24	5	1	18	998	1,187	11	4	15
Newport	24	4	1	19	883	1,333	9	0	9

2005

The winter months leading up to the 2005 season were full of problems, but as most regulars at Cowley would readily confess, they were used to it. Firstly, their stadium landlords indicated that they wanted to stage greyhound racing on Fridays, with promoter Nigel Wagstaff being offered Thursday as his race-night for speedway. The irony here was that Thursday had been the original raceday for Oxford, when they had opened for post-war racing. However, Waggy was most concerned since all his business arrangements and decisions had been made on the assumption that the club would be running on Friday evenings. Concerns over this issue dragged on, but eventually Oxford did agree to race on a Thursday.

Understandably, Nigel Wagstaff was in a buoyant mood after he had managed to agree terms with exciting American racer Billy Hamill, who had been forced out of British speedway in 2004 due to team-building restrictions. Rules and regulations had previously seen fellow countryman Greg Hancock without a British club until Oxford had paved the way for him to return midway through the 2003 campaign. Now Wagstaff had the two great Americans in tow

Oxford Silver Machine Academy celebrate their League Championship success in 2005. From left to right, back row: Marc Andrews, Sam Martin, Jamie Courtney, Ben Barker, Scott Courtney, Kyle Hughes, Bryn Williams (team manager). Front row, kneeling: Jason Newitt, Craig Branney, Chris Mills, Chris Bint (mascot).

again, the pair having forged such a devastating partnership for several seasons previously at Cradley Heath and then at Coventry. There were problems, though, and these centred on the fact that Coventry were hoping to sign the England number one, Scott Nicholls, from Ipswich. The Witches didn't want to let the rider go, so asked for full payment of a substantial transfer fee, rumoured to be of £50,000. Understandably, Coventry then demanded a full transfer fee from Oxford for both Hancock and Hamill, who were assets of the Brandon-based club. This was a body blow to Wagstaff, but after a somewhat unsettling period of time, he was eventually allowed to sign the duo on loan.

With Danish youngster Niels-Kristian Iversen and battling Aussie Travis McGowan also on board to back the Californian duo, the prospects looked good for the season ahead. Completing the side's starting line-up were Dane Tom P. Madsen and returning Czech Lukas Dryml, while Mr Wagstaff sprang a surprise when he signed reigning Latvian Champion Kjastas Puodzhuks, who was just eighteen years of age and full of promise. This was typical of the way Waggy ran his business at Oxford. He always had his eye on both his team and what was happening 'over the water', and was never afraid to bring in new riders, as would be shown on many occasions in the months that followed.

Having put together a sound Silver Machine side, attention turned to the Conference League team, as Oxford became the only club from the Elite League to also run in British speedway's third tier of racing. Bryn Williams masterminded the operation and convinced his charges that they were better than anyone else in the division. The reward was that the Silver Machine Academy went on to secure the Championship by a single point ahead of Wimbledon. Craig Branney was the team's leading rider, with 210 points from 17 league appearances giving the Cumbrian-born youngster a huge 10.80 average. Jamie Courtney also made tremendous progress to post a 9.40 average, having notched 223 points from 20 matches. Ben Barker and Chris Mills finished with impressive averages of 9.13 and 8.91 respectively, while other regulars in the side included Kyle

Hughes, John Branney (the younger sibling of Craig) and Sam Martin. In the Knock-Out Cup, the youngsters reached the quarter-final stage, before losing 96-93 on aggregate to Mildenhall. Meanwhile, in a highly successful campaign, the Oxford Academy finished as runners-up in the two other competitions in which they participated, namely the Conference League Four-Team Championship and the Conference League Pairs Championship.

Returning to the main side and the campaign began at Sandy Lane on 17 March, when Oxford entertained Wolverhampton in the first leg of the Air-Tek Trophy. Welshman Freddie Williams, who had won the World Championship in 1950 and 1953, opened the season, enjoying a ride around the track and meeting all the riders, before taking in the racing from the comfortable surroundings of the stadium restaurant with his wife Pat, a former ice skater. The Silver Machine shaded a close match 47-41, with Greg Hancock and Billy Hamill looking positively brilliant as they rolled back the years to score 12+2 and 11+1 points respectively. The return encounter took place at Monmore Green on 21 March, as the riders completed the second of a two-year agreement to offset the costs of installing air safety barriers at all Elite League venues. Wolves went on the rampage to win 55-38 and secure an aggregate success, with only Hancock offering any real resistance in tallying 16+1.

Oxford's league fixtures began with defeats at Peterborough and Swindon, with the season really hitting the buffers in the second of those two meetings at Blunsdon on 24 March. In heat nine, Billy Hamill held a comfortable lead over former Oxford rider Jonas Davidsson, when the American's chain snapped on the pits bend, sending him tumbling. With little time to react, Davidsson inadvertently hit the stricken rider and the result was sickening for both Hamill and Oxford Speedway. The American suffered broken ribs and torn muscle damage, while a large part of his back was also broken. Added to that, the broken ribs punctured a lung and he lost a lot of blood. Hamill was put into intensive care and a difficult recovery process began. He was to be out of action until the middle of June and then, understandably, took time to find his feet.

Kjastas Puodzhuks wasn't seen again after the loss at Swindon, having struggled to adapt to the pace of the Elite League, and defeat followed at home to Swindon on Good Friday, 25 March, when visiting skipper Leigh Adams romped to a 15-point maximum. Oxford registered their first league win at Arena-Essex on 30 March, when 15 points from Niels-Kristian Iversen led them to a 49-41 success. The first of what were to be many team re-declarations then saw Jesper B. Jensen brought into the side as defeat was suffered at Eastbourne. Swede Stefan Andersson followed the cheery Dane into the team at the expense of an out-of-form Lukas Dryml, with Chris Mills and Craig Branney sharing a 'doubling-up' role in one of the reserve berths. This seemed to work wonders as the Silver Machine claimed a 49-46 win against Peterborough at Cowley on 14 April, however, this was offset seven days later when Arena-Essex left Oxford with a 48-46 victory under their belts. Nigel Wagstaff reacted by dispensing with the 'doubling-up' reserves and signed veteran Swede Henrik Gustafsson, but a further home defeat came against Coventry on 5 May, the Bees cantering to a 54-40 success.

More losses occurred on the road at Coventry and Peterborough, before the Silver Machine recorded only their third league win of the season at home to Poole on 12 May. Prior to the match, Nigel Wagstaff had appointed the Reverend Hedley Feast as the club chaplain and, whether it was divine inspiration or not, this seemed to do the trick as the Silver Machine rode to a surprise 49-41 victory over the high-flying Pirates. With Greg Hancock injured, Peterborough's Peter Karlsson was an excellent guest in netting 11+1 points, while 'Henka' Gustafsson gave a vintage display to score 9+3. Hancock returned to the side four days later, but he couldn't prevent Oxford from losing heavily, 59-35, at Belle Vue in the Knock-Out Cup and, although they defeated the Manchester side 49-41 in the return leg on 19 May, they made a hasty exit from the competition. The away match at Belle Vue had marked the first appearance in the side of Pole Tomasz Bajerski, who replaced the axed Tom P. Madsen in yet another team change. The poor results continued with a defeat at Poole and whilst a welcome home win came against Wolverhampton on 2 June, further losses were encountered in the return match at the home of the Wolves and also at Arena-Essex.

Greg Hancock's 12+1 points and 10+1 from Jesper B. Jensen inspired Oxford to a 48-46 win against Ipswich in a hard-fought fixture at Cowley on 9 June. However, defeat in the corresponding meeting at Foxhall Heath was followed by another change to the line-up as the merry-go-round continued. This saw the fit-again Billy Hamill reintroduced, along with Russian racer Renat Gafurov. Meanwhile, Stefan Andersson and Jesper B. Jensen dropped out, the latter eventually relocating to Peterborough. The Silver Machine celebrated Hamill's return by defeating Arena-Essex 49-41 at Sandy Lane on 16 June. Niels-Kristian Iversen dashed to an unbeaten 14+1 points, while Hancock suffered just one loss to Mark Loram on his way to a score of 14. Although he looked a little rusty, Hamill at least recorded a race win as he tallied 6 points from four programmed starts.

Tomasz Bajerski's stint in the Oxford side didn't last long and, after a home loss to Coventry on 23 June, German youngster Tobias Kroner was introduced. Unfortunately, the loss to the Bees was to be the start of a depressing run that saw ten straight defeats, four at home and six on their travels, as the Silver Machine became rooted at the foot of the Elite League standings. During this period, Renat Gafurov wasn't seen again after making only his third appearance for the club at Swindon on 7 July, with various riders called upon to plug the gap in the side. Polish rider Pawel Staszek had been introduced to the declared line-up as the Russian's replacement towards the end of July, but in the event he didn't make an appearance until some weeks later. In the meantime, the dismal spell finally ended on 15 August, when Oxford forced a 45-45 draw at Wolverhampton, thanks to 14 points from a resurgent Billy Hamill and 11 from Greg Hancock. That seemed to galvanise the side and, with Staszek making a belated debut on 18 August, they strained every sinew to eke out a 46-44 victory over Poole at Sandy Lane. The cornerstone of the win being brilliant displays from Hamill and Niels-Kristian Iversen, with 15+1 and 13+1 points respectively. A week later, Staszek made his second and final appearance for the club in a 50-41 home success over Eastbourne, as Iversen (14) and Hamill (13+1) again starred, aided by a typically determined showing from Travis McGowan, who recorded 14+2 points.

After a home defeat against Peterborough, Nigel Wagstaff's final throw of the dice saw Freddie Eriksson and Chris Mills brought into the team to replace Tobias Kroner and Pawel Staszek. At last, the Silver Machine seemed to have the right combination, as they took victory in home matches against Eastbourne and Swindon, the only blemish being a 54-40 loss at Ipswich on 6 October.

Oxford Silver Machine salute the Cowley faithful after taking victory in the 2005 Craven Shield. From left to right, back row: Billy Hamill, Greg Hancock, Henrik Gustafsson. Front row: Nigel Wagstaff (promoter/team manager), Jamie Courtney, Travis McGowan, Niels-Kristian Iversen, Freddie Eriksson, Chris Mills, Bryn Williams (assistant team manager).

Oxford carried their good form into the Craven Shield to top their group after gaining home and away victories against Swindon, plus a Sandy Lane success over Wolverhampton. They subsequently met Eastbourne and Belle Vue in the three-legged semi-final and forged a route through after finishing level on 107 points with the Eagles, while the Aces from Manchester totalled 92. The Silver Machine, therefore, again squared up to Eastbourne in the final, with Poole being the other competing side. The first leg took place at Arlington Stadium on 22 October, when the Eagles finished first on 41 points. Oxford were only just behind on 40 though, while Poole scored 27. Four evenings later, the second leg at Poole saw the Silver Machine move ahead on aggregate courtesy of 39 points, while the Pirates totalled 35 and Eastbourne 34. Although the Eagles recorded 39 points to win amidst a great atmosphere in the deciding leg at Cowley on 28 October, it was Oxford who took overall victory thanks to their tally of 36 points. On aggregate, that totted up to 115 points for the Silver Machine, with Eastbourne in second place on 114 and Poole in third spot on 95, having totalled 33 on the night. Aptly, in a nail-biting climax, it was Billy Hamill who won the last heat, with Henka Gustafsson grabbing third position to give Oxford the glory. On an evening to really savour for the loyal supporters, in the second part of a double-header the Silver Machine then defeated Wolverhampton in their last Elite League fixture to secure the match points and the aggregate bonus, thereby handing the wooden spoon to unlucky Arena-Essex. However, no sooner were the celebrations over than Nigel Wagstaff announced he was quitting or as he put it 'taking a sabbatical' from the sport.

Looking at the rider statistics, Greg Hancock headed the league averages for the third year on the bounce, with 347 points from thirty matches giving the Californian a 9.30 figure. Billy Hamill finished as runner-up to his compatriot, as 140 points from eighteen appearances yielded a 7.95 average. This only served to emphasise what might have been for Oxford, had Hamill been able to enjoy an injury-free campaign. Freddie Eriksson's short end-of-season spell produced a 7.81 average, while Niels-Kristian Iversen (7.47), Jesper B. Jensen (6.69) and Travis McGowan (6.46) all posted useful figures. Looking briefly at the Grand Prix, Hancock enjoyed a wonderful term at the sharp edge of the sport, totalling 144 points to finish as runner-up to Jason Crump, the American's season including a brilliant victory in the Latvian round at Daugavpils on 9 September.

Aside from all the team alterations, the turbulent season had also seen several changes made to the number eight rider over the months since March, with the position held at various times by Craig Branney, Michal Makovsky, Brent Werner, Emil Kramer and Lubos Tomicek.

Finally, an off-track event that occurred during 2005 was the Oxford Cheetahs Reunion 1985-1986, which took place at the behest of Nigel Wagstaff. This was a wonderful idea and the club's former press officer Glynn Shailes was given the task of working with Waggy in tracing the riders who had helped Oxford to secure back-to-back league titles in those two glorious years. A small committee, which included Tempus Publishing's sales director Martin Palmer, were to deal with attaining sponsorship for a golf tournament and the arranging of a reunion dinner, whilst Mr Shailes assisted with the production of a special brochure for the occasion. After much hard work, the event became a reality and took place over two days, on 15 and 16 September. Regrettably, only Marvyn Cox, the late Simon Wigg and the late Nigel Sparshott were absent, yet with Wiggy's children, Abigail and Ricki, in attendance on both days, together with his widow Charlie (now happily remarried), it certainly seemed as if the former track great was present in spirit. Hans Nielsen looked as fit as ever and his children, Daisy and Daniel, showed they were both excellent golfers, just like their famous father. In addition to the riders, former presenter Peter York was also welcomed, as were the promoters of those two fabulous years, Bernard Crapper and John Payne. The event was hailed a great success, with both the local and speedway press affording it excellent coverage.

The former riders and management members who attended the Oxford Cheetahs Reunion 1985-1986, which was successfully staged as a two-day event in 2005. From left to right, back row: Peter York (presenter), Klaus Lausch, Hans Nielsen, Per Sorensen, John Tremblin (junior team manager), Bernard Crapper (co-promoter/team manager), John Payne (co-promoter), Jens Rasmussen, Phil Roberts (Oxford Cubs), Alastair Stevens. Front row, kneeling: Mel Taylor, Troy Butler, Andy Grahame, Jon Surman, Kevin Smart, Nigel De'Ath.

ELITE LEAGUE

Team	Mts	Won	Drn	Lst	For	Agn	Pts	Bon	Tot
Belle Vue	36	24	0	12	1,766	1,520	48	13	61
Coventry	36	23	0	13	1,739	1,605	46	13	59
Peterborough	36	21	2	13	1,709	1,598	44	12	56
Eastbourne	36	19	1	16	1,658	1,646	39	10	49
Poole	36	18	1	17	1,666	1,647	37	10	47
Ipswich	36	16	3	17	1,661	1,672	35	9	44
Swindon	36	17	2	17	1,617	1,675	36	7	43
Wolverhampton	36	14	2	20	1,682	1,647	30	10	40
Oxford	**36**	**11**	**1**	**24**	**1,550**	**1,773**	**23**	**3**	**26**
Arena-Essex	36	11	0	25	1,539	1,804	22	3	25

PLAY-OFFS
Semi-finals: Belle Vue 53 Eastbourne 40; Coventry 55 Peterborough 41.
Final (aggregate result): Coventry 101 Belle Vue 83.

CONFERENCE LEAGUE

Team	Mts	Won	Drn	Lst	For	Agn	Pts	Bon	Tot
Oxford	22	15	3	4	1,091	909	33	9	42
Wimbledon	22	15	0	7	1,106	932	30	11	41
Weymouth	22	13	0	9	1,075	956	26	7	33
Mildenhall	22	12	1	9	1,067	968	25	8	33
Armadale	22	12	0	10	1,025	986	24	7	31
Rye House	22	12	0	10	1,046.5	987.5	24	5	29
Stoke	22	12	0	10	1,031	982	24	5	29
Scunthorpe	22	11	0	11	1,012	1,000	22	5	27
Boston	22	11	0	11	982.5	1,055.5	22	4	26
Newport	22	9	0	13	968	1,051	18	3	21
Buxton	22	6	1	15	890	1,112	13	1	14
Sittingbourne	22	1	1	20	823	1,178	3	1	4

2006

Following the departure of Nigel Wagstaff, the rumour machine, as usual, went into overdrive. However, it wasn't long after the close of the 2005 season that Poole-based businessman Aaron Lanney successfully concluded a deal with Steve and Vanessa Purchase to take control of Oxford Speedway. Not a great deal was known about the incoming club owner, other than in his youth he had ridden cycle speedway for Swindon and that he'd been a fan of speedway all his life.

Whilst Mr Lanney was quick to reinstate the Cheetahs nickname and their royal blue and yellow colours, he had to start his team building almost from scratch, since the former Silver Machine riders began moving on to pastures new. Inspirational skipper Greg Hancock joined Reading, as the Berkshire side returned to the top league for the first time since 1996 under the new stewardship of John Postlethwaite and his company Benfield Sports International, which also had responsibility for the Grand Prix series. Taking the position of co-promoter with the rebranded Reading Bulldogs was Jim Lynch, who had been named in a similar position alongside Nigel Wagstaff at Oxford in 2005. Following Hancock to Reading was Aussie Travis McGowan, while Niels-Kristian Iversen went to Peterborough and Billy Hamill joined Wolverhampton. Oxford's Conference League side also disappeared, with the youngsters sold on to Reading. Unfortunately, in the event they never took to the track at Smallmead, which was a great pity.

With most of the previous year's line-up gone, Aaron Lanney didn't have much time to assemble a fresh side within the sport's new 40-point limit for 2006 and, in fact, the only rider with recent Oxford experience to land a team berth was to be young Czech Lubos Tomicek. The new boss quickly signed Australian Davey Watt, who had spent the year before at Eastbourne and posted a very useful 7.32 league average. It was revealed that Mr Lanney had been in talks with Piotr Protasiewicz, but in the end the Polish international was to stay at Ipswich, with whom he'd ridden in 2005. On the positive side, a double swoop saw David Howe join Oxford on loan from Wolverhampton, along with Swedish youngster Eric Andersson, whose only previous experience of British racing had been to appear in Magnus Zetterstrom's Testimonial at Poole on 30 March 2005, although, nonetheless, he was rated as a very hot prospect indeed. Sensationally, Aaron Lanney then announced that he had signed six-times World Champion Tony Rickardsson, albeit on a short-term deal until the Grand Prix series got underway. The side was completed with the acquisition of Polish riders Adam Skornicki and Adam Pietraszko, who came via Wolverhampton and Berwick respectively. With the starting line-up finalised, the last piece of the jigsaw was the appointment of former Exeter rider Graeme Gordon as team manager.

As the season got underway the talk on the terraces was the possibility that Todd Wiltshire might be tempted into a track return at Oxford as the replacement for Tony Rickardsson, once the Swede had completed his stint for the club. The Aussie was held in high esteem at Cowley and the thought that he might be seen once again in Oxford colours certainly had the regular patrons buzzing. Wiltshire had been on the comeback trail Down Under after changes in his personal life provoked a rethink on his retirement. He had competed in the three-round Australian Championship and finished as runner-up to Leigh Adams. This was a terrific performance from the thirty-seven-year-old and showed that he'd lost none of his magic.

With Wednesday becoming the race night in 2006 and David Howe skippering the side, the Cheetahs opened up by entertaining Swindon in a challenge match on 15 March, when they slipped to a 51-39 defeat. Whilst this was disappointing, it wasn't really that surprising as the Oxford seven was new and had had no time to gel together as a unit. Tony Rickardsson headed the scoring with 9 points and literally blitzed around the circuit first time out in heat four to clock 57.99 seconds. Although that was quick, it was still some way short of Hans Nielsen's long-standing track record of 56.2, which was set on 13 October 1988. Twenty-four hours later, there was worse in store for the Cheetahs when they contested the return challenge match at Blunsdon and found the Robins right on the gas. The final score was 61-28 in the Robins' favour and, although it was still early days, there were some supporters who voiced concerns that Oxford didn't possess sufficient strength in depth for the cut and thrust of the Elite League.

Adam Skornicki was a popular team member in 2006, not least for his celebration 'doughnuts' in front of the grandstand at Cowley. The Pole remained ever-present over the 40-match league programme to tot up 266 points and finish with a satisfactory 6.55 average.

The Cheetahs kicked-off their league campaign at home to Ipswich on 22 March and again suffered defeat, losing by 51 points to 42. It was a good meeting, but for Oxford fans it was the wrong result. Tony Rickardsson was in excellent form with 16 points, while Davey Watt netted 9+1. Beyond those two, however, the scoring faded away, giving those who doubted the side's make-up more ammunition. A hammering followed at Ipswich, before the Cheetahs were dumped from the Knock-Out Cup, losing both at home and away to Wolverhampton. Returning to Elite League business, Oxford then lost a further two home matches against Peterborough and Eastbourne, taking their record for the season to eight straight defeats.

With such a desperate run of results, the talk about Todd Wiltshire had gathered pace, since the Australian had a lower green sheet average than Tony Rickardsson and his arrival would allow Aaron Lanney the scope to make changes that would strengthen the team. As things turned out, Rickardsson was to depart before his proposed six-week spell had concluded, which paved the return for Wiltshire and another former Cowley favourite, Freddie Eriksson, who was drafted in to replace the struggling Adam Pietraszko. However, prior to this the Cheetahs had produced one of the shock results of the season on Good Friday, 14 April, when they defeated league leaders Reading 50-44 at Sandy Lane. Over 2,000 fans packed into the stadium for the 12.30p.m. start time and they saw Rickardsson at his brilliant best, as he ripped through the card to register a 15-point maximum. Adam Skornicki also had a good meeting in scoring 11+1 points, while, Pietraszko apart, the rest of the team showed a greater solidity than that previously witnessed by the faithful supporters. The victory was greeted by the sight of Mr Lanney circumnavigating half a lap of the track in his underpants! Apparently, he had stated that he would do this prior to the match if Oxford won and he was 100 per cent true to his word. The corresponding Elite League fixture took place at Smallmead later that evening, when Rickardsson made his final appearance for the Cheetahs. There was to be no repeat of what had happened earlier, though, as Reading ran riot to triumph 67-28. Rickardsson signed off by again heading the scorechart on 11 points, while Aaron Lanney described the performance of his side as 'totally inept'.

Todd Wiltshire's much-anticipated return occurred at Eastbourne on 21 April, when Oxford were thumped 60-32. The Aussie's contribution was just 3+1 points, but he soon got back in the groove after that and was to be nothing short of a revelation as the season unravelled. Following a loss at Peterborough, the Cheetahs claimed only their second win of the season at Cowley on 26 April, when Coventry were beaten 47-43. Wiltshire shone like a beacon, leading his side to victory with a sparkling 11+1 points from five starts. Unfortunately, success was to be scarce for the club in 2006 and a run of five defeats followed, including a 56-38 reverse at Swindon on 4 May. However, there was great joy on 31 May, when the side returned to winning ways against the Robins. The Oxford fans have always enjoyed putting one over their local rivals and, of course, this works both ways, but the win was even sweeter given the club's position at the foot of the league table and the fact that Swindon had been such convincing victors on their previous visit at the start of the season. On a rare night to savour, Adam Skornicki recorded a brace of wins over visiting number one Leigh Adams and generally performed wonders to head the scoring with 12 points. Meanwhile, Wiltshire and the ever-improving Eric Andersson supplied the Pole with great backing to register tallies of 11 and 9+3 respectively.

June began with two league matches against Poole, beginning with the away clash at Wimborne Road, where the Cheetahs lost 55-40 despite a quite brilliant 15 points from Todd Wiltshire. A day later, on 8 June, Oxford pulled out all the stops to gain revenge courtesy of a 50-43 scoreline. The remarkable Wiltshire again starred with 12+1 points, while David Howe plundered an identical tally in what was one of his best showings of the year. More defeats came at Reading and at home to Coventry, but Aaron Lanney hadn't been complacent and realised the team needed more tweaking. Freddie Eriksson had shown plenty of effort, but hadn't really got amongst the points in the desired fashion and it was he who made way for the return of the much loved Ales Dryml. The Czech international impressed with 12 points in his first meeting back against Reading at Sandy Lane on 21 June, and whilst Adam Skornicki tallied 14, the duo couldn't stop the Bulldogs from winning 54-39. Another defeat followed at Peterborough, before disaster struck against Wolverhampton in a home match on 12 July. Although the Cheetahs lost 51-41, the meeting was overshadowed by a serious heat seven accident involving Dryml, which left the rider fighting for his life in an intensive care unit at the John Radcliffe Hospital. Remarkably, and against all the odds, the Czech recovered from his severe head injuries and was, thankfully, able to return to his homeland where he began his recuperation.

Strangely, despite their problems, Oxford were to have a better second half to the season results-wise than they had enjoyed in the first part of the campaign. One of the reasons for this was that they could choose good guest replacements for Ales Dryml, although, of course, they would have preferred to track the Czech rider himself. Original club number eight Mathieu Tresarrieu was replaced by Pole Stanislaw Burza and first linked with the side for a league match at home to Eastbourne on 26 July. The Cheetahs collected a 50-42 victory and their first bonus point of the season, having gone down 50-45 against the Eagles at Arlington three days previously. Adam Skornicki and Todd Wiltshire scored 13+1 points apiece, while a little lower down the line, Burza gave a very good account to tally 6+2. A couple of other changes around this time saw Aaron Lanney take over the team managing duties from Graeme Gordon in order to cut down on expenses, while Wiltshire replaced David Howe as captain of the side.

As the season petered out, Oxford were to win seven of their last fifteen fixtures and, for the second year running, somehow managed to leapfrog Arena-Essex and avoid the dreaded cellar position. In an unsatisfactory conclusion, despite being the holders of the Craven Shield, the Cheetahs weren't able to participate in the competition as new rules meant that the bottom two clubs in the Elite League table were precluded from entry.

At the club's final home meeting there was a pleasant happening, which could have easily been overlooked. The date was 27 September and Oxford had beaten Arena-Essex 55-37. Jim Gregory, who had been a star for the Cheetahs back in the 1950s, had visited Cowley on many occasions during the intervening years to provide displays on vintage speedway machines. However, at the age of seventy-nine, he intended to finally retire. Before bringing the curtain down, Gregory had been keen to race once again at Oxford and, after the Cheetahs had defeated the Hammers, he accomplished his wish, but only just. He had enjoyed just one outing, when down came the rain and the rest of the vintage troupes' outings were cancelled. At least he had fulfilled his desire, which, after all, was the important thing.

The rider statistics for a difficult term saw Tony Rickardsson top the league averages, his six matches yielding 70 points and a 9.66 average. The Swede incidentally announced his retirement from the sport, with immediate effect, in the lead-up to the Scandinavian Grand Prix in August. At the time, he had participated in five rounds of the series, recording 41 points. Next in line for the Cheetahs was Todd Wiltshire, who totalled 302 points from 33 matches for a highly satisfactory 7.98 figure. Meanwhile, Davey Watt had a steady year to finish on a 6.99 average, having scored 241 points from 36 appearances. Delving a little deeper, Adam Skornicki remained ever-present over the 40-match programme to average 6.55, while David Howe also completed all of the club's fixtures to end up with a 6.26 figure.

So ended the 2006 season under Aaron Lanney and shortly after its conclusion, it was announced that Colin Horton, the businessman behind Peterborough Speedway, had agreed a deal to also become the club owner of Oxford. Mr Horton appointed Trevor Swales as general manager and Colin Meredith as meeting coordinator, though he was quick to stress that Mr Lanney would also be staying on as co-promoter. Thus 2007 will become yet another new era for the fans of the Oxford Cheetahs.

At the age of seventy-nine years, Jim Gregory fulfilled his wish to race on the Cowley circuit one final time in 2006, before finally retiring from the vintage troupe.

ELITE LEAGUE

Team	Mts	Won	Drn	Lst	For	Agn	Pts	Bon	Tot
Peterborough	40	24	0	16	1,942	1,731	48	16	64
Reading	40	25	1	14	1,934	1,756	51	13	64
Swindon	40	23	1	16	1,893	1,786	47	14	61
Coventry	40	23	1	16	1,856	1,835	47	11	58
Belle Vue	40	21	0	19	1,880	1,761	42	15	57
Wolverhampton	40	20	2	18	1,827	1,840	42	10	52
Poole	40	19	0	21	1,880	1,806	38	13	51
Ipswich	40	19	0	21	1,847	1,837	38	8	46
Eastbourne	40	20	1	19	1,791	1,860	41	5	46
Oxford	**40**	**12**	**0**	**28**	**1,696**	**1,989**	**24**	**2**	**26**
Arena-Essex	40	11	0	29	1,658	2,003	22	3	25

PLAY-OFFS
Semi-finals: Peterborough 52 Coventry 40; Reading 51 Swindon 43.
Final (aggregate result): Peterborough 95 Reading 94.

If you are interested in purchasing other books published by Stadia, or in case you have difficulty finding any Stadia books in your local bookshop, you can also place orders directly through the Tempus Publishing website
www.tempus-publishing.com